Praise for
Hitler's German Enemies

"It is vital that we be reminded by legendary historian Snyder of some of the fine traditions and recent martyrs of a highly gifted people."
—PROFESSOR BERNARD BELLUSH

"Snyder, an eminent authority on nationalism and recent German history, tells their stories with clarity and emotion."
—BOYD C. SHAFER, former editor of
the *American Historical Review*

"An excellent reference source."
—American Library Association,
Booklist

"A fitting monument to the martyrs described in its pages."
—PROFESSOR HANS L. TREFOUSSE

Berkley Books by Louis L. Snyder

HITLER'S ELITE
HITLER'S GERMAN ENEMIES

HITLER'S GERMAN ENEMIES

Portraits of Heroes Who Fought the Nazis

Louis L. Snyder

BERKLEY BOOKS, NEW YORK

This Berkley book contains the complete text
of the original hardcover edition. It has been
completely reset in a typeface designed
for easy reading and was printed from new film.

HITLER'S GERMAN ENEMIES

A Berkley Book / published by arrangement with
Hippocrene Books, Inc.

PRINTING HISTORY
Hippocrene Books edition published 1990
Berkley edition / February 1992

ISBN: 0-425-13080-0

A BERKLEY BOOK®TM 757,375
Berkley Books are published by The Berkley Publishing Group,
200 Madison Avenue, New York, New York 10016.
The name "BERKLEY" and the "B" logo
are trademarks belonging to Berkley Publishing Corporation.

PRINTED IN THE UNITED STATES OF AMERICA

10 9 8 7 6 5 4 3 2 1

To the Snyders of Rolling House Road

DOLORES, HAROLD, JULIE ANN and
TERRY, MAL and KAREN, DOUGLAS and CARY,
SANDRA, and JORDAN

The Third Reich was the greatest failure of civilization on the planet. In Freudian terms, it was as if the superego had gone crashing into the dark, wild id. . . . Germany represented one of the farthest advances of the culture, yet the Third Reich profoundly perverted the entire heritage of Western civilization. It was as if Goethe had taken to eating human flesh.

—Lance Morrow

The men of the Resistance were the greatest and most noble political group of our times.

—Winston Churchill

Contents

Preface

FROM 1928 TO 1931 I WAS A STUDENT AT THE UNIVERSITY OF FRANK-
furt am Main as a German-American Exchange Fellow and then
stipendiary of the Alexander von Humboldt Foundation. Those
were happy days in the delightful atmosphere of German university life, years in which enduring friendships were made.
The Germans I knew and learned to admire were decent folk
subject to the concern and anxieties of all people living in a
troubled world. At that time they were depressed by the gory
battle of the streets between upcoming Nazis and convinced
Communists, but few suspected that their lives would be burdened later by an inhuman dictatorship.

From 1933 on, after Hitler came to political power, the German name was besmirched by a descent into vulgarity such as
the nation had never before seen in its history. I had the feeling
at the time that my friends in Germany could not possibly
succumb to the nihilism of Hitler and his gang of cutthroats. In
1934 I learned to my dismay that Dr. Kurt Rheindorf, *Privatdozent* at Frankfurt and a magnificent human being who had
sponsored my doctoral dissertation on Bismarck and Americans, was killed by the Nazis in their Blood Purge. It was a
tragic loss of a good man.

There were Germans who refused to remain silent as Hitler
consolidated his regime and prepared the country for war. But
there was little word from Germany to the outside world about
opposition, resistance, and conspiracy. After the war much evidence emerged about Germans from all walks of life, who,
motivated by Kant's categorical imperative, sacrificed their
lives in the struggle against a half-demented tyrant.

I was not surprised.

This book of psychobiographical vignettes and profiles seeks to honor those Germans. These are token chapters—there were others who took part in that struggle between good and evil.

I wish to express my thanks to Nana Wiessler and Tony Wells of the Wiener Library in London, that treasure trove and repository of information on all phases of National Socialism and the Third Reich. I owe much to the staff of the New York Public Library. My thanks also to Eric Greenfeldt of the Princeton Public Library, an institution devoted to the non-university residents of Princeton without concern for the profit motive. For Ida Mae Brown Snyder, my lifelong companion, I can only express my humble appreciation once again for her expert editorial eye, her valuable suggestions, and her unfailing help in the agonies faced by the harried writer.

Louis L. Snyder
Princeton, N.J.

Introduction

IN A GLOW OF EUPHORIA ADOLF HITLER ASSERTED THAT HIS THIRD Reich would last for a thousand years. Fortunately for the inhabitants of this globe there were only twelve years, but they were years of fear and foreboding. Nazi Germany was a monstrous abomination, a terrible throwback in civilization, a retreat into barbarism. There were, indeed, tyrants and dictators in the past—Nero, Attila the Hun, and Ivan the Terrible—but this was something unique in history. An entire nation, proud of its contributions to civilization and culture, became victims of a neurotic Austrian and his henchmen.

Nazi Germany had its rogues' gallery of scoundrels, misfits, and thugs—from Goebbels to Eichmann, from Goering to Himmler. However, in this maelstrom of evil there were Germans worthy of honor, those who asserted their conscience over the demands of the state, courageous heroes who chose to be throttled by Nazi executioners rather than give in to a regime they detested. These Germans acted on the assumption that a fireman should not be afraid of fire. That such Germans could even exist and cry out against the terror of Nazi dictatorship is testimony to the fact that the decent human spirit is unquenchable and persists despite every effort to stamp it out.

Many Germans were dissatisfied with the Hitler regime but they were reluctant to criticize it or stand in its way. Not the Germans described in this book. Motivated by love of country and appalled by the excesses of Nazism, they did what they could to rescue their fellow countrymen from the abyss. They faced Hitler's police with deserved contempt. These were humans who placed right, honor, and justice beyond the value of their own lives. By sheer moral spirit they acquired something of the aura of the lives of saints.

The great German poet Goethe, a universal mind, understood his people. "The Germans," he said, "are really a strange people. With their profound thoughts and ideas which they seek everywhere and project into everything, they make things harder for themselves than they should." Goethe also contributed his version of the Faust legend, a poetic epitome expressing the deepest conflict of human experience—the eternal struggle between good and evil. In this crowning achievement of his literary life, the poet closed with a mystery theme in which the centenarian Faust finally triumphs over the powers of evil.

The men and the woman described in this book represent Goethe's spirit of decency in a troubled society. These were the good Germans who acted against a regime whose power was maintained by lies, treachery, and murder.

It has been said that evil flourishes when good men do nothing. These heroes in Naziland did what they could to banish the evil. They deserve our attention, respect, and admiration. That they were unsuccessful, that it took a global coalition of outraged humanity to bring down the dictator, should not lessen our sense of esteem.

They came from all classes and from all parts of the country. A common thread ran through their minds—they could not and would not accept the injustices of a monstrous regime. Their consciences were outraged. They moved from resentment to rebellion. They suffered under the Nazi terror. Most of them lost their lives in the unequal struggle against the totalitarian state. They are remembered reverently and gratefully as champions of decency, as martyrs for the sake of humanity.

All honor to these magnificent human beings.

HITLER'S GERMAN ENEMIES

1 *

Dietrich Bonhoeffer:
Pastor As Hero

———————

Death is the supreme festival on the road to freedom.

Only by defeat can we atone for the horrible crimes that we have committed against Europe and the world.

Christian Martyr

"DIETRICH WAS NO SAINT. BUT CHRIST WAS HIS LIFE AND THEREFORE his conscience."

Millions of people throughout the world would be inclined gently to disagree with Sabine Bonhoeffer-Leibholz, twin sister of Dietrich Bonhoeffer, German Protestant pastor hanged for high treason three weeks before Hitler's suicide in the bunker below the ruins of Berlin. But they would differ only with the first part of her judgment. They see him not only as a saint but as charismatic patriot and hero who by his words and actions provided a ray of light in the darkness of the Nazi Third Reich.

If ever there was a man of Christlike character on this earth it was Dietrich Bonhoeffer. Many who saw him in his days of trial were impressed by his noble bearing and cheerfulness under painful conditions. Here was a human being of extraordinary humility and sweetness of character, known for his sensitiveness and deep awareness. With passionate faith in his theology he endured in the hellhole of Nazism and took up the struggle against it.

There was triumph and there was tragedy in the life of this remarkable man. As a youngster of distinguished family background, he chose the career of academic theology, and quickly established himself as one of the most quoted theologians of the

1

day. Horrified when he saw what Hitler was attempting to do
with religion in Germany, he rebelled against the institutional
Church which was willing to coöperate with the *Fuehrer*. Unable to countenance what was happening to his country, he
became a double agent and a courier making contacts abroad in
Sweden and Switzerland. He went to Sweden in 1942 carrying
proposals from conspirators for peace terms with the Allies.
With little regard for his own safety, he promoted Operation
Seven, which enabled seven Jews to escape from Nazi Germany
to Switzerland—an action which at the time nearly cost him his
life.

And then tragedy. Only a few days before he could be rescued by triumphant Allied forces, this remarkable young
Lutheran pastor was executed on a Nazi gallows.

The life of this extraordinary man reflects the dilemma of
thousands of other Germans who had to face the realities of an
atavistic regime. Bonhoeffer found it impossible to stand aside
while the reputation of his beloved Fatherland was being
smeared by Nazi crimes. In the ongoing conflict between good
and evil in Hitler's Third Reich, Bonhoeffer represented what
was left of decency in that troubled land.

Throughout his life from child to adult Bonhoeffer was well
known for his ardent, emotional personality. Friend and
biographer Eberhard Bethge recognized his quality: "He remained intense in the way he set about everything: reading,
writing, making decisions, and going into the reasons for
them, helping people or warning them—in short, dealing with
whatever was presented to and asked of him throughout his
career."

Most of all, Bonhoeffer remained true to his religious
identity. He was convinced that the ideology of National Socialism conflicted with the principles of Christianity. Biographer
Mary Bosanquet caught the essence of his life: "It was lived
with God and for God, with men and for men, ever more
fearlessly exposed by the multifarious world, and it is by his
life as much as by his words that he spoke and can speak
today."

Early Career

Dietrich Bonhoeffer was born on February 4, 1906, together with twin sister Sabine, the children of Dr. Karl Bonhoeffer, Professor of Psychiatry and Neurology and Director of the University Hospital for Nervous Diseases at Breslau. In 1912 the family moved from the quiet provincial university town to Berlin. Parents and eight children enjoyed a happy family life. All the offspring were high-spirited but never rude or ill-mannered. Dietrich was known as a handsome boy, with fair hair, ruddy skin, and gazing blue eyes. He enjoyed excellent health and unusual vitality of mind and body. Those who knew him predicted a most successful life.

In 1913 Dietrich started school at the *Friedrich-Werder Gymnasium* (grammar school). An early reader, he was captivated by a German translation of *Uncle Tom's Cabin*, and soon was absorbing the German classics, especially the works of Goethe and Schiller. He was an accomplished pianist—for a time the family expected that he might become a professional musician.

The loss of older brother Walther had a disturbing effect on young Dietrich. The boy grew up in the unhappy days of the early Weimar Republic, a time when the nation was plunged into resentment and despair. Influenced by Christian ethical standards strongly established in his family, Dietrich decided to read theology at the university. As an adult he made a most favorable impression, standing over six feet tall, with wide shoulders, and forearms covered with muscles. His large head was crowned with a shock of unruly blond hair.

In 1923 Dietrich studied theology at the University of Tübingen. In the spring of 1924 he and brother Klaus made a three months' visit to Rome, where both were impressed by their first sight of the ancient city. Although profoundly moved by the Roman Catholic Church "as a world in herself," Dietrich saw uncertainties in its greatness. Possibly Catholicism had lost its role as a signpost to God and had become a burden on the road. He returned home anxious to resume his studies in Protestant theology. In the summer of 1924 he went to Berlin.

Dietrich studied under liberal theologian Adolf von Harnack. With his independent judgment he showed a preference for the work of Göttingen's Karl Barth, whose theology called for a single-minded search for burning central truth through the so-called dialectic school. A fellow-student testified to Dietrich's attitude in theology: "I had the experience of hearing a young, fairhaired student contradict the revered historian, his Excellency von Harnack, contradict him politely but clearly on positive theological grounds. Harnack answered, but the student contradicted him again and again. The talk was of Karl Barth."

At the end of 1927 Dietrich presented his doctoral thesis, *Sanctorum Communio,* and defended it in public debate. In this early thesis, product of a precocious young theology student, Dietrich tried to understand the relationship of the Church from a sociological point of view, as a group of sinning human beings, with the Church in its divine aspect as the body of Christ on earth. In one of his first sermons, delivered a few months later, Bonhoeffer reiterated this thesis: "It is perhaps the most serious calamity of the present time that we do not know what the 'Church' means, which burned so passionately in the heart of Jesus at the time of his farewell. . . . We need ourselves to become the Church. . . . Paul calls it the body of Christ. . . . Sacrifice, intercession, absolution, these are the wonderful powers of the Christian community, which are all contained in the word Love, Love as God has shown it to us, in becoming Christ to the other person. . . . The Church, that is our faith—I believe in a holy Church; Church, that is the significance of the human society; Church, that is our hope for the present and the future. In the words sung once by the ancient Father of the Church: God our Father, the Church, our Mother, Jesus Christ our Lord, that is our Faith. Amen."

With the doctorate won, Bonhoeffer's next stage in becoming a pastor required that he spend a year as curate under a parish minister. Offered a post in the German Lutheran Community in Spain, he went to Barcelona. Serving an elderly chaplain in a community of German families, he soon doubled the size of the congregation.

Returning to Berlin in February 1929, Bonhoeffer worked on his habilitation thesis, *Akt und Sein (Act and Being),* which he finished in early 1930. Its acceptance the following July won him an appointment to the theological faculty at Berlin as *Privatdozent* (instructor). He delivered his inaugural lecture, "An Enquiry into Man in Contemporary Philosophy and Theology," in the great hall at the University of Berlin. Thus began a distinguished academic career for the young theologian.

Meanwhile, Bonhoeffer decided that he would like to spend some time abroad. Given the opportunity for a year at New York's Union Theological Seminary, he took a sabbatical leave and left Germany in September 1930. A few days after he arrived in New York, elections for the *Reichstag* produced a surprising result: the number of National Socialist deputies rose from twelve to a hundred and seven. Although he made some close friends at Union Theological Seminary, Bonhoeffer was not impressed by the work being done there. In a letter to a friend he wrote: "A theology is not to be found here. I attend what are theoretically lectures and seminars on dogmatics and religious philosophy, but the impression remains annihilating. They chatter until all is blue without any factual foundation or any criteria of thought becoming visible. The students, who are mostly twenty-five to thirty years old, have not the faintest notion of what dogmatic theology is about. They do not know how to ask themselves the simplest questions. They intoxicate themselves with liberal and humanistic expressions, laugh at the fundamentalists, and basically they are not even a match for them." The mind remained critical and blunt.

Returning to Germany, Bonhoeffer resumed his lectures at Berlin in the winter semester of 1931–1932, and he continued for two years through the summer session of 1933. So effective was his work that a group of interested and loyal students formed around him. The word was passed among students that here was a highly gifted and promising theologian, a virile, independent thinker, way beyond the intellectually flaccid successor to the recently deceased Harnack.

Ethical Theologian

Dietrich Bonhoeffer was only thirty-nine when he became victim to Hitler's vengeance. But his work made him a major figure in contemporary theology. The final twelve years of his life coincided exactly with the rise and fall of Hitler's Third Reich. During his short life he produced theological insights that were to make his name known throughout the world.

At the base of Bonhoeffer's teaching was a deep passion for the life of the Church. It was that dominant emotion that led him to the Confessional Church, a part of German Protestantism which resisted the Nazi effort to control and exploit it. He became involved in the struggle and eventually sacrificed his life for it.

First and foremost, Bonhoeffer's Christology was grounded in his belief in the uniqueness and significance of Jesus Christ. This was the unifying element of his theology. In his fragmentary book, *Ethics*, he reached the conclusion that Christ and reality go inextricably together. His close juxtaposition of Christ and reality remained at the heart of his teaching—that Christ is the point at which God and the world must be discussed together:

> No man can look with undivided vision at God and at the
> world of reality so long as God and the world are torn
> asunder. Try as he may, he can only let his eyes wander
> distractedly from one to the other. But there is a place at
> which God and the cosmic reality are reconciled, a place at
> which God and man must become one. That and that alone
> is what enables man to set his eyes upon God and the world
> at the same time. This place does not lie somewhere out
> beyond reality in the realm of ideas. It lies in the midst of
> history as a divine miracle. It lies in Jesus Christ, the Recon-
> ciler of the world. . . .Whoever sees Jesus Christ, does in-
> deed see God and the world as one. He can henceforward no

longer see God without the world or the world without God."*

Bonhoeffer saw the commandment of God as the element in which one could live without always being conscious of it. Thus, it implied freedom of movement and of action, freedom from fear of decision, freedom from fear to act; it implied certainty, quietude, confidence, balance, and peace. One could honor one's parents, be faithful in marriage, respect the lives and property of others not because at the frontiers of his life there is a threatening "thou shalt not," but because he accepts as holy institutions of God these realities—parents, marriage, life, and property, all of which confront him in the midst and fullness of life. One can recognize in Bonhoeffer's theology the reason for this extraordinary man's involvement in the struggle against Hitler and the Third Reich. Bonhoeffer was not crippled by fear to act against abysmal despotism.

In prison at Tegel, Bonhoeffer on August 3, 1944, sent a letter in which he outlined a book "of not more than 100 pages" that he would write in the future. "All this is very crude and condensed, but there are certain things I am anxious to say simply and clearly—things that we so often like to shirk." There would be three chapters: 1. A Stocktaking of Christianity; 2. The Real Meaning of Christian Faith; and 3. Conclusions.

In Chapter 1 Bonhoeffer intended to discuss the question: What protects us against the menace of organization? "Man is again thrown back on himself. He has managed to deal with everything, only not with himself. We can insure against everything only not against man. In the last respect it all turns on man." He would treat the Protestant Church; Pietism as a last attempt to maintain evangelical Christianity as a religion; Lutheran orthodoxy as an attempt to rescue the Church as an institution for salvation; and the Confessional Church as the Church on the defensive.

---

*Dietrich Bonhoeffer, *Ethics,* ed. Eberhard Bethge, trans. by Neville Horton Smith (New York: The Macmillan Co., 1965), pp. 69–70.

In Chapter 2, "The Real Meaning of the Christian Faith," Bonhoeffer intended to write of God and the secular. The transformation of all human life was given in the fact that "Jesus is there only for others," the experience of transcendence. That was the ground of Christ's omnipotence, omniscience, and omnipresence. Faith was participation in the being of Jesus (incarnation, cross, and resurrection). "The transcendental is not infinite and unattainable tasks, but the neighbor who is within reach in any given situation. God in human form—not, as in oriental religions, in animal form, monstrous, chaotic, remote and terrifying, nor in the conceptual forms of the absolute, metaphysical, infinite, etc., nor yet in the Greek divine-human form of man in himself, but "the man for others.'"

In Chapter 3, "Conclusion," Bonhoeffer gave essence to his belief:

> The Church is the Church only when it can exist for others. To make a start, it should give away all its property to those in need. The clergy should live solely on the free-will offerings of their congregations, or possibly engage in some secular calling. The Church must share in the secular problem of ordinary human life, not dominating, but helping and serving. It must tell men of every calling what it means to live in Christ, to exist for others. In particular, our own Church will have to take the field against the vices of hubris, power-worship, envy, and humbug, as the roots of all evil.*

Advent of Hitler

January 30, 1933—an extraordinarily important date in the troubled history of the German people. On that fateful day Adolf Hitler became Chancellor of Germany—and a new tragedy began for the Germans. Within a few months a totalitarian state was set up with the National Socialist German Workers' Party (NSDAP) the only legal political party. The process

*Dietrich Bonhoeffer, *Letters and Papers from Prison*, ed. by Eberhard Bethge (New York: The Macmillan Co., 1953), p. 211.

of coördination *(Gleichschaltung)* was begun quickly as every institution in the state was molded into the Nazi pattern.

Bonhoeffer, as well as millions of other Germans, did not know it at the time, but the event signalled the end of their stay on this planet. A shameful episode began in German history, a reversion to primitive, brutal barbarity. A band of savage nihilists had taken full charge over the destiny of a highly gifted people.

The young pastor had no intention of bending in the Nazi whirlwind. Others of his status in German society reluctantly accepted a situation they deemed to be inevitable: give the flamboyant Austrian a chance, for he could do no worse than the bumbling Weimar politicians. Besides, it was all very colorful—the raging oratory, the bread-and-circuses, the goose-stepping on asphalt, the patriotic songs. The loud-mouth politician might bring an end to the iniquitous system of Versailles. Give the brown-shirted battalions a chance. There was little to lose and much to gain.

But not Dietrich Bonhoeffer, activist pastor. Every grain in his body rebelled against this barking demagogue and his thick-headed comrades. Bonhoeffer was repelled by Nazi philosophy as an unacceptable assault on decency. He would not sit back and do nothing. He would not rest while the good name of his Fatherland was being besmirched before all the world.

The young theologian was nauseated by the anti-Semitism of the Nazi movement and its threat against the Jewish people. He saw such bigotry as shameful. He was delighted when, in 1926 his much-loved twin sister Sabine was married to Gerhard Leibholz, a brilliant young lawyer, who was Jewish by birth. While studying theology, Dietrich met Franz Hildebrandt, the son of Hildebrandt the art historian and a Jewish mother, and enjoyed a long, unbroken friendship with him. Moreover, Bonhoeffer saw nothing in his Christian heritage to call for the kind of anti-Semitism promoted by Hitler and his entourage of Jew-haters. In his mind this was contemptible prejudice and he would have none of it.

Bonhoeffer was quick to make his sense of opposition to Nazism known. On February 1, 1933, only two days after the

Nazis came to power, he spoke on the radio in the Potsdamer Broadcasting House on "The Concept of Leadership." Moderate in tone, the talk analyzed the development of the idea of a *Fuehrer* and the changes it had undergone in the postwar Youth Movement. He asked whether the popular desire for a leader meant a psychological need of youth or a political need of the nation as a whole. "To what point is leading and being led healthy and genuine, and when does it become pathological and extreme? It is only when a man has answered these questions clearly in his own mind that he can grasp something of the essence of 'leadership' and something of the nature of the younger generation."

Clue to the future. Already the tentacles of Nazism were beginning to spread. Before his last sentences could be broadcast, Bonhoeffer's microphone was cut off. The choking of free speech in Nazi Germany had already begun.

Bonhoeffer had no intention of retreating into silence. Like other members of his own family, he regarded the triumph of National Socialism as a misfortune. Distaste arose from Hitler's demagogic methods of propaganda, his motor drives through the countryside with whip in hand, and the *Fuehrer*'s choice of confederates. The young pastor was annoyed by repressive measures against Jews, the boycott of Jewish shops, and street scenes of disgusting inhumanity. In an address in Berlin toward the end of April 1933 he protested on behalf of Jews who had been converted to Christianity.

Meanwhile, Bonhoeffer began to have fears about the status of Christianity in the Third Reich. By July 1933 the *Reichstag* formally recognized a new "Reich Church," to be under the leadership of a "Reich Bishop," who would be charged to unify diverse German Protestant sects into a single ecclesiastical institution which would support Hitler's Third Reich. Within two months the new "German Christians" at a national synod elected the notorious Ludwig Müller as Reich Bishop.

There was opposition as the German Church struggle began. Bonhoeffer was involved in the dissenting movement from its inception. With friend Franz Hildebrandt he urged the formation of a new Free Church, whose form and constitution might be considered at an Ecumenical Council of all the Protestant Churches. The Confessional Church came into existence with the Barmen Declaration of May 1934, which, unfortunately for its promoters, was never adopted by German Protestantism as a whole. Bonhoeffer fought hard for its tenets. He said repeatedly that to be a Christian in Germany meant to be a member of the Confessional Church. Scores of Germans were to sacrifice their lives for their loyalty to the Confessional Church. Ultimately, only a small group acted in the way Bonhoeffer wanted. From then on, the development of his theology ran parallel to his role in the German church struggle.

Already, Bonhoeffer, along with Martin Niemoeller and Franz Hildebrandt, had formed an Emergency League of Pastors, dedicated to four goals:

1. To renew allegiance to the Scriptures and the Creed.

2. To resist any attack upon them.

3. To give material and financial help to those who suffered through repressive laws or violence.

4. To repudiate the Aryan Paragraph, which required that the civil service would be purged of all those who were either Jewish or of partly Jewish descent.

More than a thousand Prussian pastors signed the protest. Resistance among Protestant theologians was gathering strength. But very few had any notion of the extent of the danger. Bonhoeffer himself saw the problem as immediate and absolute. The Church, he warned, was moving toward a future of appalling moral danger. He spoke again and again of state measures against Jews, which he believed to be a denial of ''the explicit teaching and spirit of the Gospel of Jesus Christ,'' as well as a blot upon the good name of the German people.

The German dictator, busy in the task of consolidating his totalitarian state, began to hear damaging details about the activities of the militant young pastor. Who was this loudmouth who dared challenge the regeneration of Germany? He would not take back talk from this holy medicine man of God. He would keep a close watch on Bonhoeffer and prevent him from infecting the new Nazi ''Positive Christianity,'' a Christianity

molded to Nazi doctrine. There was danger in the theological
air.

The Years Abroad

During the first nine months of the Hitler regime, Bonhoeffer
became estranged from his colleagues, with whom he differed
about the way to oppose National Socialism. He was a pacifist,
his comrades-in-arms shared Hitler's aggressiveness. He denounced anti-Semitism as un-Christian; his colleagues kept silent. He decided that it was "about time to go into the
wilderness for a spell."

On October 17, 1933, Bonhoeffer interrupted his teaching at
the university and left Germany to take up a post of pastor in the
South London suburb of Forest Hill. He became vicar for two
German congregations—the Reformed Church of St. Paul and
the German Evangelical Church in Sydenham. This was his first
regular pastorate and the only one he ever held. During the next
year he lived in two countries simultaneously, traveling to Germany to assist as much as he could in religious opposition to
Hitler, and to England where he hoped to receive the strongest
possible support for the clerical resistance to Nazism. Settled in
an uncomfortable Victorian house, he, despite his strong constitution, was adversely affected by the British weather and suffered from colds and influenza. He fought a losing battle against
an invasion of British mice. A month after he came to London,
Franz Hildebrandt arrived to share his bachelor's existence.

At first, Bonhoeffer's opposition to the Nazi steam roller was
strictly a matter of theological differences without the critical
political dimension it later assumed. He spent the time from the
fall of 1933 to the spring of 1935 in London. Within a few
months he came to know Dr. George Bell, the Bishop of
Chichester, whom he urged to do what he could to recognize the
new Confessional Church as the only authentic Protestant body
in Germany.

In the winter of 1935, Bonhoeffer received a summons from
the leadership of the Confessional Church urging him to return
to Germany to become head of one of its Preachers' Seminaries.

In the strict Nazi scheme of cöordination these seminaries remained the only means by which future ministers could be trained. Of the five established, Bonhoeffer would direct one, first at Zingst and then at Finkenwalde, near Stettin on the Baltic coast. He began his work in late April 1935 with some twenty-three students under his guidance.

Bonhoeffer threw himself zealously into his work with students. At the same time he began to publish books outlining his theology. When the seminary at Finkenwalde was closed in 1937 by the police, the project went underground. Bonhoeffer continued to teach in dispersed locations until the operation was stopped by the *Gestapo* in March 1940. Abandon the struggle, never!

From Opposition to Conspiracy

The exact moment when Bonhoeffer decided to join the conspiracy against Hitler is not known. He must have had a terrible bout with his conscience. Here he was, a man of God, dedicated to peace and non-violence, contemplating joining the plot against the life of the *Fuehrer* and moving over the line between opposition and conspiracy. But the stakes were enormous. The Nazi dictator was in Bonhoeffer's eyes so dangerous to the Fatherland that he must be removed. Let other pastors quake in their boots and try to appease the monster. He would do what his conscience demanded. Did not an angry Jesus seek to drive the money-changers from the temple? This was more than a money-changer—this Austrian interloper would mean the ruination of the country.

In mid-March 1938 Hitler won another bloodless victory in the crisis over Czechoslovakia. Bonhoeffer and his friends were now convinced that a European war would be the end result of the *Fuehrer*'s policies. For Pastor Bonhoeffer this was a serious problem. He was not the sort of person who refused battle under any circumstances, but to fight for this contemptible man was altogether impossible for him. His age group was to be called for national service in 1939.

For the time being, Bonhoeffer decided to find some academic occupation in America. He could at least live in freedom there and follow his theological calling without the political pressures of Nazi Germany. He never gave a moment's thought of escaping from danger—that was not in his character. When a radiogram came offering him a combination post of theological lectureship and work in summer conferences and universities, he made a second trip to the United States.

Bonhoeffer soon decided that he had made an error. In a letter to theologian Reinhold Niebuhr dated July 1939, he wrote: "Sitting here in Dr. Coffin's garden I have had the time to think and pray about my situation to have God's will clarified. I have come to the conclusion that I have made a mistake in coming to America. I must live through this difficult period of our national history with the people of Germany." Bonhoeffer wrote that he would have no right to participate in the reconstruction of Christian life in Germany after Hitler if he did not share the trials at this time with his people. His brothers in the Confessional Synod had wanted him to go, "but I was wrong in going."

For Bonhoeffer that decision was followed by four years of a double life, two years in prison, and then the gallows.

When the war broke out in 1939, Bonhoeffer had already taken his stand—the removal of Hitler. He believed implicitly that what was treason in the eyes of the *Fuehrer* was in reality true love of country. Bonhoeffer's life at this time wavered between his theological work and the rising tempo of the conspiracy. The plot against Hitler was led by legal expert Hans von Dohnanyi, Dietrich's brother-in-law, and Hans Oster, chief of staff of the *Abwehr*, the counterintelligence department of the High Command of the Armed Forces.

Meanwhile, despite pressure from the *Gestapo*, Bonhoeffer combined his theological pursuits with clandestine operations. In September 1940 he was forbidden to speak in public or publish anything, and he was to report regularly to the police. He was placed beyond the reach of conscription when, in October 1940, Hans Oster saw to it that he was appointed as a counterintelligence agent of German Military Intelligence. He worked in the *Abwehr* office in Munich and stayed there through February 1941.

One of the most important goals of the conspirators was to contact Allied governments. A *coup d'état* was in their eyes basic, but the Allies must recognize any government replacing the Nazis. This was Bonhoeffer's assignment in the conspiracy. He had the required papers to get across the borders, ostensibly on missions for German counterintelligence, but in reality to inform Allied officials about the conspiracy.

Bonhoeffer's clandestine diplomacy began in the spring of 1941. In all he made six trips outside Germany, the first two to Switzerland in 1941 and the remainder to Norway, Switzerland, Sweden, and Italy in 1942. The most important mission was to Sweden from May 30 to June 2, 1942. The conspirators learned that Dr. George Bell, Bishop of Chichester, would be in Stockholm. Obtaining a courier-passport from the Foreign Office, Bonhoeffer flew to Sweden. He gave Bell, whom he had known during his stay in England, full details of the plot including names of its key figures. Bell was to relay this information to the British Foreign Office.

Bonhoeffer's desire for a public declaration by the Allied governments was not successful. In taking his leave from the bishop, the German pastor spoke of the spirit of fellowship and Christian brotherhood needed to carry them through the dark hours. Agreeing, Bishop Bell returned to London and did his best to persuade Anthony Eden and others in the government that a positive response must be made to the conspirators. The bishop called passionately for a rational formulation of peace aims and the proclamation of a new European order in which Germany, liberated from the stains of National Socialism, would have its status without the mistakes of the Treaty of Versailles.

Neither personal contact nor a public campaign was productive for the zealous bishop. The Allied policy of unconditional surrender was already formulated. Apparently, the good bishop had a far clearer grasp of grand strategy than the statesmen.

Meanwhile, Bonhoeffer and Dohnanyi went to Rome in the

hope that a favorable decision by the British might be encouraged by the Vatican. Again disappointment.

There was serious trouble ahead. In October 1942 an *Abwehr* agent from Munich was arrested for trying to take foreign currency across the border to Jewish refugees in Switzerland. Under *Gestapo* questioning he broke down and talked. The interrogators learned about Bonhoeffer's trip to Sweden. On April 5, 1943, the *Gestapo* arrested Bonhoeffer and Dohnanyi. *Abwehr* chief Hans Oster was forced to resign and was placed under house arrest. The *Gestapo* did not know that it had struck at the heart of the conspiracy.

Bonhoeffer was taken to the military prison at Tegel in Berlin as a counterintelligence agent under suspicion. At first he misled his questioners. Only later was he to be implicated in the plot against Hitler.

Tegel Prison

In *Letters and Papers from Prison*, most widely read and quoted of his works, Bonhoeffer wrote sensitively about the problems of identification which face the Christian in the present century. He also gave an extraordinary picture of the military prison at Tegel.

For the first night he was locked in an admission cell. The blankets on his bed had so foul a smell that, even though it was cold, it was impossible to use them. The next morning a piece of bread was thrown into Bonhoeffer's cell: he had to pick it up from the floor. Every day from morning to night he heard the sound of beatings of prisoners held for interrogation.

"After 48 hours they returned my Bible to me. It had been searched to see whether I had smuggled inside it a saw, razor blades, or the like. For the next twelve days the door was opened only for bringing food in and putting the bucket out."

Placed in a more spacious cell, Bonhoeffer was offered larger rations, but he refused because "that would have been at the expense of other prisoners."

The tone set by the warders, Bonhoeffer reported, was to act in the most evil and brutal way. The building resounded with their vile and insulting abuse. They ranted and raved at the unfortunates in their charge. The pastor tried to have a quiet word about treatment of others but he had no success.

There were 700 prisoners to be fed and the food was inadequate. When doctors or officers inspected the quality of rations, there was always a nourishing sauce made of meat or cream added to the plates. But usually the meat intended for prisoners had all the goodness boiled out of it in the cauldrons where the staff food was cooked. Relatives who visited the prison were strictly forbidden to bring in any articles of food.

Although most prisoners asked for work, many of those detained for investigation spent the days without any activity. They were allowed three books a week from a mediocre library. Games of every kind, including chess, were forbidden. There were no religious services. During the winter months, the inmates often had to sit in the dark for several hours because the guards were too lazy to switch on the cell lights. They were not allowed to lie on their beds until the last call so that they had to sit for hours in the dark.

The prisoners were exposed to air raids with no protection whatever. During such raids, frantic inmates shouted and screamed in terror. The only way a prisoner could communicate with the staff in case of emergency was by putting out a flag. The signal was often ignored for hours. If a prisoner knocked on the door he was given a volley of abuse. Bonhoeffer reported that he had known prisoners to be kicked into sick bay—one had acute appendicitis and the other was suffering from prolonged hysterical convulsions. Some were bound in chains for their interrogation and trial. "The men who empty the buckets and bring around the food receive the same small amount of soap for washing as the ordinary prisoners and even for the latter it is hardly enough."

Bonhoeffer from experience described the degrading punishments, food, and living conditions of the prisoners, most of whom were intended to return to the front as combatants. Some to the left and right of his cell were condemned to death and were awaiting execution. The sympathetic pastor did his best for these unfortunates. Most he could help only through his prayers:

> I heard outside a hasty, muffled tread,
> Near my cell it suddenly stops dead.
> I go all cold and hot,
> I know, oh, I know what. . . .
> I go with you, brother, to that place
> And hear your last words, face to face:
> 'Brother, when I cease to be,
> Pray for me.'

Bonhoeffer's fellow-prisoners were enormously impressed by the humane pastor in their midst. When one inmate let fall an anti-Semitic remark, Bonhoeffer immediately cut him off. He developed a close relationship with Italian Professor Gaetano Latmiral, who had been arrested in Germany after the Badoglio *Putsch* as a bearer of "technical secrets." After the war Latmiral described his relationship with Bonhoeffer at Tegel: "He explained to me the meaning of many passages in the Gospel and told me that he was writing a poem on the death of Moses, when Moses climbed Mount Nebo and God showed him, before he died, the land that would one day belong to his people, but that he would enter. He loved the theme. . . . He also spoke of the tragic fate of the German people, whose qualities and short-comings he knew. He told me that it was difficult to desire its defeat, but that it was necessary. . . . He observed that Wagner's music was for him an expression of barbarous pagan psychology. . . . The leading German families had in part expiated their guilt by trying to remove Hitler, though far too late. He said he was not sure that he would see the end. . . . He hoped that he would be able to accept death without fear, in the belief that it was in a just cause. . . . He was always so interesting and good-humored. He was the best man and the most gifted man I have ever met."

Letters to His Parents

The pastor's notes to his parents sent from Tegel Prison from April 14, 1943, on, give a clear picture of warm relationships in the Bonhoeffer family. Dietrich was allowed to write only every ten days. He was anxious to calm their fears. In his first letter he informed them that strangely enough the discomforts one generally associated with prison life, the physical hardships, hardly bothered him at all. He had enough to eat in the mornings, even with dry bread. The hard prison bed did not worry him a bit, and he got plenty of sleep. "A violent mental upheaval, such as a sudden arrest, brings with it a need to take one's own mental bearings, and come to terms with an entirely new situation. ... I am not so unused to being alone as other people are, and it turns out to be a good spiritual Turkish bath. The only thing that disturbs me or would bother me is the thought that you would be tormented by anxiety about me, and that you are not sleeping or eating properly. Forgive me for causing you so much worry. It seems that a hostile fate is more to blame than I am."

Here the good pastor was caught in the coils of a gangster state and his main worry was about the reaction of his parents. Spring was coming and the prisoner was happy that his father and mother would have plenty to do in the garden.

On April 25 Dietrich, now allowed a letter, wrote that he was having a happy Easter. "Good Friday and Easter free us to think about other things far beyond our own personal destiny, about the ultimate meaning of life, suffering, and events. Things are all right, and I am well."

On May 5, after four weeks in prison, Dietrich wrote that he was now getting used to prison in a kind of natural and unconscious way, though he had been able from the outset to accept his lot consciously. He told how he spent his time reading, learning, and working. He told of reading in Jean Paul that "the only joys that can stand the fires of adversity are the joys of home." "Thank you again very much for remembering me every day, and for all that you are doing and putting up with on my account.'' The obedient son, clamped into prison, was thinking of his parents and the effect of his imprisonment on them.

In his letter of May 15, 1943, Dietrich told his parents what prison life was like:

> The situation in itself—that is every single moment—is, perhaps, no different here from anywhere else. I read, meditate, write, walk up and down my cell—taking care not to rub myself against the walls like a polar bear. The important thing is to do what one still has and can do—there is plenty left—and not be dominated by the thought of what one cannot do, or by feelings of resentment or discontent.

> I am sure I never realized as clearly as I do here what the Bible and Luther meant by 'temptation.' Suddenly, and for no apparent physical or psychological reason, the peace and composure that were supporting one are jarred, and the heart becomes, in Jeremiah's expressive words, 'deceitful above all things, and desperately corrupt.' Who can understand it?. . .

> One of my predecessors here has scribbled on the cell door: 'In 100 years it will be all over.' That was his way of trying to counteract the feeling that life spent here is a blank. . . . 'My times are in thy hand' [Ps. 13.15] is the answer of the Bible. But in the Bible there is also the quotation that threatens to dominate everything here: 'How long, O Lord?' [Ps. 13].*

Again and again Dietrich spoke of what a blessing it was to belong to a large, closely knit family where each trusted the other and stood by him. He thanks his parents for their flowers, ''always a great blessing,'' for they bring color and life into his dreary cell. ''Above all,'' he wrote on August 17, 1943, ''don't worry about me more than you can help. I am keeping my end up, and my mind is quite calm. How good it is to know from previous experience that we are really not too upset at all by the

*Letters and Papers from Prison, op. cit., pp. 45–46.

air raids. Anyway, you, even as I, have something better to do than be thinking about possible air raids. Prison life gives one, almost as a matter of course, a kind of detachment from the cares and excitements of the day.''

The dutiful son kept his parents informed about his health. He reported that on Sunday night he had ''stupidly'' gotten gastric catarrh and had a temperature, but now it was normal again. He would go to bed as a precaution. ''I do not want to be ill on any account.'' He reported an important event in his prison life when he was given a knife and fork instead of the everpresent spoon for his meals.

At Christmas time, eight and one half months after he was taken to Tegel Prison, Dietrich assured his parents that he was not going to be depressed by a lonely Christmas. It would always take its place, he wrote, among the unusual Christmases he had spent in Spain, America, and England. In later years, he would look back on his time in prison, not with shame, but with a certain pride. ''That is the only thing no one can take from me.'' He warned his parents that the New Year would bring a great deal of anxiety and disturbance.

Disturbance, indeed! The New Year was to be the last year of Dietrich's life on earth.

Road to the Gallows

The death of Dietrich Bonhoeffer was a tragedy of heart-breaking import. Liberating American troops were only a few miles away with the Third Reich in its death throes. Adolf Hitler, quintessential heel as always, was in a state of hysteria, virtually a raving lunatic in his Berlin bunker, moving inexorably toward his special *Götterdämmerung,* his Wagnerian Twilight of the Gods. The Brown Napoleon, on the verge of utter defeat, railed against his fate. The German people, unworthy of his genius, had abandoned him. Again the nihilist reaction. Destroy everything, make Germany a wasteland, let the onrushing Allies capture nothing of value! And at this late date, Hitler denounced those German ''traitors'' who had failed to support him in his ''noble'' work. Send more victims to the hangman's noose—better late than never! Gentle humanitarian Dietrich Bonhoeffer was included among the unfortunates.

February 7, 1945. Twenty of the most important prisoners in the Prinz Albrecht Strasse in Berlin were ordered to assemble in the prison yard. Two trucks were ready for departure. Among the victims readied for slaughter were Adm. Wilhelm Canaris, head of the *Abwehr* and one of the most important conspirators; Kurt von Schuschnigg, one-time Chancellor of Austria (later freed), and Bonhoeffer. One truck was bound for the concentration camp at Buchenwald, the other for dreaded Flossenbürg.

The truck on which Bonhoeffer was placed headed for Buchenwald. Here Bonhoeffer, spending the last weeks of his life, met Captain S. Payne Best, a British officer arrested on the border of Holland as a consequence of a German Intelligence hoax. (See below.) Best had been a prisoner in Sachsenwald during the last year and had been transferred to Buchenwald just two weeks after Bonhoeffer was brought there.

At Buchenwald the British intelligence officer and the German pastor had cells opposite each other. The Briton soon developed a deep respect for his fellow-prisoner, of whom he painted an extraordinary picture. "Bonhoeffer," he wrote, "was different, just quite calm and normal, seemingly perfect at his ease. His soul really shone in the dark desperation of prison." And again: "Bonhoeffer was all humility and sweetness. He always seemed to diffuse an atmosphere of happiness, of joy in every smallest event in life, and of deep gratitude for the mere fact that he was still alive. He was one of the very few men I have ever met to whom his god was real, and ever close to him."

Bonhoeffer and Best, German and Briton, became good friends. The pastor was fascinated by Best's war career. In early September 1939, British intelligence agents at The Hague received word from a German refugee in the Netherlands that German officers representing a military conspiracy against the Nazis wanted to make contact with British authorities. London assigned Capt. Best and Maj. T. H. Stevens to meet the Germans. After complicated secret maneuvers, the two British agents met three German officers, including a Major Schaemel.

The latter told them that high officers in Germany were appalled by the losses suffered in Poland, that they wanted peace, and that they were prepared to capture Hitler and open negotiations for peace.

Best and Stevens arrived at the little frontier town of Venlo on November 8, 1939, where they were supposed to meet an important German general high in the ranks of the conspirators. Instead, they were taken into custody by a detachment of armed German troops from across the frontier and brought to Berlin. There they learned to their dismay that "Major Schaemel" was actually Walter Schellenberg, chief of the counterespionage division of the *Gestapo*.

The Venlo incident was important for Hitler because he could claim that Dutchmen were involved and that the Netherlands had violated neutrality. The *Fuehrer* now had his excuse for invading the Netherlands. Best remained a prisoner of the Germans for the remainder of the war.

Best did what he could to help his fellow-prisoner. He adopted an imperious manner toward his guards, an attitude he had perfected after five years' imprisonment in Sachsenhausen. He shared his possessions, including two small pocket chess sets, with fellow-inmates and freely lent his books and playing cards to others. Most of all, he admired Bonhoeffer, who had "thrown himself into the hands of God, taking seriously not our own sufferings, but the sufferings of God in the world."

On Easter Sunday, April 1, 1945, the prisoners could hear American guns in the distance. Hitler's Reich was collapsing in grim chaos. For prisoners at Buchenwald it had become a race between liberation or summary execution. They knew that the camp commandant had received standing orders—before the guards abandoned the camp all political prisoners were to be shot, or they would be moved on twenty minutes' notice.

For forty-eight hours the prisoners listened to guns booming in the distance. Their thoughts may well be imagined. Then, late on the evening of Tuesday, April 3, 1945, seventeen inmates held in a windowless cellar in Buchenwald, including Bonhoeffer and Best, were packed into a van driven by gas generated by burning wood. There was scarcely room enough for eight men.

The driver stopped the truck every hour in order to clean the generator. There was nothing to eat or drink.

Then began a strange odyssey as the truck headed southeast. The three guards were in a quandary as to what to do with their charges, who themselves were mystified by their fate. Stopping at a village close to Flossenbürg, the guards were told that the camp was full and the commandant would not take them.

Meanwhile in Berlin, Hitler was told of the discovery of Adm. Canaris's diary, which named Bonhoeffer as one of the conspirators. Infuriated, he ordered Ernst Kaltenbrunner, chief of the Security Service, to see to "the immediate execution of the traitors." The next day the three guards from Buchenwald on the wandering truck were relieved and ten security guards of the *SD* took over. "Prisoner Bonhoeffer," said one of the *SD* men, "come with us."

Bonhoeffer took leave of his companions. Aware now of his fate, he turned to Best and said: "If you get home safely, I would like you to take a message to my friend George Bell, the Bishop of Chichester. Tell him that for me this is the end but also the beginning. With him I believe in the principle of our universal Christian brotherhood, which rises above all national interests, and that our victory is certain. Tell him, too, that I have never forgotten his words at our last meeting." The two men shook hands and Bonhoeffer walked with the waiting *SD* men to their car.

After driving all day, the guards and their prisoners reached Flossenbürg in the late evening. At midnight two uniformed guards brought Bonhoeffer along with five others before a summary court-martial. The "trial" continued throughout the night. All the prisoners were found guilty of treason.

The executions took place at dawn on Monday, April 9, 1945. A decade later the camp doctor described the last moments of Bonhoeffer and his fellow prisoners:

On the morning of the day between five and six o'clock the prisoners, among them Adm. Canaris, General Oster, and Judge Advocate General Sack, were led out of their cells and the verdicts read to them. Through the half-open door in one room of the huts I saw Pastor Bonhoeffer, still in his prison clothes, taking off his prison garb, kneeling on the floor in fervent prayer to God.

I was most deeply moved by the way this lovable man prayed, so pious and so convinced that God was hearing his prayers. At the place of execution, he again said a short prayer and then climbed the steps to the gallows. He was courageous and composed. His death came in a few seconds. I have seldom seen a man die so completely submissive to the will of God.

Like the others, Bonhoeffer was ordered to strip. He walked naked down the stone steps through the trees to the gallows. After kneeling for a few moments to touch the earth, he mounted the steps. A guard removed his glasses before placing the noose around his neck.

The body was taken down and burned.

Aftermath

In London, hatred of Germans was still at a peak. But on July 27, 1945, Bishop Bell led a memorial service for Bonhoeffer at Holy Trinity Church, Kingsway. This public ceremony in honor of a German was an unusual event in those stirring days. In his sermon, Bishop Bell spoke sadly of Bonhoeffer's martyrdom:

> His death is a death for Germany—indeed for Europe, too . . . his death, like his life, made a fact of the deepest value in the witness of the Confessional Church. As one of a noble company of martyrs of differing traditions, he represents both the resistance of the believing soul, in the name of God, to the assault of evil, and also the moral and political revolt of the human conscience against injustice and cruelty. He and his fellow prisoners are indeed built upon the foundation of the Apostles and the Prophets. . . .

> For him . . . there is the resurrection from the dead; for Germany redemption and resurrection, if God pleases to

lead the nation through men animated by his spirit, holy and
humble and brave like him; for the Church, not only in that
Germany which he loved, but the Church Universal which
was greater to him than nations, the hope of a new life.

The difference in character between the brooding Nazi dictator and the gracious evangelical theologian reveals a striking
contrast in man's nature. On the one hand, a disgruntled, fanatical Austrian, the personification of evil in this world, wielding
complete political power without the slightest regard for human
decency. On the other hand, a benevolent young pastor, a
Christlike personality, the epitome of the Good German, who
placed his life on the line to serve his compatriots.

Both men were destined for a violent death—Hitler by his
own hand, Bonhoeffer by order of the *Fuehrer* who had lost all
control of himself. Adolf Hitler's legacy is a dark one—that of
a mass murderer responsible for the death of millions. The Nazi
Fuehrer earned the contempt not only of his countrymen but of
people everywhere who suffered from his machinations. In contrast, Dietrich Bonhoeffer has won a global reputation as the
gentle soul who refused to accept Nazi barbarism.

The business of living in this world is at best a precarious
one. The lives of millions were snuffed out during the grotesque
era of the Third Reich. Joseph Conrad said it best: "Life makes
me feel like a cornered blind rat waiting to be clubbed." The
Hitler era, with its deplorable excesses, gave meaning to Conrad's judgment. Bonhoeffer's life was a ray of light in the dark
days of a cruel and brutal regime.

Bonhoeffer's "religionless Christianity," bolstered by his
martyrdom, had an important effect on postwar Protestantism
throughout the world. The ideas of this magnificent man survived his death.

2*

GEN. LUDWIG BECK:
The Military

I don't understand politics very well, but I don't have to understand in order to know what has to be done.

Man of Conscience

I swear by God this sacred oath that I shall render unconditional obedience to Adolf Hitler, the Fuehrer of the German Reich, Supreme Commander of the Armed Forces, and that I shall at all times be prepared, as a brave soldier, to give my life for this oath.

ON AUGUST 2, 1934, THE DAY ON WHICH PRESIDENT PAUL VON Hindenburg died, Hitler required every officer and soldier in the German Armed Forces to make this solemn declaration of loyalty to his person instead of to the Constitution. Any deviation from this pledge was to be regarded as treason.

At that time Ludwig Beck was serving as *Chef des Truppenamtes* (Adjutant General), a key post in the *Reichswehr* Ministry. Like many other officers he felt shackled by this personal oath of allegiance to Hitler, and he resented its imposition.

Beck was tall and thin with chiseled, straight features and a kind of benevolent expression. But behind the bland exterior was an inflexible will and, unlike many of his fellow-officers, a man of unusually high intelligence and culture. Both in appearance and personality he gave the impression of a mild-mannered university professor or a scholar devoted to a lifetime of research on some esoteric subject. As a career army officer he believed in war only as a necessary last resort and hoped to conduct it in the Bismarckian way—overwhelming force and a quick end to hostilities.

For three years, from 1935 to 1938, Beck was chief of the Army General Staff, the élite of leadership responsible for over-all military planning and preparation for emergencies. In this key position he could make critical decisions about manpower and the implementation of land warfare. He was aware of Hitler's suspicions about the loyalty of the officers' corps and about his efforts to increase Party influence at the expense of professional officers. He came into increasing conflict with a leader he suspected of advocating a war of conquest instead of a defensive stance based on moral principles. The *Fuehrer* rejected Beck's repeated advice that Germany was not really ready for war. This was precisely the kind of general Hitler did not want. Hitler willingly accepted Beck's resignation in 1938.

From the beginning Beck was nauseated by Nazi ideology. To him it was horrendous. More important, as a professional officer he opposed the *Fuehrer*'s obvious intention of using the military to serve his own political goals. As a patriot he had no intention of fading away at a time when he believed his country to be in danger. Instead, he became the only general who did everything possible to obstruct or retard Hitler's plans. The quiet, introverted army officer eventually became the acknowledged leader of the German Resistance.

Beck was noted for his careful study of any matter before him before acting on it. He came to the conclusion that the spell cast upon the German people could only be maintained as long as Hitler was alive. He was convinced that a bold stroke was necessary, one that would at the same time relieve the German army of its oath of loyalty. He urged his fellow-conspirators to drop their plans to take Hitler alive. After some debate in the fall of 1942, the plotters agreed with Beck and went ahead with plans for assassinating Hitler.

Moral and religious convictions compelled Beck to take his stand. ''A moral man,'' he said, ''is the maker and conductor of policy, a man who in the final analysis is ruled by the inner moral law of conscience.'' For him the Nazi regime was inexpressibly wicked, and militarily it could lead only to disaster for the Fatherland. In his mind, assassination was the only means of saving the country from destruction. It was Hitler's life against millions of others, and only his death could put an end to the senseless killing.

An irrevocable decision—and it was to cost Beck his own life.

The True Professional

Ludwig Beck was born on June 29, 1880, in Biebrich in the Rhineland. Not a Junker or even a Prussian by birth, he was descended from a line of Hessian army officers. His father, abandoning the military tradition of the family, became a civil engineer and eventually an industrialist in metallurgy with ownership of an iron mine in the Rhineland. With his two brothers Ludwig grew up in a home in which the moral virtues were stressed. After finishing secondary school in Wiesbaden, he decided to revive the family tradition and chose the career of professional soldier.

In 1911 Beck was attached to the General Staff. During World War I he served in various capacities. After the war he was rapidly promoted with various commands in the *Reichswehr*. Among his colleagues he had the reputation of a good officer, a man of integrity and of wide-ranging cultural interests. They saw him as a heavy-thinking philosopher who often spoke in terms of the Kantian categorical imperative even for the fighting man—one's behavior should be governed by principles which one would have govern the conduct of all people. There was no hint that this moral man would one day become the nerve center of the German Resistance.

In 1930, at the height of the Weimar Republic, Beck appeared as a witness for the defense at the trial of three lieutenants who were accused of spreading Nazi propaganda in the *Reichswehr*. The subaltern officers were indicted before the Supreme Court at Leipzig on a charge of high treason. The trial aroused great interest because Hitler was also a witness. British historian John W. Wheeler-Bennett implied that Beck's testimony revealed that he was infected with Nazi doctrines and that he was guilty of ''cynical casuistry.'' From the viewpoint of subsequent developments, there was really little basis for the charge. Beck's testimony may well have been no more than the expected concern of a senior officer for his subordinates.

During the first few years of the Hitler regime, Beck believed that it would work out well for Germany. The *Fuehrer* sensed that he had won Beck's confidence when in 1935 he elevated Beck to Chief of the Army General Staff. Beck accepted because, although from the beginning he was suspicious of Nazi ideology, he could work from the inside to prevent any moves to aggressive war. He would make the army an instrument of defense, so strong that no enemy would be inclined to attack Germany. This, in Beck's view, would prevent a general European war.

For a time Beck was inclined to see Hitler as a victim rather than the promoter of illegal acts committed by the Nazis. He had the mistaken belief that it might be possible to get rid of the *Gestapo* and other Nazi organizations and restore law and order, while at the same time retaining Hitler as chief of state. Beck would change his mind.

Alienation

Beck became more and more uncomfortable with the actions of Hitler. His frustration turned to anger in early 1938 with the Blomberg-Fritsch crisis, when the *Fuehrer* dismissed two of his leading generals after distasteful personal scandals. Field Marshal Werner von Blomberg, Minister of Defense and Supreme Commander of the *Wehrmacht*, the new armed forces, and Col. Gen. Werner Freiherr von Fritsch, Commander-in-Chief of the Army, were two of the highest officers in the Third Reich. Both were present at the historic Hossbach Conference on November 5, 1937, when Hitler made clear his intention of winning *Lebensraum* (living space) by force. Both officers were appalled and shaken by Hitler's objectives, and both were out of office within three months. In each case the dismissal was accompanied by a scandal, manipulated and used to destroy the careers of the two officers.

In the late months of 1937 Blomberg, a widower, began to consider seriously the thought of marrying his secretary, a Fräulein Eva Gruhn, despite what was said to be her questionable past. The wedding took place on January 12, 1938, with Hitler himself and Hermann Goering present as witnesses. Almost immediately gossipmongers began to attack the new *Frau Generalfeldmarschall*. There were complaints about Blomberg's "disgracing the officers' corps." Unhappily for Blomberg and his bride, there may have been some truth to the rumors.

The Berlin police gathered a dossier on the field marshal's new wife and it was not a favorable one. Goering brought it to Hitler's attention. Angered because he had attended the wedding, the *Fuehrer* ordered Blomberg's dismissal, which came on February 4, 1938. He also sent a letter thanking Blomberg for his services during the past five years in helping build the new *Wehrmacht*. Blomberg and his bride disappeared from the military scene in Berlin and went into exile at Capri.

Fritsch was involved in an even uglier situation. He also had opposed Hitler at the Hossbach Conference and he, too, was slated for dismissal. He had to be eliminated in one way or another, and the means were soon found. Fritsch's dossier included what was said to be evidence that he was guilty of homosexual offenses under Section 175 of the Criminal Code. He was called before Hitler, Goering, and Himmler to answer the charges. Himmler produced an obscure witness named Schmidt who was prepared to testify that he had observed Fritsch commit a homosexual offense with a young boy *(Lustknabe)* named Bavarian Joe near the Potsdam Railroad Station in November 1934.

Stunned and humiliated, Fritsch hotly denied the charge. A lifelong bachelor who had little to do with the opposite sex, he was especially vulnerable to accusations of this sort. He demanded and obtained a trial before an army court of honor, which acquitted him "for proven innocence." His personal honor was vindicated, but his career was ended. On February 4, 1938, the same day on which he had written a cordial letter to the dismissed Blomberg, Hitler sent an icy communication to Fritsch accepting his resignation.

On August 11, 1938, Fritsch was publicly rehabilitated. Only a few days after the outbreak of World War II, he was hit by a Polish machine-gun bullet while in a field on the outskirts of Warsaw. Colleagues believed that, mortified beyond endurance, he had deliberately sought death.

After these two resignations, Hitler named himself Supreme Commander of the Armed Forces, a post which allowed him to solidify his control over the military and embark upon his program of aggression. The lowly dispatch runner of World War I was now top man of Germany's armed forces.

Meanwhile, Beck was becoming thoroughly disgusted with Hitler's policies and specifically with his handling of military matters. He found it altogether unacceptable that the officer corps should submit to the what he believed to be outrageous humiliation that had been accorded Gen. von Fritsch. It appeared to him to be an impossible situation—honorable professional officers, bloated with stipends and decorations, had accepted the Fritsch dismissal, a matter which Beck could not reconcile with his own conscience.

Even more, Beck was dismayed by Hitler's obvious intention of invading Czechoslovakia, which he saw as a part of the *Fuehrer*'s adventurous policies based on dangerous intuition instead of careful military planning. There was some reason for his concern. On May 30, 1938, Hitler had called his senior officers of the armed forces to a secret meeting and informed them of his "unalterable decision . . . to smash Czechoslovakia in the foreseeable future by military action." Beck immediately raised strong objection. If that were done, he said, the inevitable result would be a larger war for which the armed forces, still in the process of being built up, would not be able to cope with, especially in view of the precarious economic situation in the country.

Then came a strike at Hitler's raw nerves. When it came to a military commitment of the armed forces, Beck said, it was essential that the leadership of the Reich take into consideration the opinion of military experts. "Differences of opinion about the relationship between policy and the conduct of war, as well as gaps between political claims and goals on the one hand and the military capacity of the state on the other hand, can be the first and perhaps decisive step toward the loss of a war. History has told us that often enough wars have been lost before they began. The favorable or unfavorable outcome of a war can almost always be laid at the door of policy.''

Angry reaction by the *Fuehrer*. He resented the frankness of his Chief of the General Staff of the Army. He was the master of Germany and he had no intention of allowing anyone, even a top military man, to dictate policy to the Leader.

As a means of winning support for his views, Beck sought a meeting with Gen. Walther von Brauchitsch, new Commander-in-Chief of the Army as successor to Fritsch. Brauchitsch avoided him and went on leave. Beck believed it to be inconceivable that Hitler might involve Germany in this adventure without consulting his General Staff. On Brauchitsch's return to Berlin, Beck sent him a memorandum, already shown to fellow-generals, holding that the army simply was not ready for war and that economic collapse would surely follow for Germany and all Europe. Beck had two aims: he wanted to convince not only Brauchitsch but also others that as professional soldiers it was important that they do everything possible to avoid a war for which Germany was not prepared.

Beck's memorandum, dated July 16, 1938, issued a serious warning:

> Final decisions involving the survival of the nation are involved. History will surely place a blood guilt on these leaders if they do not follow their professional and political conscience. As soldiers the obedience has its limit at the point where their knowledge, conscience, and responsibility forbid execution of an order.
>
> If their advice or warnings are not listened to in such a situation, then they have not only the right, but also the duty to the people and history, to resign. If all of them act together, the implementation of a war action becomes impossible. It is possible for them to save their country from the worst possible fate of complete ruin.
>
> Lack of greatness and comprehension of his task is shown when a soldier in a high position during these times sees his

duty only in the limited scope of his military duties, without
realizing his ultimate responsibility before the entire nation.
Unusual times demand unusual action.

Measured words—revealing the character of the man.
Clearly Beck was hoping for agreement from his fellow-gener-
als to halt Hitler in his plans for aggression. But he failed.
Brauchitsch had no intention of following what he regarded as
a dangerous sentiment. In any event, word got to Hitler about
Beck's memorandum.

Indignation and rage from the summit. Hitler ordered Beck to
retract his opinion. He would grant an audience. The *Fuehrer*
was adamant—he would not allow Beck or any of his generals
to step beyond their military duties and dictate foreign policy.
He would put this loud-mouthed officer in his place and show
him who was guiding the country's destiny. There was only one
Fuehrer and these pipsqueak generals must follow him.

The interview was stormy. Beck urged the *Fuehrer* to
promise that there would be no diplomatic provocations without
previous consultation with the General Staff. Hitler, convinced
that he was only helping "ethnic Germans" in the endangered
Sudetenland, said curtly that Beck's role as Chief of the General
Staff was simply to follow orders and suggested that he do so
without any further discussion. "All this talk about 'shared
responsibilities' has gone on far too long. The General Staff
reports on matters of military command—and nothing more.
That goes for its chief as well."

Beck replied that it was impossible for him to pass on an
order of which he disapproved. He, therefore, was submitting
his resignation. Hitler was angered: he did not like the idea of
any officer who had taken his oath of loyalty to resign of his
own free will. He, the Leader, would himself dismiss anyone
who no longer merited his confidence. He asked Brauchitsch to
intercede with Beck and have him withdraw his resignation.
Beck said that he had merely intended his offer of resignation
as a gesture of protest—he wanted to maintain the right of the
General Staff for consultation and to stop the diminution of the
generals' authority.

There was no meeting of minds. Beck resigned his post on August 18, 1938. He had hoped that more officers would follow his lead, but he was disappointed. The other generals did not follow suit.

The *Fuehrer* was relieved by the resignation of the blunt-spoken Beck. At one time he had thought highly of the man, but now he was glad to get rid of "the old sniveler" and "the barracks-room lawyer."

Keitel on Beck

A complicating factor was that Beck was not popular with other officers at his level. They tended to regard him as an impractical agitator always seeking listeners among his colleagues. They saw him as a once flawless officer who had some good virtues but was "too intellectual" and had developed into an incorrigible defeatist. Among those who were irked by him was Gen. Wilhelm Keitel, Chief State of the German High Command of the Armed Forces between 1938 and 1945 and second only to Hitler in directing German forces in World War II. In his memoirs Keitel told how he had interviews with Beck in 1937 for hours on end but was never able to move him. "He was annoyed that anyone should dare to issue directives to his Army."

Keitel, who was destined to hang at Nuremberg after the war, expressed his contempt on the occasion of Beck's resignation in 1938. The judgment came from one of Hitler's most loyal officers:

> I wept no tears over Beck in view of the shameless way he had treated me; I was always the first to recognize his great virtues, and I would never have thought him capable of selling his soul to treasonable intriguers as early as 1938, or of being their spiritual leader from that point on. One can seek his motives only in his injured vanity and his abysmal hatred for Hitler; that was why this formerly impeccable officer made common cause with our enemies and stiffened

their resolve while awaiting our overthrow, something Beck was impotent to bring about himself.

He was no leader, as he was to show as a conspirator by his pathetic behavior when there was still time to act and when the plot—even though it had gone wrong—demanded a man of action and not the *cunctator* [a person who delays] that he has always been; witness his three futile attempts at putting a bullet into his head while sitting in a chair!*

Forum of the Conspiracy

After his resignation Beck returned to his home in the Goethestrasse in Berlin. Here he became a popular figure in the neighborhood—the tall, stiff general who always looked straight ahead and who always seemed to have a mournful expression on his face. He read for hours in his many-volumed library and puttered around in his garden. He seemed to be the perfect example of the inactive, retired general. He had done his level best to thwart Hitler in the Nazi plans for aggression. He had failed—and in his view only destruction and chaos could follow.

But the 58-year-old retired general was by no means ready to fade away. Always interested in philosophy and the art of conversation, he turned his interest toward the Wednesday Club *(Mittwochsgesellschaft)*, an exclusive honorary society and discussion group which had been formed in the 18th century as an informal adjunct of the Prussian Academy of Sciences. Later, the salon attracted scholars and intellectuals as well as right-wing conservatives who delighted in talking about history, art, science, and literature. The group was limited to about seventeen members and a new member was admitted only on the death of one of their number. Meetings were held on the second Wednesday of every month. The host of each session would read a paper in the field in which he was an expert. The meal

*The Memoirs of Field-Marshal Keitel, ed. by Walter Gorlitz (New York: Stein and Day, 1966), p. 68.

was almost modest according to club rules, so that even the poorest scholar could entertain his guests in the same style.

Even more, the academics, industrialists, civil servants, and military officers of the Wednesday Club were much concerned by Hitler's policies, which they were sure were leading the country to an unwanted war. In time the Wednesday Club became a theoretical forum of resistance to the Hitler regime. Such members as diplomat Christian Albrecht Ulrich von Hassell, Prussian Minister of Finance Johannes Popitz, and Beck were intellectuals who later formed an inner circle of opposition and conspiracy. The men of the Wednesday Club did not hesitate to show their distaste for Hitler and his regime.

Gestapo authorities suspected members of the Wednesday Club and held most of them under surveillance. Hitler sensed that it was best not to interfere with the proceedings of the society, even though he held all its members in contempt. They spoke freely among themselves and from their ranks came several of the most important conspirators against Hitler.

Beck was frank in the Wednesday Club sessions. He denied the justification for total war. The wisest course in warfare, he said, was to seek a moderate political purpose, end the war quickly, and always "lead to a good peace in the sense expressed by the great Chancellor Bismarck." Modern warfare, he insisted, could be limited in its aims and development. There must be a strong ethical policy behind the war effort and the technical conduct of hostilities must be promoted along ethical lines. War must be "a political instrument, a means kept subordinate to policy." It must be grounded on a new moral idealism within the state and within its relationship to other peoples. Above all, the responsible political leader must be a moral human being.

Beck told his colleagues at the Wednesday Club that Hitler was the wrong man in the wrong position. They were inclined to agree with him. The man was not a moral human being controlled by his inner conscience, but a dangerous political adventurer who was sure to drag the nation to the edge of destruction. He had no sense of fairness, justice, or wisdom. He was unable to look beyond narrow military considerations to the

goal of ethical idealism. His policies had harmed the good name
of Germany. Germans must rid themselves of this dictator.

From Dissent to Conspiracy

Beck resigned his army post because he was convinced that
Hitler, on the excuse that Germany needed living space, had
decided on a war that was not grounded on absolute necessity.
Furthermore, with his knowledge of the nature of war, Beck
believed that Hitler's "local war" was bound to lead to world
conflict that would inevitably end in German defeat. At first
Beck tried desperately to get other generals to make common
cause with him to ward off the danger that a small war would
lead to total war, a conflict which Germany was not prepared to
fight and which she would surely lose. In his view it was madness to misuse the *Wehrmacht* as the tool of an adventurous
foreign policy.

Beck the military officer was the exact opposite of the National Socialist ideal. A man of integrity and intellectual refine-
ment, he had worked hard in the defense of his country. His
colleagues noted that he would often miss lunch rather than
leave his desk and at times did not quit his office until the early
hours of the morning. He was the type of officer who tried to see
both sides of a problem and often, because he had his doubts
would take his time in making a decision. He was completely
trustworthy: his word was his bond.

These characteristics carried over into Beck's days of conspiracy after his resignation. Once his conscience brought him
into opposition, he had no intention of sitting idly by while
Hitler recklessly pursued his dangerous course.

Beck found a kindred spirit in Gen. Franz Halder, who in
1938 succeeded him as Chief of the General Staff of the Army
and held that post until 1942. Soon after his installation Halder
informed Beck that he would have no part in any movement
opposing Hitler unless it was based on a firm legal and moral
foundation. Halder was torn between his opposition to Nazism
and his oath of loyalty. He indicated that he was inclined to
favor a *coup d'état*, but he would not hear of assassination.

Even before the Czechoslovak crisis he spoke of his contempt for Hitler. Diplomat Hans Bernd Gisevius, a member of the conspiracy, quoted Halder's estimate: "The criminal Hitler is deliberately dragging us into a war, no doubt to gratify his pathological sexual impulses and blood lust. He is one of those revolutionary absolutists who feel that everything he sees around him must be destroyed." Halder could not reconcile his beliefs as a Catholic with Hitler's amorality and disposition to repeat one lie after another. This man, he said, was "the gravedigger of his country as well as the incarnation of evil in the world."

At the time of the Czechoslovak crisis, Halder, joined by Beck and other high-ranking officers, proposed to seize the government by a military *Putsch* in Berlin and install a parliamentary regime. But the plot never went beyond the discussion stage. Halder felt that the overthrow of the Nazi regime would have to await some outstanding reversal—a diplomatic or military defeat that would destroy the *Fuehrer's* prestige.

The plot soon collapsed. Halder made his views clear: "A breach of my oath to the *Fuehrer* is not justified." It was difficult for him to reconcile any immediate solution with his oath of allegiance. Furthermore, he was opposed to any idea of killing Hitler. The *Fuehrer*, he said, could be arrested and made to answer for his crimes before a tribunal; better yet, be sequestered in an insane asylum. Halder was agreeable when another of the conspirators said that he had the coöperation of a well-known psychiatrist who was prepared to commit Hitler involuntarily and sign a certificate stating that the *Fuehrer* was insane.

Beck, in his abrupt way, felt that this proposed solution had little to recommend it. He saw Hitler as a cancerous growth on the German body politic and the only way to get rid of his barbaric influence was to remove him from this earth. The man must be handled as he had treated thousands of others. In the fall of 1942, this view, sponsored mainly by Beck, won through. The conspirators dropped all plans to take Hitler alive and decided on his assassination.

Both the military and civilian leaders of the conspiracy saw assassination as unethical and to be used only under the most extreme circumstances. They did not want to appear as revolutionary terrorists using assassination as a means of winning power. Nevertheless, under Beck's urging, even those who were opposed on religious grounds to the act of killing Hitler finally agreed to go along with the decision. In their minds there was just no other way left: every day thousands of soldiers were dying on the battlefields as well as many victims in the concentration camps. It was Hitler's life against the lives of millions.

"Appeal to the German People"

Although there were many differences among the conspirators, understandable enough considering the pressure they were under, such frictions were cast aside when basic problems were faced. During the course of the year 1943–44 the plotters reached agreement on the naming of a shadow government. Beck was chosen to be provisional Head of State after the elimination of Hitler.

In addition, there was an "Appeal to the German People," a statement which was to be signed by Beck. This document never came into force because of the failure of the July 20th *Putsch*. It took on importance because it expressed in dramatic terms the stand taken by Beck and his colleagues. Here were Germans speaking to Germans:

Germans!

In recent years terrible things have taken place before our very eyes. Against the advice of experts Hitler has sacrificed whole armies for *his* passion for glory, *his* megalomania, *his* blasphemous delusion that he was the chosen and favored instrument of Providence.

Not called to power by the German people, but becoming the Head of the Government by intrigues of the worst kind, he has spread confusion by his devilish arts and lies and by tremendous extravagance which on the surface seemed to bring prosperity to all, but which in reality plunged the German people into terrible debt. In order to remain in power, he added to this an unbridled reign of terror, destroyed law, outlawed decency, scorned the divine commands of pure humanity and destroyed the happiness of millions of human beings.

His insane disregard for all mankind could not fail to bring our nation to misfortune with deadly certainty; his self-imagined supremacy could not but bring ruin to our brave sons, fathers, husbands and brothers and his bloody terror against the defenseless could not but bring shame to the German name. His enormous lawlessness, oppression of conscience, crime and corruption in our Fatherland which has always been proud of its integrity and honesty. Truthfulness and veracity, virtues which even the simplest people think it their duty to inculcate in their children, are punished and persecuted. Thus public life and private activity are threatened by a deadly poison.

This must not be, this cannot go on. The lives and deaths of our men, women and children must no longer be abused for this purpose. We would not be worthy of our fathers, we would be despised by our children if we had not the courage to do everything, I repeat everything, to ward off this danger from ourselves and to achieve self-respect again. . . .

Germans!

Hitler's despotism has been broken. . . . Hitler has confused the minds and souls of the people by his devilish arts and lies, and by his tremendous extravagance, which seemed to bring prosperity to all; but which in reality has plunged us into debt and want, and has caused fatal disappointment, even outside of Germany. In order to remain in power he set up a reign of terror. There was a time when our people could be proud of its honesty and integrity. But Hitler scorned the divine commandments, destroyed the law, outlawed decency and ruined the happiness of millions. He disregarded honor and dignity, and the freedom and lives of other men. Countless Germans, as well as members of other nations, have for years been languishing in concentration camps, submitted to the most terrible torments and often to frightful torture. Many of them have perished. Our good name has been sullied by cruel mass murders.

With blood-stained hands Hitler has pursued his madman's course, leaving tears, sorrow and misery in his train.

With deadly certainty his lunatic disregard for all human impulses has brought misfortune to our people, and his self-imagined military genius has brought ruin to our brave soldiers. . . . This must not go on! We would not be worthy of our fathers, we would be despised by our children if we had not the courage to do everything, I repeat everything, to ward off this frightful danger from ourselves and to regain our self-respect.

Time without number Hitler has broken his oath he made to the people ten years ago by violating divine and human law. Therefore, no soldier, no civil servant, in fact no citizen is any longer bound to him by oath. . . .

Have courage and confidence! The task is a very heavy one. I cannot and will not make you empty promises. By hard work we will have to struggle in order once more to make our way forward and upward. But we will go this way in decency as free men and again find peace of conscience.

Let each one of you do his duty! Let each help to save the Fatherland!
Colonel-General Beck*

Forced Suicide

When Col. Count Claus von Stauffenberg returned to the War Ministry in the Bendlerstrasse in Berlin on the evening of July

*Constantine FitzGibbon, *Officers' Plot to Kill Hitler* (New York: Avon, 1956), Appendix, pp. 202–205.

20, 1944, he was certain that Hitler had been killed in the guest barracks of the field headquarters at Rastenburg, East Prussia. He was convinced that it was impossible for anyone to survive that tremendous blast which shattered the barracks room. Bodies had flown out of the smashed windows and thick clouds of smoke rose from the scene.

Then shock, amazement, and horror. Stauffenberg and his colleagues learned to their dismay that Hitler would soon speak over the radio. The intended victim had survived!

It was a dramatic scene as power slipped from the hands of those who planned to eliminate Hitler and his regime.

For the conspirators the key factor was the desertion of one of their number, though it was probable that they were doomed anyhow. Gen. Friedrich Fromm, Commander-in-Chief of the German Reserve Army (Home Army) and Chief of Armaments from the beginning of the war, was aware of the July Plot against Hitler, but he was undecided whether or not to participate actively in it. He decided that he would join the conspirators at the point when they could demonstrate their success. He was at the War Ministry when news came about the bombing attempt on Hitler's life.

Fromm immediately called Rastenburg and learned from Gen. Keitel that the plot had failed and Hitler was alive. Self-preservation took over. With that piece of vital news Fromm turned on the conspirators. He ordered Stauffenberg's arrest. The latter said coldly: "General Fromm, I myself detonated the bomb. No one in that room could possibly be alive." Fromm replied "Count Stauffenberg, the assassination attempt has failed. You should shoot yourself at once." Stauffenberg said: "I shall do nothing of the kind."

Then followed a tragic comedy of errors amid shouting and gunfire in the corridors. The plotters arrested Fromm, but officers loyal to Hitler quickly freed him and took the conspirators into custody. Fromm, with his own head at stake, ordered summary execution of Stauffenberg and three of his immediate entourage.

Fromm, hurrying to redeem himself in Hitler's eyes, spoke

acidly to the plotters: "Gentlemen, I am now going to treat you as you treated me. You are under arrest. Lay down your arms."

He turned to Beck. Eyewitnesses described the encounter:

"Surely," said Beck, "you won't ask me, your old commanding officer, to do that." He asked to be allowed to keep his pistol "for private purposes." Now he added: "You would not deprive an old comrade of this privilege."

Fromm: "Very well, do so. But at once."

Beck took his pistol and loaded it.

Fromm: "Don't point it at me."

Beck: "At this moment I am thinking of earlier days."

Fromm (interrupting): "It is not necessary to go into that now. Please, will you kindly go ahead."

Beck, uncertain in this moment of despair, glanced in farewell at his friends, pointed the gun toward his temple and fired. The bullet grazed the top of his head and drew blood.

Beck (reeling): "Did it fire properly?" Suffering from shock, he collapsed into a chair.

Fromm (in an order to two officers): "Take his gun from him."

Beck: "No, no. I want to keep it!"

Fromm: "Take the gun away. He hasn't the strength."

Beck pleaded to be allowed the chance to take a second shot. Fromm then went to the other conspirators and gave them a few minutes to write down any last words. After five minutes he gave the order to take the prisoners downstairs into the yard and execute them at once. The four were led away.

Fromm returned to Beck.

Fromm: "Well, what about it?"

Beck (stunned, half-dazed, sitting in the chair, blood running over his face): "Give me another pistol."

Fromm: "Very well, you have time for a second shot."

Beck (barely conscious): "Please help me if it doesn't work this time."

Beck fired, but he was again unsuccessful.

Fromm (turning to a sergeant): "Help the old man."

The sergeant approached the now unconscious Beck and shot him in the neck.

Fromm was pushing zealously for his life. Once the slaughter was under way, he mounted a military vehicle in the courtyard and made an enthusiastic speech to the soldiers of the guard battalion on duty at the War Office. He spoke of his "beloved *Fuehrer*" and about how Providence had saved Hitler's life. He called for three loud *"Sieg Heils!"* for the Leader and then drove off to report to Propaganda Minister Goebbels.

Fromm's fellow-officers deemed his actions as cowardly. He was not able to save his life. Eventually, in March 1945, he was arrested on the orders of Heinrich Himmler, who had replaced him as head of the Reserve Army and was anxious to implicate him in the plot against Hitler. Fromm was sentenced to death by the People's Court and executed by firing squad on March 19, 1945.

Conscience in Rebellion

The career of Ludwig Beck provides an excellent example of the psychology of conscience in revolt. As a military man he saw final decisions about the continuity of the nation at stake. He saw history as burdening the nation's leaders with blood guilt if they failed to act according to their knowledge and their conscience as members of the state.

Beck knew well the importance of soldiery obedience, but in his mind such obedience had its limit at that point where responsibility forbade the execution of an order.

The recalcitrant general understood well the mystique of Nazism. "One must not live," he said, "in the intoxication of an ideology."

3 *

CARL GOERDELER:
Lord Mayor of Leipzig

"To seek our fate not in the stars but in ourselves."

The Unifying Spokesman

HE WOULD HAVE BEEN CHANCELLOR OF GERMANY HAD THE CONspiracy against Hitler been successful. Lord Mayor of Leipzig in the turbulent 1930s, he was the energetic leader of the civilian Resistance movement, the man of action who spoke for the circle of Germans disgusted by what the Nazis had done to their Fatherland—for government administrators, churchmen, businessmen, professors, and industrialists. He was the conscience of a troubled Germany at a time when her soil and soul were rotted by the Nazi blight.

Carl Friedrich Goerdeler, tall, broad-shouldered, always distinguishable by his broad-rimmed hat, toured the homeland as a kind of itinerant evangelist on a mission to enlighten his countrymen about the evils of National Socialism. He was a passionate advocate of right against wrong, of honor and justice. Totally absorbed in his purpose, he worked inside the grip of a slave state. He never relinquished his drive for decency.

It was a troubled life that ended in execution—the fate of many heroes in the struggle against tyranny. Goerdeler's name became honored in the postwar Bonn Republic and at the same time won global respect for his courage in dangerous times.

Goerdeler was the heart of the civilian opposition, resistance, and conspiracy against entrenched Nazism. Where others surrendered in the unequal battle with the *Fuehrer's* rogues and scoundrels, he never wavered. He maintained close personal contact with all those who were opposed to the Hitler regime and was tireless in recruiting others for the cause. He criticized those generals who had succumbed to Hitler, while at the same time he urged other high officers to join the civilian conspiracy.

Goerdeler was the human engine destined to drive resistance forward. Nothing discouraged him, not even the many obstacles in his path. Where lesser men gave up in despair, he never even thought of abandoning the struggle. With his shrewd political knowledge and especially with his understanding of the German economy, he gave direction and hope to those who looked for an end to the Third Reich. Again and again many Germans, concerned by what has happened to their country, were won over by the tall, gangling East Prussian who refused to knuckle under to Nazism. Here was the irrepressible political activist.

Goerdeler always looked beyond the Third Reich, which he regarded as a temporary aberration in German history. He issued one draft after another of plans for state reorganization after Hitler's fall. He even composed speeches for the future Chancellor—a post for which Resistance leaders regarded him as the outstanding candidate. His eagerness to plan for a successor state brought him into conflict with others, but he never ceased his work for a new government stripped of Nazi stains.

Those who worked with Goerdeler regarded him as a kind of latter-day saint. Considering the number of individuals won over by him, Goerdeler's effect on others was in all probability greater than any of those other Germans taking part in the campaign against Hitler and his regime.

For the dictator, always worried about opposition and determined to destroy it without a tinge of mercy, the former mayor of Leipzig was a rotten traitor. For Hitler, Goerdeler was more than an annoying gadabout or busybody traveling around the country criticizing the Third Reich—he was a dangerous animal to be destroyed—if National Socialism was to live. The tyrant succeeded in exterminating the man but not his message.

Not for one moment did Goerdeler agree that he was working for a lost cause. It is a reasonable judgment that the history of the Resistance movement in Nazi Germany is a story of seeming failure. The dictator was overthrown from outside, not inside, Germany. The Allies, determined to end the Hitler regime, had to sacrifice millions of lives in the process. The German Resistance movement found it impossible to win the mass support required to smash Hitler's career. The dictator and his cohorts had far too powerful a grip on the machinery of state to be dislodged. Opposition was throttled at its source. Foreign governments, appalled by the excesses of Hitlerism, nevertheless did little to encourage those inside Germany who opposed the regime. They were convinced that this would-be Napoleon could be removed only in the crucible of war.

Despite the failure of Goerdeler and his fellow dissenters in their struggle, they earned global respect for their efforts under most trying circumstances. The dissenters in Naziland should not be written off as obscure utopians, as men who lacked the will to power and who have become historically irrelevant. Goerdeler was destined to lose his life as an idealist in the process, but it was not a battle fought in vain. In the larger context of the struggle between good and evil, the name of Carl Friedrich Goerdeler takes an honored place.

From Bureaucrat to Center Stage

The future anti-Nazi gadfly was born on July 31, 1884, in Schneidemühl, the son of a conservative Prussian family, many of whom had been civil service officials. His father was legal adviser in the public banking institution and later took up the post of district judge in nearby Marienwerder. The young boy grew up in comfortable circumstances in a large and intimate circle of relatives. The family's political affiliation was always Free Conservative, the party of the great Chancellor Otto von Bismarck. In 1899 the senior Goerdeler became a deputy in the Prussian Diet.

After attendance at the Humanities *Gymnasium* in Marienwerder, young Goerdeler studied jurisprudence and political science at the University of Tübingen in Swabia. He passed his first legal examination and began his career as a junior barrister. The young lawyer soon won a reputation for his puritanical character and his way of bringing others to his point of view.

At this stage of his career Goerdeler was attracted by municipal administration, which he favored because of its many problems of organization and its close relations with economic life. He demonstrated a special ability in administration and regularly won testimonials from superiors for his "really eminent talent for organization." He gained experience as a certified assistant judge, as a banking expert in Königsberg and Berlin, and as an assessor in the steel town of Solingen.

The World War beginning in 1914 gave Goerdeler the opportunity to demonstrate his talent for administration by service on several fronts. In 1918 he was assigned to organize the financial administration of a large part of White Russia and Lithuania, which the Germans had appropriated under the terms of the Treaty of Brest-Litovsk. But that same year brought the fall of the monarchy with the abdication of William II and the critical events of the German revolution. Devoted as he was to the old monarchical institutions, Goerdeler was severely shaken by these events, and for a time was not certain whether or not he wanted to serve as a public official in the new republican Germany.

Devoted to high political ideals and dedicated to moral principles in public life, Goerdeler moved to Königsberg to continue his public career there. With his attractive personality and his ability to get things done, he quickly became deputy to the Lord Mayor of Königsberg and began to introduce reforms for the local administration. At first, as Deputy Mayor, conservative, monarchist and nationalist, he incurred the hostility of suspicious Social Democrats, but so winning was his personality and so impressive were his achievements that he even received their approbation and good will. There was little doubt that his reforms worked. Labor union officials were impressed by Goerdeler's scrupulous fairness in negotiations, by his willingness to listen, and by his preference for compromise. It was clear by this time that the able young Prussian was destined for higher office.

Goerdeler served as Deputy Mayor of Königsberg for ten years from 1920 to 1930. On May 30, 1930, he was elected to the post of chief *Bürgermeister* (Lord Mayor) of Leipzig, the first town of Saxony in size and commercial importance. In trade and industries Leipzig ranked among German cities immediately after Berlin and Hamburg. Its importance as a commercial center derived mainly from its great fairs, which annually attracted merchants from all over the world. It was also a German cultural center: in his *Faust,* Goethe called Leipzig "Paris in miniature"—*"klein Paris."*

The war of 1914–18 brought impoverishment to the Saxon city and its finances were in chaos. The city government worsened the situation by its reckless borrowing of foreign capital. The new Mayor quickly embarked on a program to restore the crumbled municipal finances. He demanded a new austerity based on the puritanical principle of thrift, an end to construction of luxurious public buildings, and a halt in increases of wages and salaries. These reforms made him highly unpopular among many citizens of Leipzig, but his measures worked. During the next several years of Goerdeler's activities as Mayor, Leipzig managed to retain its status as a prosperous German city and as a center of world commerce.

In his work as Mayor, Goerdeler was able to demonstrate his talent for administration. He maintained close contacts not only with local officials but also with state and national leaders as well as with important public officials outside Germany. He was successful in his work despite his tendency toward authoritarianism: he mistrusted the type of parliamentary government in the Western democracies and his political position was frankly conservative. He was not really popular with the public, which resented his somewhat overbearing behavior. But there was reluctant approval of his measures: the citizens of Leipzig were convinced that he was giving them bitter medicine but agreed that it was good for them.

Goerdeler's success as Lord Mayor of Leipzig brought him to the attention of Reich President Paul von Hindenburg, the venerable hero of the World War now turned father of his Fatherland. Anxious to obtain Goerdeler's talents for the national government, the President in mid-December 1931 appointed him Reich Commissioner of Prices with the special task of administering national price controls. So successful was Goerdeler in this special post that he won national attention and acclaim. He even seemed on the verge of succession to the chancellorship at the time when Chancellor Heinrich Brüning was driven from office by the intrigues of Gen. Kurt von Schleicher and Franz von Papen (''devil in top hat'').

By early 1933 Goerdeler had come a long way in his public career. The forty-nine-year-old Prussian had won attention as a top-flight administrator. Devoted to God, family, and home, enthusiastic nationalist and patriot, father of three sons and two daughters, he had surged to a position of national prominence in the Weimar Republic, a government which at first he, as conservative monarchist, had mistrusted. There were many Germans who believed this man of honor, this man of principle, to be an ideal candidate for the country's top political post.

And then came the catastrophe of Nazism and the brown dictatorship. They were to cost Goerdeler his life.

In the Shadow of the Swastika

January 30, 1933. With some reluctance and distaste, President von Hindenburg named Adolf Hitler German Chancellor with a coalition cabinet, but refused him extraordinary powers which the Nazi leader had expected. It was a great moment for the little man who had been an unwashed tramp on the streets of Vienna. He had won his way to political power without a *Putsch,* without revolution, in the legal, constitutional way that he had promised.

Goerdeler watched in dismay as Hitler, supported by Dr. Joseph Goebbels's propaganda blitz, elbowed his way past rivals to the topmost post in German government. The highly civilized but apolitical German public had been sold a soiled set of goods. The neurotic Austrian, apotheosis of the little man, had tricked the Germans in a spectacular display of nationalism gone berserk.

Not for a single moment was Goerdeler taken in by the fanaticism of Hitler and his brown battalions. As an experienced politician he knew well the futility of Hitler's promises and he was certain that the country was headed for disaster under this new regime. In Berlin he witnessed the spectacle of Nazi triumph. He spoke up and issued warnings about what was in store for his countrymen. He disagreed with those of his friends who thought it best to give Hitler a chance to fulfill his grandiose promises. Perhaps the Austrian spellbinder might turn out to be just what the country needed.

Goerdeler denounced that point of view as false reasoning and even stupid. The government, he said, was on an evil course, which could only result in disaster for the German people as well as for the whole world. Hitler's understanding of mass psychology and his willingness to work with the far right had brought him to political power, but the country was in dangerous hands. Goerdeler warned: one day it would pay for its confidence in an irresponsible and unstable leader.

What to do? Goerdeler at first decided that it was best to work inside the new regime to do what he could to ease the damage to the country. In November 1934, appointed because of his past experience, he accepted a call to take office again as Reich Commissioner for Price Control. He had no intention of working for the glory of the Third Reich. Quite the opposite. From his key position he could plan for the removal of a man leading Germany to ruin. It was a tragic mistake. There was no stopping the Nazi steam roller.

In his new post Goerdeler recommended orthodox economic and financial measures, including an end to wasteful expenditures, revision of the faulty debt structure, and absolutely accurate financial statements by the government. He soon came into conflict with Dr. Hjalmar Horace Greeley Schacht, President of the *Reichsbank*, a stiff egomaniac, who resented any interference in what he regarded as his personal sphere of influence and who at first supported the *Fuehrer's* unorthodox economic principles. Goerdeler's official position quickly became untenable.

Hitler began his policy of *Gleichschaltung* (coördination), designed to fuse every element of German life into the Nazi social machine, obviously a means to consolidate his dictatorship. Though he knew he was treading on dangerous ground, Goerdeler dared to speak out against the Nazi policy of coördination. Others said nothing, but not Goerdeler. At the Leipzig

Spring Fair of 1935 he was the only one who dared to criticize *Gleichschaltung*. He was clear and forceful:

"Only through a system which allows fully for individuality, with a minimum amount of regimentation can a people live in harmony and obtain for itself a rightful place in the world. The best energies of a nation can be developed only when discipline and freedom prevail, in a situation in which each individual can do his best." Brave but futile words.

Goerdeler's was the voice of reason crying out in perilous times. He had no doubts about the real nature of the Nazi regime. Everything he cherished in government—economy, justice, decency—was being violated by the dictator and his cohorts. He was sure that Hitler's hectic pace of rearmament would lead to disaster. All reforms Goerdeler had introduced in his political career were being torn to pieces in this rampaging totalitarian state.

Goerdeler was especially troubled by Hitler's cascading campaign of anti-Semitism. The Lord Mayor of Leipzig was no special friend of the Jews. In the conservative monarchist tradition he was sympathetic to the argument that Jews had won too much influence in Germany and that too many of them were active in the upper echelons of the Social Democratic Party. He even looked with favor upon some of the premises of the Nuremberg Laws on Citizenship and Race, also called the Ghetto Laws, designed to define the status of Jews in Germany and to restrict them in political, social, and cultural life. The series of edicts in late 1935 aimed to deprive Jews of German citizenship and remove them from the professional and cultural life of the nation.

Goerdeler believed it necessary to lessen the influence of Jews in national life, but it was another thing to step beyond the bounds of decency. He was appalled to see the Nazi campaign against Jews develop into persecution and atrocity. He was disgusted by the practice of assaulting and beating Jews, by the humiliation of forcing them to clean the streets, by the smashing of their windows and shops. This was uncivilized behavior which should not be countenanced by decent people. The good name of Germany was being besmirched before the whole world. Put an end to the atavistic barbarism.

Nazis in Leipzig, well aware of the sentiments of their Lord Mayor, decided to test him in their own special way. They demanded that he remove the monument to Jewish composer Felix Mendelssohn, which stood in front of the Gewandhaus, the City Hall. Goerdeler refused to grant that request. Culture, he said, recognized neither race nor creed, and it was essential that it be allowed to flow freely.

Furious reaction from zealous Nazis. The Mayor was a Jew-lover! He failed utterly to understand the *Fuehrer's* goal of cleansing Germany of the Jewish pestilence. Nazis waited until Goerdeler left the city on a business trip and surreptitiously removed the monument.

That was too much for Goerdeler. On his return to Leipzig, he resigned his office as Lord Mayor. His official career in public service for the Nazi regime was now at an end. He had served in his post for seven years, and he was in no mood to continue.

For a man of Goerdeler's energetic disposition, permanent retirement was impossible. He would not rest as long as Hitler remained in power. He would lose all his self-respect if he did not fight against what he saw as the fatal flowering of absolute evil. In the process he emerged as civilian leader of the Resistance.

How could the dictator be overthrown? Goerdeler decided that it was just not enough to work inside the country—the conspirators would have to have help from the outside. He would go to America on a mission for aid—from newspaper owners, editors, businessmen, and United States Senators. Before he left Germany and while in the United States he completed what he called his "Political Testament," in which he summarized his condemnation of Nazi ideology. He began by describing Hitler's desertion of Christianity:

> Even the love and loyalty of an animal cannot be won by force. Yet the Nazi Party lives by the false notion that through compulsion, it can fashion the beliefs of men and

make their way of life conform to a definite pattern. In particular, the Christian religion in all its forms must increasingly oppose this tendency. . . .

With inevitable logic, the Party is now compelled, if it wishes to retain its authority, to eradicate Christian principles from the nation's way of life. The fight against individual Christian churches was only a beginning. The real fight is against Christianity itself.

The more the party realizes its fundamental opposition to the true nature of man, the more it must reserve for itself the final decision in all things. 'The *Fuehrer* is always right,' becomes the watchword of the Party. Already some believe that the *Fuehrer* governs by a Divine right, and is the founder of a new religion called Nazism. Such a religion is demonstrably absurd.

Goerdeler the critic admitted that Hitler's position on the Treaty of Versailles was correct. "That fearful happening," he wrote, " was a dictate of peace born really of hate, self-interest, and the desire to destroy." But—and this was the important issue to Goerdeler—Hitler's response to Versailles was just as foolish in "hate, self-interest, and the desire to destroy." This was not the way to right the wrong of Versailles:

So Germany finds herself in a condition of outlawry, of moral decay, of economic fantasy and financial wantonness. Nobody but the German Nation itself can rescue it from this condition. Nobody else can save it from a real collapse. In the face of the determination of the National Socialist rulers to remain in power and use every means, even the most brutal, to this end, the German Nation has a difficult path of suffering before it.

The outside world must expect every atrocity and every frightfulness. For National Socialism has masterfully deceived at least eighty percent of the German people, and much of the outside world. It is a poor sign that so many educated men in Germany have allowed themselves to be deceived. But there is an explanation for this, and this too the world should know.

From this time on, Goerdeler became the heart of the Resistance movement, which was soon to move from opposition to conspiracy. On his return to Germany, he took a position as financial adviser to the Stuttgart firm Robert Bosch, primarily because the industrialist himself was anti-Nazi. In his travels Goerdeler became a tireless propagandist against National Socialism. His sense of moral indignation formed the essence of the Resistance movement. In the tradition of Kant, Humboldt, and Stein, he kept alive the spiritual heritage of German idealism. For him it all boiled down to a single issue—a matter of decency. This Nazi regime was an aberration, a throwback to uncivilized behavior, a stain on the good German name. He would have none of it and he would continue to fight it—even if it meant sacrifice of his life.

The Nazi regime, Goerdeler said, was a system "of financial craziness, of industrial violence, or political terror, unjust and immoral." It could not possibly last. Sooner or later it would head for collapse. In the midst of the war he sent a round-robin letter denouncing the Hitler government: "How is it possible that so decent a people as the Germans have borne so unacceptable a system for so long? The answer is simple—by the force of terror. That can be changed by one stroke—by the light of truth. The German people must be told in clear-cut fashion in the open (as it has known in secret) about the results of incompetent leadership, the widespread corruption, the countless crimes, all of which is not compatible with our honor."

Goerdeler insisted that it was a great error to suppose that the soul of the German people had been destroyed: to him it was damaged only temporarily. The country must be rescued from secrecy and terror. "Right and justice must be restored. The powerful soul of the Germans must be made free. Justice and truth must be restored. That day will come." Thus spoke the voice of Germany shamed.

Plans for the New Germany

Goerdeler was tireless in putting his thoughts down in writing. He drafted memoranda, appeals, and declarations. He was especially sensitive about the future, about what kind of government Germany would have after the collapse of the dictatorship. He presented comprehensive plans of what had to be done for the New Germany, how to right the wrongs committed by Hitler and the Nazis, how to set up a stable government which would merit the respect and confidence of a world assaulted by the stench of Hitlerism. His plans were regarded with such favor by his followers that most of them saw him as their future Chancellor.

In the late summer to autumn 1943 Goerdeler issued a comprehensive peace plan in which he urged his countrymen to restore justice and decency again at home. In view of monstrous Nazi crimes, "unique in history," Goerdeler insisted that the Germans themselves, not a third party or an international court, must punish the offenders against both German and international law. And Germany must become sufficiently strong again:

We start with these premises:

1. That Germany must be morally and sufficiently strong for the sake of the German people, the peoples of Europe, and the peace of the world.
2. That between England and Russia there are conflicts of interest, from East Asia to the Mediterranean, from the Mediterranean to the North Atlantic, that are based on circumstances.
3. That Europe needs security against the superior force of Russia.
4. That at present this security can only be underwritten for any length of time by England or Germany.
5. That it is doubtful whether America will make available permanent forces to provide this security.
6. That it therefore is reasonable and necessary to imple-

ment the natural community of interests between England and Germany, as fulfilling all the prerequisites.

7. That this implementation can only be possible if the European peoples come together in an eternal league of peace in freedom and independence, with neither Germany nor any other power claiming supremacy.

8. That no white nationality may contribute to enabling Japan to expand at the expense of other white nationalities or of China.

9. And that, moreover, the whole world is in need of economic cooperation in order to bring its finances into order, to assure employment, and to re-establish the foundation of prosperity.

Germany must restore justice and decency at home. She owes this to her own honor and to others. She can regain her spiritual health only if she herself punishes offenders against the law, and also the offenses against international law. Therefore an urgent admonition must be sounded against any thought of leaving this punishment to be administered by a third party or by an international court. Even the Germans who hate and despise the violation of Germany's good name by Germans, and who are ready to impose every just penalty—or, rather, precisely those Germans—will persistently reject participation in the administration of such penalties by a third party. The feelings of the victimized peoples are quite understandable to these Germans, in view of the monstrous crimes, unique in history, that HITLER and his henchmen have committed. But reason, and a re-sponsibility toward the future, demand that these feelings be kept in check. Anyone in the world, of course, and any government, is free to lodge a charge against German criminals, and the complainant will be informed about the measures that are taken thereupon. Nor can there be any objection to the presence of an official representative of the victimized nation during the public trial. Moreover, the public nature of such trials will be guaranteed, thus ensuring an opportunity to verify that they are genuine. After the enormous misfortune into which

HITLER has plunged the German people, there is no doubt that the German courts will tend more to severity than to softness.

In this memorandum Goerdeler urged that "no white nationality may contribute to enabling Japan to expand at the expense of other white nationalities or of China." This racist remark indicated that Goerdeler had his own prejudices. His famous memorandums outlining his plans for a post-Hitler Germany were marked by traditional claims of power politics, nationalist and racialist undertones, and illiberal views. Those were his beliefs and one can take issue with them. But the kind of society he envisioned, flawed as it was, could not in any way be compared with the views of Hitler. Goerdeler advocated traditional German authoritarianism in the Bismarckian sense, certainly not the nihilist ideology of the Nazi *Fuehrer*.

Road to Martyrdom

For Nazi authorities the very existence of Goerdeler was anathema. They would see to it that this dangerous Prussian would be put out of action. They could not tolerate this kind of dissenter. Morever, they learned from the *Gestapo* that the Resistance was regarding Goerdeler as a future Chancellor. That kind of talk could not be allowed.

The *Gestapo* worked feverishly but by mid-July 1944 it had learned nothing definite about Goerdeler, at least not enough to justify taking him into custody. Nevertheless, on July 17 it issued a warrant for his arrest. Goerdeler went into hiding. The *Gestapo*, angered by the unsuccessful bomb attempt on Hitler's life on July 20, redoubled its efforts to find Goerdeler. He became one of the most wanted men in the Third Reich. A million-mark reward was offered for his head.

Goerdeler was now in the underground, but he had no intention of stopping his work. Convinced that the war was lost, he still had some hope of turning to Himmler or Goebbels as possible allies who might desert the *Fuehrer*. Himmler? That was possible. The former chicken-farmer turned government terrorist had a high opinion of his own skin and might offer his aid to the Allies as the successor to Hitler. But Goebbels? The little mouse-doctor, master of propaganda, would probably never betray his leader, as was the case later when he committed suicide after arranging to have his six children poisoned.

Goerdeler's friends warned him to leave Berlin as soon as possible. The city was a danger spot for anyone taking part in the conspiracy. At first Goerdeler refused to listen to those who worried about him. He relied on Gerhard Wolf, a close friend, who worked in the Police Traffic Control and who previously had provided him with police cars as an escort. Wolf, though in grave danger himself, gave Goerdeler a police car to take him into hiding.

Then the dramatic race for life. Goerdeler spent the night of July 20 at the Rahnsdorf estate of Baron Palomini, a trusted friend, whose home was used as a rendezvous by the conspirators. The next day, when *Gestapo* agents appeared in the vicinity, Goerdeler fled to another estate a dozen miles away. He was by now a marked man: the *Gestapo* had found a projected list of names for a new cabinet in the safe of a conspirator. Goerdeler's name was on it.

The fugitive remained in hiding until July 24, when he went back to Berlin. Here, comparatively safe in the busy streets of the capital, he changed quarters each night. On the night of July 29–30 he stayed with his cousin in a Berlin suburb. His cousin advised him, in view of his desperate situation, to disguise himself and try to escape to the Russians. It was the only way, said the cousin, for Goerdeler to save himself.

Goerdeler was not convinced enough to take that drastic move. He tried unsuccessfully to establish contact with the Swedish Embassy—to him the Swedes were preferable to the vengeful Russians. He then went to Potsdam to stay with a university friend, who, in the midst of the dangerous hegira, found time to celebrate Goerdeler's sixtieth birthday on July 31. With the *Gestapo* on his heels, he moved again, leaving Berlin and staying in Friedrichshagen in the home of a friendly junior clerk.

By this time all Germany knew of the hunt for Goerdeler. Notice of the reward of a million marks for his capture was printed in all German newspapers. Hitler was on a vengeance spree for the attempt on his life and Goerdeler was one man he wanted in a *Gestapo* dungeon.

The fugitive was in a cruel dilemma. Each time he contacted a friend for sanctuary he placed that person in mortal danger. Anyone who helped him in any way placed his own life in jeopardy. Goerdeler thought of fleeing the country, but he knew well that that would endanger his family and close relatives. In any event he had no passport and no means of getting one. He was aware that no real escape was possible.

Then came an unfortunate decision. Convinced that sooner or later he would fall into the hands of the *Gestapo*, he decided to make a farewell visit to the graves of his parents in Marien-werder. On the evening of August 8, with rucksack on his back and walking stick in hand, he set out on his dangerous journey. Taking a roundabout course, avoiding control posts, he arrived two days later in Marienwerder.

It was pure folly—everyone in Marienwerder knew Go-erdeler. On the way to the cemetery he was recognized by a woman, an enthusiastic Nazi anxious to play the role of heroine. Goerdeler, knowing that she was following him, did not dare go on to his parents' graves. Instead, he walked for several hours to Stuhnsdorf, where he passed the night in the open alongside a lake.

The next morning, worn out, he walked into an inn, where he hoped to have breakfast. He did not know that the inn was the pay office for a nearby *Luftwaffe* airfield. When he noted a *Luftwaffe* woman staring at him, he left the inn for the safety of a neighboring woods.

It was too late. The woman, who had known the Goerdeler family for years, informed two pay-office men that the stranger was the wanted Goerdeler. The chase ended as Goerdeler was placed under arrest. The fugitive did not blame his captors. Later he said that if they had not arrested him, they would have been severely punished, in all probability with execution.

Trial and Death

Goerdeler's behavior during the time between his arrest and execution reflected a strong character. He remained the man of high moral sense. From the beginning of his imprisonment he admitted that he was aware of the preparations for the plot of July 20, but at the same time he rejected the very idea of assassination as a political policy. He believed that it was possible to get rid of Hitler without the ultimate step of murder.

In the clutches of the *Gestapo*, Goerdeler began a game of planned deception. He gave his captors one statement after another which could easily be substantiated but which had to be investigated fully. It was his way of stalling for time. Certain that the end of the war was near, he worked carefully to prolong his life as long as possible. On one matter he did his best to confuse his interrogators: to protect those who helped him on his flight he gave either false or incomplete information. He would not betray his comrades.

Goerdeler's jailers did everything possible to break his spirit. Week after week they deprived him of sleep in an attempt to drive him to distraction. They rigged a bright light to shine continually in his eyes through the day and night and cut his food to a point designed only to keep him alive. He accepted the abuse without complaint in the hope that Anglo-American and Russian invasions were imminent.

Goerdeler held fast to his principles. He thought it a great mistake to assume that the moral force of the German people was exhausted. He saw the only hope of salvation in sweeping away the terror and secrecy, in restoring justice and decent government and thereby paving the way for a great moral revival.

Feigning concern, Goerdeler sent a petition to Hitler: "If we place the Fatherland above all, we must consider July 20 the final judgment of God. The *Fuehrer* has been saved from almost certain death. God did not wish the preservation of Germany to be bought by an act of blood. He has given that task once again to the *Fuehrer*. This is within the ancient German tradition. Every German who has been in the Opposition is now obliged to stand behind the *Fuehrer* whom God has preserved.''

Hypocritical calculation. In the past Goerdeler had never made a secret of his utter contempt for Hitler. Now, understandably, he was seeking to preserve his own life. There was no reply to his petition.

In early September 1944 Goerdeler was brought before the dreaded People's Court. The courtroom in the plenary chamber of the Berlin Law Courts was decorated with three large swastikas and busts of Frederick the Great and Hitler. Bright lights blazed for the benefit of film cameras. At a long table sat two professional judges and five others selected from among Party officials, the *SS*, and the armed forces. Sessions were held *in camera*, and there was no possibility of appeal.

Presiding was ''Hanging Judge'' Roland Freisler, merciless and cold-blooded monster who heaped abuse upon prisoners brought before him and who took special joy in sending them to the gallows. Goerdeler stared straight ahead as the satanic judge denounced him as a traitor. On September 7, 1944, came the expected verdict—death.

There followed five months of tortured waiting. Not even the threat of imminent execution could stifle Goerdeler's compulsion to put his thoughts on paper. After receiving the death sentence he wrote a memorandum in his cell titled: ''Thoughts of a Person Sentenced to Death—September 1944.'' In it he described eight points about Germany's future domestic situation:

> . . . I would now have to describe the European situation which I foresee (as a future goal) and which includes the situation of our fatherland as well. But as I don't know whether I will still have enough time at my disposal, I will first sketch the domestic situation that is necessary in order for Germany to recover and to exist; for without it the basis for foreign policy and the necessary basis for life could not be attained and kept.
> 1. Justice must be entrusted to independent courts. These may make rulings only according to the law and not accord-

ing to a philosophy of life (Weltanschauung). At all levels of the courts, respected laymen must be called in. Moreover, lawyers in goodly number must be recruited to fill the judgeships, in order to keep the legal proceedings closely linked with life. And always two courts!

2. The personal rights—freedom of opinion, of conscience, of religion, of teaching, of life—must be protected against any interference that is not ordered by a judge acting by authority of the law. These rights must be soundly incorporated into the life of the community by constitution and by law.

3. The press should not have unrestrained freedom; the duty to be truthful must be imposed on it. Untruthfulness has to be punished even if it is not insulting, for the misuse of the freedom of opinion in the press is unbearable. Responsibility of the press to honorary boards whose composition and competence are determined by law.

4. Basis of civic activities to be decency and purity of character; on the same basis the relations of the people among themselves must be regulated in all fields of endeavor.

5. The family, as the nucleus of the edifice of the state and the community, deserves special protection. This is extended by giving it educational support and by the establishment of a fund to allot pensions to families with many children, by levying charges on families with few or no children. Moreover, in the case of a married couple with at least three children the father gets a double vote at elections.

6. The educational system must be simplified: three years of primary school, five years of elementary school, three years of continuation school, nine years of secondary school, or six years of lower-grade secondary school (Mittelschule). In secondary schools, in order to obtain uniformity and to ease things for parents and children, only: Gymnasium (lycée) based on the humanities and classics, plus alternate secondary school (Oberrealschule) based on modern languages. In all schools, social science beginning from age 15, with the use of a simple book (already drafted) so that all Germans are inoculated against the plague of the present, against economic illusions. Universities and technical academies are merged in order to restore the unity of education and its

comprehensive scope. They and the students receive the
right to self-administration under state supervision. One university (Heidelberg) is tentatively established along the lines
of the English college system. The full-time positions of
curators will be abolished for economy. Supervision is by
the state executive power. Highest demands are set in all
educational institutions in order to obtain highest accomplishments. Religious instruction up to the 14th year if the
parents do not reject it, so that the young people learn the
Ten Commandments once more, and take them to heart.
Parents decide about the children's religion until the 18th
year. Religious lessons may only be given by those teachers
who are prepared to do so or by clergymen.
7. The churches receive the right of self-administration and
lose their state subsidies; they finance themselves. The
Protestant church receives the right to benefit from a church
tax only if it organizes according to the synodal system (with
participation of laymen).

The Catholic church only if it appoints a German primate
who will be competent to certify assignments to the higher
positions in the church organization. The churches are
granted freedom of activity to implement their doctrine in
practice, especially in the fields of welfare, nursing, education. Their establishments are to be active side by side with
those of state, the districts and the communities.
8. The constitution is founded on the self-administration of
large regions (*Gaue*), districts and communities. These re-
gional and local authorities are responsible for all activities
that are not the necessary function of the *Reich* because of
the unity of the *Reich*. . . .

Neither the Anglo-Americans nor Russians came in time to
rescue Goerdeler from his captors. He was hanged on February
2, 1945, at the Prinz Albrecht Strasse prison.

Champion of Decency

For the psychologist, headstrong Goerdeler provides a case
history on the effects of youthful environment. A devout Protestant, Goerdeler never deviated in his lifetime from a deep re-

spect for the Christian ethic and for simple justice in human affairs. He was not the type to remain silent in the face of injustice and terror. A man of principle, he fought back.

Fellow-countryman Eberhard Zeller paid emotional tribute to the executed prisoner: "Goerdeler's effect on human personalities was perhaps the greatest possessed by any working against Hitler. His stimulating influence on all around him was a talent that could only ripen to such a degree in the rotting soul of the governmental and private circumstances in which he and his colleagues lived. These circumstances aroused him from his normal human limitations to pursue a great mission, developed the power to appeal to consciences and turn them toward a fear of God and a passion for honesty, right, law and decency."

Decency! The final word of this encomium—"decency"—was the precise term Goerdeler used again and again throughout the years of his struggle against Nazism.

4*

BAMBERGER REITER STAUFFENBERG:
Fulcrum

—————

We wish for a new order which will make all Germans responsible for the state, and which will guarantee them right and justice.

Germanic Hero

SO HANDSOME WAS THE YOUNG GERMAN OFFICER THAT HE WAS called the Bamberger Reiter because of his resemblance to the famous thirteenth-century statue in the Cathedral at Bamberg, Bavarian seat of a bishropic. His courage resembled that of Richard the Lion-Hearted. This leading conspirator was driven by an almost mystical sense of purpose.

Claus Schenck Graf von Stauffenberg was appalled by the personality, character, and activities of the scruffy Austrian who had come to political power in Germany along with his crowd of assorted ruffians, scoundrels, and misfits. Stauffenberg saw Hitler as anti-Christ, as a master of vermin, a disreputable human being unworthy of the good name of the German people. The young officer was adamant: this grotesque politician must be removed from German life. "We have put ourselves to the test before God and before our consciences; it must be done, for this man is evil incarnate." Others thought the same way, but few had the special combination of ethics and energy sufficient to go ahead with the task.

Stauffenberg struggled with his own conscience. As a new officer with a great future before him, it seemed certain that he would advance into the upper hierarchy of the military, especially after a brilliant start in his career. But that was not enough for a man who understood the difference between right and wrong. Where others pouted and talked and criticized, Stauffenberg went ahead with plans for a move he believed to be absolutely necessary. He was aware of the consequences of failure, but he was willing to accept the danger.

Claus von Stauffenberg was born in Greifenstein Castle, Upper Franconia, on November 15, 1907. A member of the Swabian aristocracy, he was related on his mother's side to the Yorck family. He was a descendant of Prussian Field Marshal August Wilhelm von Gneisenau, key figure in rebuilding the Prussian army shattered by Napoleon in 1806, and the architect of its triumphs during the Wars of Liberation (1813–15). His father was Privy Chamberlain to the last King of Württemberg and his family loyally served several royal houses.

As a subaltern Stauffenberg was regarded by his superiors as an officer with a great future. He was given the accolade of "the new Schlieffen" because of the originality of his military thinking (Alfred Graf von Schlieffen, head of the German General Staff in 1911, had delivered a famous plan for strategy against France and Russia in a two-front war). This promising young officer, it was said, would inspire the Army beyond its old narrow military spirit.

At the outbreak of World War II, Stauffenberg served with distinction as a 1st Lieutenant in a Bavarian armored division in Poland and in the French campaign in 1940. He saw himself as a combat officer willing to offer his life for the Fatherland. He was both disappointed and displeased when he was ordered back to headquarters, for he was reluctant to leave his troops. His superior officers regarded him as an excellent strategist and recommended that he be placed in a post of authority where he could contribute more to the final goal of victory.

In early 1943 Stauffenberg was transferred to North Africa to make better use of his military talents. In April he was wounded in the face, both hands, and one knee by fire from a low-flying Allied plane. He feared that he might lose his sight completely, but he kept one eye. His right hand was missing, half his left hand and part of his leg. He was saved by the expert medical supervision of Dr. Ferdinand Sauerbruch, a distinguished and well-known physician practicing in Munich. Reporting back for service, Stauffenberg was appointed Chief of Staff of the Army Ordnance Department.

During his convalescence, Stauffenberg had a lot of time to think about himself, his country, and the Hitler regime. Reared in an atmosphere of monarchist conservatism and Catholic piety, he had turned against his heritage and tended to prefer a socialist society to that of the bourgeois Weimar Republic. Indeed, like other Germans, for a time he saw hope for his country in Hitler's National Socialism.

But Stauffenberg was now uncomfortable with Nazism and its implications. He was disillusioned with Hitler and his disreputable minions. Other senior officers had the same feeling and condemned the Nazi regime, but only among themselves. Stauffenberg was made of sterner stuff. There must be an end to the new totalitarianism and the Nazi terror. It was necessary in Stauffenberg's mind to eliminate Hitler's dictatorship and start "a new state combining ethical socialism with aristocratic traditions."

The dissatisfied officer got in touch with various dissident groups, including Moltke's Kreisau Circle. Impelled by Christian morality and angered by the excesses of Nazism, Stauffenberg decide to devote his life to the task of overthrowing this shameful regime. He moved from opposition to resistance to conspiracy.

Failed Attentats

The prey was elusive. Several attempts had been made inside the Third Reich to rid the nation of its monster, but they had all failed. Disgusted officers, diplomats, politicians, and ecclesiastics agreed that Nazism was shameful and disgraceful and that Hitler had to be removed. The conspirators were few in number, but they were a determined lot.

The first attempt, the Potsdam *Putsch,* came in January 1933 just before Hitler became Chancellor. During these critical weeks the generals who hated Nazism planned to proclaim a state of emergency, declare martial law, and set up a military dictatorship for a limited time. They would use Hitler and a modified form of National Socialism to win the support of the masses and then drive him out of power. Indifferently organized, this early contemplated *coup d'état* turned out to be unsuccessful. Hitler came to power on January 30, 1933. The man seemed to have a charmed life.

Disgusted generals and civilians tried again in the Berlin *Putsch* of September 1938. By this time, opposition to Hitler had emerged in a Resistance movement. Army leaders were infuriated by the Blomberg-Fritsch crisis, when Hitler removed two of his leading generals after distasteful personal scandals. Among the plotters were Col. Gen. Ludwig Beck; members of the *Abwehr*, the foreign and counterintelligence department of the High Command of the Armed Forces, including Adm. Wilhelm Canaris and Maj. Gen. Oster; such high-placed individuals as Carl Friedrich Goerdeler, jurist and Lord Mayor of Leipzig; and a group of young civilians, among them Pastor Dietrich Bonhoeffer, Fabian von Schlabrendorff, Hans von Dohnanyi, and Otto Jahn. After resigning his post as Chief of the General Staff, Beck became active as leader of the conspiracy. The plan was to seize the *Fuehrer* as soon as he gave the order for Operation Green directed against Czechoslovakia. The idea was to capture Hitler alive, bring him before a People's Court, certify him as insane, and put him away in a lunatic asylum. Unsuccessful attempts were made to contact London for assistance. Plans for the *Putsch* were shattered due to irresolute leadership, inept organization, and failure to act at precisely the right moment. The visits to Germany of Prime Minister Neville Chamberlain in his appeasement crusade lessened hope of success for the plotters.

The next attempt came shortly after the outbreak of the war with the Zossen *Putsch* of November 1939. Though disheartened by the failure of the Berlin attentat, the conspirators resolved to try again. Named after the village of Zossen, where the plotters met, the attempt again failed because of hesitancy and poor planning. Officers who were supposed to lead the move backed down after Hitler angrily berated his generals for cowardice and defeatism.

Within a few days there was another attempt to kill Hitler in the Beer-Hall plot of November 8, 1939. On the sixteenth anniversary of the 1923 Beer-Hall *Putsch*, Hitler ordered a great celebration in Munich. Conspirators planted in the hall a bomb that could be operated by a push button. The plot misfired when Hitler completed his speech and left the hall earlier than expected. The roof collapsed on the audience, killing seven people and injuring sixty-three more.

On March 13, 1943, came the Smolensk attempt on Hitler's life. Maj. Gen. Henning von Treschkow and his staff officer 1st Lieut. Fabian von Schlabrendorff planned to kill Hitler with a delayed action bomb concealed in the *Fuehrer's* private plane during a return flight from Smolensk to his field headquarters in Rastenburg. The bomb, which had been placed in a bottle of brandy, failed to go off and had to be retrieved. (See chapter 8 on Hans von Dohnanyi for a more detailed description of the Treschkow plot.)

Eight days later came another attempt on Hitler's life. In a suicide mission two bombs were to be placed in the *Fuehrer's* overcoat pocket. Once again the plot failed when the intended victim changed his schedule. Foiled again!

The conspirators were frustrated by what they regarded as bad luck. Again and again they saw their man escape. Dispirited, disgruntled, they were determined to try again. Their most important effort came in the summer of 1944 in a plot which received global attention. But again the quarry was to emerge alive, wounded, infuriated, and intent on savage revenge.

The Plot Continues

By the summer of 1944 there was much dissatisfaction in military circles with Hitler and his regime, though the upper brackets of the High Command of the Armed Forces, stationed in the Bendlerstrasse in Berlin, remained loyal. Such leading officers as Field Marshal Wilhelm Keitel, Gen. Alfred Jodl, and Gen. Walther Warlimont took seriously their oath to the *Fuehrer*. There was little disaffection by others. Among senior officers favorable to the conspiracy were Field Marshal Erwin von Witzleben, who retired from active service in 1942; Col. Gen. Heinrich von Stuelpnagel, Military Governor in France; Col. Gen. Erich Hoepner, the armored forces commander who had been dismissed by Hitler in 1941: Col. Gen. Friedrich Olbricht, head of the Supply Section of the Reserve Army; Maj. Gen. Hans Oster, Chief of Staff of the *Abwehr;* and Maj. Gen. Heinrich von Treschkow, Chief of Staff of Army Group Center on the Russian front.

Also central to the plot were several younger officers, who were willing to stake their lives in the goal of ridding the Fatherland of Hitler. Among them were 1st Lieut. Fabian von Schlabrendorff, staff officer under Gen. von Treschkow, and Col. von Stauffenberg.

In early 1944 Stauffenberg emerged as leader of the anti-Hitler conspirators. His motive was clear—he and his fellow-conspirators must prove to the world and to future generations that the men of the German Resistance were willing to take the decisive step.

Key appointment—July 1, 1944. Stauffenberg was made Chief of Staff to Col. Gen. Friedrich Fromm, Commander-in-Chief of the Reserve, or Home Army. Great importance for the plotters—Stauffenberg now had access to army briefings. He was assigned to give interim reports to the *Fuehrer* himself. That very day Stauffenberg was visited by a stranger, a junior officer from the East. To this man whom he scarcely knew, Stauffenberg said: "There is no point in beating around the bush. I am employing all the means at my disposal for the purpose of committing high treason." The nonplussed young officer, not knowing what to make of this strange remark, kept it to himself. Temporary good fortune for the conspirator.

Three days later Stauffenberg met several of his friends at his home in Wannsee. He asked them whether it was now too late. Would it not be wiser to wait until the inevitable defeat in order to preserve their strength for the post-Nazi era? His friends demurred—the ultimate act must be completed for the benefit of future German generations.

On July 6 Stauffenberg flew to Berchtesgaden to discuss

the possibility of someone in Hitler's retinue carrying out the assassination. His discreet inquiries there made it certain that he must do it himself. There was a problem—the twin role of assassin and *Putsch* leader might well be too much for any one man. No use to worry about that now—the key issue was immediate removal of Hitler. The tyrant must be struck down.

Meanwile, Russian tanks were moving inexorably on Berlin. Some twenty-seven German divisions had ceased to exist. The Soviets were preparing a new massive offensive. The Allies were on the verge of a breakthrough in the West. Stauffenberg flew once again to Berchtesgaden, but the circumstances were still just not right for the attentat.

On July 14 Hitler moved his headquarters from Berchtesgaden to Rastenburg. At this time Fromm and Stauffenberg were summoned to field headquarters to attend a conference on the following day to discuss the important matter of new divisions needed for Army Group Center. This was a key matter in Hitler's overall strategy.

Excitement among the conspirators. This was the signal for Operation Valkyrie. In Norse-Teutonic mythology the Valkyrie were beautiful, awe-inspiring maidens who were said to have hovered over the ancient battlefields, choosing those who were to be killed. Hitler had already set up an Operation Valkyrie designating that the Home Army take over the security of Berlin and other large cities in the event of a revolt by millions of imported foreign workers. With his trusted troops on the front lines the suspicious *Fuehrer* feared a rebellion on the home front.

The conspirators gave Valkyrie a second meaning. For them it was the perfect cover name. In their view the Valkyrie maidens had already chosen Hitler for death.

Another meeting at Stauffenberg's home. As soon as Hitler was dead, negotiations would begin with the Russians. Matters were now critical: the Russians had begun their offensive and the Western Allies were about to take Caen after the Normandy invasion.

July 20, 1944

At 8 P.M. on the evening of July 19 Stauffenberg left his office and drove to his home in Wannsee. Early the next morning, along with his adjutant Lieut. Werner von Haeften, he flew from the airfield at Rangsdorf, south of Berlin, to Rastenburg. The men carried two bombs. Stauffenberg had an English bomb with a silent fuse which could be operated by breaking a glass capsule filled with acid and which could dissolve the wire and release the firing pin. The acid would eat through in ten minutes. Stauffenberg wrapped the bomb in a shirt and placed it in his brief case holding reports for Hitler. There was a second bomb in Haeften's brief case.

Rastenburg was 350 miles northeast of Berlin on the Prussian plains. The plotters' aircraft landed just after ten o'clock. The compound was protected by numerous electric fences and barbed wire, as well as blockhouses and check-points. Hitler had called the conference in the *Gästebaracke*, the guest barracks, a large wooden hut built on concrete and stone pillars with a roof of tarred felt. There were three windows. At each end of the room there was a small table. In the center was a large table covered by situation maps.

Impending drama. Shortly after 10 A.M. Stauffenberg was admitted after giving the proper password. His task was routine: he was to give a report on the status of the Home Army. Present were twenty-four officers of Hitler's entourage.

Stauffenberg set the timer on the bomb just as he entered the staff room. That gave him exactly ten minutes to place the device where it could do the most damage.

The young officer greeted the *Fuehrer* and then silently placed the brief case on the floor beside Hitler. He excused himself: "I must make a phone call." Then came one of those fortuitous events which affects the course of history. Col. Heinz Brandt, deputy to Gen. Adolf Heusinger, feeling the brief case to be in the way, pushed it from his chair under the map table in such a manner that it rested against the heavy upright support on the side farthest from Hitler. That casual move saved the *Fuehrer's* life.

Gen. Heusinger rose to his feet to give a gloomy report on the situation on the Russian front. He was in the final stage of his presentation: "The Russians are pressing with strong forces westward. Their forward troops are already south-west of Dünsburg. If we do not at least withdraw the Army Group from Peipusse [Lake Peipus], there will be a disaster."

12:42 P.M. The bomb exploded with a deafening impact. One end of the conference building simply disintegrated. The roar of the explosion shook the ordinarily quiet area of Rastenburg as if a rocket had fallen. Black smoke poured from the interior of the hut. It was a macabre sight—several bodies flew out of the smashed windows. Screams of terror pierced the air.

Of the two dozen men present, Berger, the stenographer, was killed outright. Three others died of their wounds later.

Hitler, supported by Field Marshal Keitel, staggered out of the hut to move to his quarters for immediate medical attention. His hair was on fire, his right arm partially paralyzed, his right leg burned, and his ear-drum damaged.

The *Fuehrer* was badly hurt—but he was alive.

Chaos at the Bendlerstrasse

Stauffenberg and adjutant Haeften were at their staff car several hundred yards from the conference building when the bomb exploded with a thunderous roar. They saw the hut disintegrate and heard the cries, screams, and shouts. Success! Surely Hitler, the intended victim, close to the brief case containing the explosive, was dead.

Stauffenberg was euphoric. His immediate concern was to bluff his way through the check-points of the Rastenburg complex, speed to the airport, and get back to Berlin. There he would race to the Ministry of War in the Bendlerstrasse, where his fellow-conspirators were ready to take over control of the government.

The staff car sped around the circuit of the inner section of the compound. Within two minutes Stauffenberg reached the first control unit. Jumping out of the car, he did not wait for the challenge he expected after that tremendous blast. Instead, in a loud voice he demanded use of the telephone. He turned to the duty officer and roared: "*Herr Leutnant!* I have permission to pass!" It was sheer gall but it worked. The astonished guard let the escape-automobile pass.

Stauffenberg, adjutant Haeften, and their driver sped to the outer perimeter. Again the same ruse. Stauffenberg rushed to the telephone and demanded to speak to the adjutant of the camp commander. The *SS* sergeant on duty refused to accept Stauffenberg's word: he had orders to let no one pass in or out. Only when the commandant's adjutant confirmed the request were the three men allowed to proceed.

The staff car reached the airport about twenty minutes after the bomb explosion. The conspirators were airborne by 13:15, flying in a slow Heinkel plane from East Prussia to the capital.

After landing at Rangsdorf, Stauffenberg and his adjutant commandeered a staff car and in three-quarters of an hour were at the Bendlerstrasse. As soon as he reached the War Office, he was told that there had been a call from Field Marshal Wilhelm Keitel, Hitler's Chief of Staff, who was at Rastenburg with the *Fuehrer*. Stauffenberg, anxious to take charge of the coup, reported to his fellow-conspirators what he had seen. He was told that Keitel had declared the report of Hitler's death as nonsense. "Quite true," Keitel said, "an attempt has been made on the *Fuehrer*'s life, but, fortunately, it has failed. The *Fuehrer* is alive and only slightly injured. Incidentally, where is your Chief of Staff, Colonel Stauffenberg?"

Stauffenberg was shocked, dismayed, and confused. Surely Keitel was lying. Even if Hitler had escaped death, the *coup d'état* must go on. "Impossible!" he cried. "I saw the whole thing myself. I was standing nearby when the explosion took place. It was as if a 150-millimeter shell had hit the barracks. It is just impossible that anyone could have survived. Keitel is lying! Keitel is lying!"

Muddle at the Bendlerstrasse. On the one side were the conspirators, anxious to announce the formation of a new government now that Hitler was presumed dead. But there were also officers who decided to remain loyal after word had come that the *Fuehrer* was wounded but still alive. Among them was Col. Gen. Friedrich Fromm, Stauffenberg's immediate superior, who now refused to support the plot.

When Stauffenberg informed Fromm that no one who was in that room at Rastenburg could have possibly survived, Fromm turned on him and told him that because the assassination had failed he must shoot himself. ''I shall do nothing of the kind,'' was the angry reply.

Late that afternoon Stauffenberg countersigned two proclamations designed to get the new government under way. The first one was issued under the signature of Field Marshal Erwin Witzleben, who had been retired from active service since 1942, and who was designated by the conspirators to become Commander-in-Chief of the new German Army:

General Order of the Day to the Armed Forces of the German Reich

THE *FUEHRER* ADOLF HITLER IS DEAD. [This opening sentence was omitted from later copies.]

An irresponsible clique of party leaders, strangers to the front, have tried to exploit this situation, and to stab the hard-fighting army in the back in order to seek power for their own selfish needs. In this hour of supreme danger, the Reich Government, in order to preserve law and order, has proclaimed a state of military emergency and has entrusted to me both the supreme command of the armed forces and the executive authority in the Reich.

In this capacity, I now issue these orders:

1. I transfer executive power, with the right of delegation, to the territorial commanders in the home territory, to the

Commander-in-Chief of the Home Army, who has been promoted to Commander-in-Chief of the home front . . .

2. To the holders of executive authority are subordinated:
(a) all army officers in their districts and army units, including the *Waffen-SS*, the Reich Labor Service and the Todt organization;
(b) the entire civil service of the Reich, the provinces, and the parishes, the entire security and public order police and police administration;
(c) all officials and branches of the NSDAP *[National Socialist German Workers' Party]* and associations belonging to it;
(d) all lines of communication and supply areas.

3. The holders of executive power are responsible for the maintenance of order and public security;
(a) the security of signal installations;
(b) the elimination of the *Sicherheitsdienst [Nazi Security Service]*; Any resistance to the military executive power is to be suppressed relentlessly.

4. In this time of great danger to our country, close unity in the armed sources and the maintenance of discipline is of prime importance.
I, therefore, order all Commanders-in-Chief of the army, the navy, and the *Luftwaffe [Air Force]* to give all their support to the holders of executive power in the fulfillment of their important duties, and to obtain compliance to their orders from all subordinates. A historic task is now entrusted to the German soldier. Whether Germany is to be saved depends on his energy and morale.
(Signed) The Commander-in-Chief of the *Wehrmacht*

VON WITZLEBEN, Field Marshal
(Countersigned) Count Stauffenberg

A second general order was issued to *Wehrkreis* (district of an army corps) commanders. Issued in the name of Col. Gen. Fromm, it was not shown to him for the very good reason that, though stationed at the War Office, he was not a member of the conspiracy. Again, the order was countersigned by Stauffenberg:

General Order to Wehrkreis Commanders

1. In virtue of the authority given to me by the Commander-in-Chief of the Armed Forces, I invest the Commanding General with executive power in all military districts. The functions of the Reich Defense Commission are hereby transferred to the *Wehrkreis* commanders.

2. The following steps are to be taken at once:

(a) *Signals Installations.* Occupation of all transport and communications centers; all radio amplifiers and broadcasting stations; all gas-works, power stations and water-works *[listed];*

(b) *Arrests.* The following are to be relieved of office immediately and placed in solitary confinement: all *Gauleiters [district leaders], Reichstatthalters [Reich district Governors],* Ministers, Provincial Governors, Police Presidents, all senior *SS* and Police Chiefs, heads of the *Gestapo [Secret State Police],* members of the *SS* administration and the propaganda bureaus, all Nazi district leaders. Exceptions only by my command.

(c) *Concentration Camps.* Concentration camps are to be seized at once, the camp commanders arrested, the guards disarmed and confined to barracks. Political prisoners are to be instructed that they should, pending liberation, abstain from demonstrations and independent action.

(d) *[Waffen-SS [Armed SS].* If compliance by leaders of the *Waffen-SS* seems doubtful, or if they seem to be unsuitable they are to be taken into protective custody, and replaced by officers of the army. Units of the *Waffen-SS,* whose unconditional obedience seems in doubt, are to be ruthlessly disarmed. Energetic action with overwhelming force will prevent greater bloodshed.

(e) *Police.* All offices of the *Gestapo* and *Sicherheits-dienst [Security Service]* are to be occupied. In implementing this order, the public order police will to a great extent

replace units of the armed forces. The necessary papers will
be issued by the Chief of the German Police through official
police channels.

(f) *Navy and Air Force*. Contact is to be made with senior
naval and air commanders. Unity of action must be insured.

3. In order to deal with all political questions arising from
the state of emergency, a political officer will be attached to
every military district commander. Until further notice this
political officer will take over the duties of chief of administration: He will act as advisor to the *Wehrmacht* commander
in all political matters.

4. The effective operational command post of the Commander-in-Chief, Home Area Command, is the Home Command Staff. For purpose of mutual information concerning
situation and intents, he will dispatch to each *Wehrkreis*
commander a liaison officer.

5. The executive power will tolerate no arbitrary or re-
vengeful acts in the exercise of its authority. The public
must be aware of the difference from the wanton acts of their
former rulers.

> The Commander-in-Chief of the Home Arena
> FROMM, Colonel-General
> *(Countersigned)* Count Stauffenberg

There were other proclamations, including a stirring one addressed as "Appeal to the German people," signed by Gen.
Ludwig Beck, regarded by the military conspirators as their
leader: "Hitler has sacrificed whole armies for *his* passion for
glory, for *his* megalomania, *his* blasphemous delusion that he is
the chosen and favored instrument of 'Providence.' " And
again: "Our good name has been sullied by cruel mass murders.
With blood-stained hands Hitler has pursued his madman's
course, leaving tears, sorrow and misery in his train. With
deadly certainty his lunatic desire for all human impulses has
brought misfortune for our people, and his self-imagined mili-

tary genius has brought ruin to our brave soldiers.'' A similar statement to the press was signed by Carl Friedrich Goerdeler, former Lord Mayor of Leipzig, civilian leader of the Resistance, and proposed Chancellor of the post-Hitler government.

All in vain.

"Nest of Vipers"

Winds of rage in Rastenburg. Recovering from the blast, Hitler gave way to violent frenzy. The miserable traitors! Here he, ''the greatest German of all time,'' had devoted his life to a sacred cause, and these filthy pigs were trying to assassinate him. Vengeance! Vengeance! ''I will crush and destroy the criminals who have dared oppose themselves to Providence and to me. These traitors to their own people deserve ignominious death and that is what they shall have. This nest of vipers who have tried to sabotage the grandeur of my Germany will be exterminated once and for all time.''

Meanwhile, the conspirators were literally fighting for their lives at the Bendlerstrasse. Loyal Nazis gradually won the upper hand. They released Fromm, who had been arrested by the plotters and confined to a small room. Fromm quickly turned on the conspirators.

It was a state of siege. The War Office was surrounded by troops loyal to the *Fuehrer*. Stauffenberg and his comrades fought a rear-guard action by using the telephone to plead for help. At 10 P.M. it was all over—troops stormed the building and seized the plotters.

Brandishing a revolver, Fromm faced his captives. ''I am now going to treat you as you have treated me.'' He announced immediate death sentences. He left the room to arrange for a firing squad of ten men under command of a lieutenant.

Stauffenberg and three others were led into the courtyard where an army truck used its hooded lights to illuminate the scene.

The four prisoners were struck down by shots from the execution squad.

"Long live our sacred Germany!" Stauffenberg cried as he fell.

Spirit of the Resistance

"We have examined ourselves before God and our conscience. It has to happen, for the man is Evil itself."

This was the thought motivating Claus von Stauffenberg—to dare everything, to attempt everything to remove Hitler. The *Fuehrer* was like a rat catcher who had led the howling, applauding masses, conquering nations, and destroying cities. He was responsible for an unending chain of mass graves. The grandson of Gneisenau would risk his life to destroy the menace.

The July 20, 1944, attentat was not a political revolt but rather the rebellion of senior officers, high officials, and respected public figures who felt themselves morally bound to put an end to the Nazi monstrosity. In all some two hundred Germans were executed or done to death after that momentous day, including 21 generals, 33 colonels and lieutenant-colonels, two ambassadors, seven ministers, three state secretaries, and other political and government officials.

Stauffenberg was the spearhead of the revolt.

On July 20, 1984, on the fortieth anniversary of the explosion at Rastenburg, celebrations were held throughout the Bonn Republic in honor of those who tried to kill Hitler. A special ceremony was held in the courtyard of the Bendlerstrasse Army Command Headquarters at the spot where Stauffenberg and his three brother officers were executed.

Chancellor Helmut Kohl described the plot of July 20, 1944, as "the moment of truth" for Germans which made it possible "for us to preserve our dignity." Speaking in a solemn, measured tone to those gathered at the Bendlerstrasse, now renamed Stauffenbergstrasse, he said that the plot "was necessary to show the world that the German people were not just collaborators of Hitler."

The Chancellor described the motives of the Resistance:

The common ground of those who prepared the coup was their ethical-moral conviction. In their printed statements and programs we find the commitment to human dignity, to freedom of belief and conscience, to protection of the family, to the rule of law, to social justice and to peaceful cooperation among peoples in Europe. The idea and tradition of German legal thought and the commitment to the rule of law were driving forces which led to action.

That same sentiment had been expressed some thirty-eight years earlier when Winston Churchill spoke before the House of Commons: "This resistance ranks among the noblest and greatest actions in the history of all peoples. Their deeds and sacrifice are the indestructible foundation of a new reconstruction."

5*

HANS AND SOPHIE SCHOLL:
Students of the White Rose

Isn't it a fact today that every German is ashamed of his Government?

"A Noble Treason"

WHEN IN 1979 RICHARD HANSER, CHRONICLER OF THE NAZI ERA, published his fascinating account of the revolt of the Munich students against Hitler, he came up with the perfect title. "A Noble Treason" he called his book.

Ordinarily, noun "treason" and adjective "noble" indicate repulsion of meaning, with divergence instead of confluence. In its clear-cut sense, treason simply means betrayal of one's country. For centuries it has been regarded as the ultimate of crimes. "Great Caesar fell," wrote The Bard, "whilst bloody treason flourish'd over us." And Thomas Moore judged it to be "a deadly blight." Most people denounce the traitor as an ignoble lout, as one who has betrayed his birthright and is beyond redemption.

But on occasion the dissenter is driven to distraction and strikes back at what is regarded as insufferable persecution. Before the Virginia Convention of 1765, Patrick Henry, American patriot and orator, shouted: "Caesar had his Brutus; Charles the First, his Cromwell; and George the Third ['Treason' cried the Speaker]—*may profit by their example*. If *this* be treason, make the most of it."

At five o'clock on the morning of February 22, 1943, six members of the White Rose, a clandestine group of students at the University of Munich, were rushed to the guillotine after being found guilty of treason against the Nazi regime. They had earned the enraged anger of Hitler by their "dangerous" act of distributing leaflets denouncing him and his government. From the *Fuehrer's* viewpoint, these were wretched scoundrels who were waging war against a Germany fighting for life and were giving aid and comfort to the enemy at a critical time in history. Eradicate the rotten traitors!

But for decent human beings inside Germany and throughout the world this was a classic case of the eternal struggle between idealism and tyranny. These were young patriots who loved their country, who were disgusted by the excesses of the Hitler regime, and who refused to bow low before the tyrant. Unlike others who accepted their lot under the ordeal, this handful of youngsters in the prime of life, their best years before them, dared to raise their voices in dissent, and did what they could to warn their fellow-Germans of the consequences of National Socialism.

The students of Munich, members of the White Rose, knew well what they were doing. They willingly placed their lives in jeopardy. What they did required courage far beyond the normal. The odds leaned toward a vicious death.

Other Germans accused them of being naïve in believing that they could abolish the dictatorship. But they never wavered in their determination to oppose the twisted world of Nazism. They knew that Hitler had grabbed power in a chaotic milieu of conspiracy, mob psychology, and astute political maneuvering. They were convinced that it was necessary to fight back as a matter of conscience. There was true nobility of character among these students of the White Rose.

These students were not alone. They expressed in a very real way the psychological nuances of German resistance against the tyrant. In a typical distortion of history, Hitler excoriated the Resistance as confined to "a small clique of ambitious officers." Again the Hitlerian lie—opposition to Nazism inside Germany was by no means confined to one dissatisfied segment of the population but to many levels and classes.

Resistance against the police state inside Germany never developed into a mass movement, but it certainly attracted many classes impelled by a variety of motives. There were officers in the military, administrative officials, churchmen, intellectuals, labor leaders, diplomats, scientists, artists, and students. All saw themselves as prisoners in a national penitentiary.

The young people who voiced their rebellion—good, decent, honorable young people, simply refused to stand aside and be silent while their beloved Fatherland was being shamed before the world. With their whole life before them, they were willing to be sacrificed for what they regarded as a holy cause. They saw the German name as being disgraced forever if German youth did not rise. This was not mere fanaticism, but measured reaction and obeisance to and respect for the Kantian categorical imperative.

These were the extraordinary young people who represented the spirit of atonement in a tragic era of German history.

Hans and Sophie Scholl, brother and sister, representing the best of German youth, were among the original six White Rose students who were destined for a Nazi guillotine.

Youth, Idealism, Rebellion

Hans Fritz Scholl was born in 1918, sister Sophie in 1921, children of the local mayor in Forchtenberg, Württemberg. The Scholls later moved to Ulm, a larger town in Swabia. The five Scholl children, with Hans the eldest, formed a closely knit family. Big brother Hans, tall, thin, happy in disposition, was dominant among the siblings, but loved for his open and gregarious disposition. Sophie was popular because of her sense of humor. Mother Scholl, who had been associated with a Protestant nursing order, did not insist that the children attend church regularly, but they often read the Bible at home.

The Scholls, like every other family in Germany in 1933, were affected by the revolutionary changes resulting from the advent of Nazism. From the beginning, the father was opposed to Hitler, whom he dismissed as "the scourge of God," and, indeed, spent some time in jail for his beliefs. Fifteen-year-old Hans, on the other hand, was at first attracted by Hitler's appeal to youth, "tough as leather, hard as Krupp steel." This was a great new movement designed for the regeneration of the Fatherland. Hans saw his father as a reactionary who just underestimated the great wave of the future. The typical adolescent, he would break with his parent, who just did not understand, and defy his authority. He joined the Hitler Youth organizations and his brothers and sisters followed. The old man, said the kids, was old-fashioned.

Hans and Sophie, especially, were attracted by the *Fuehrer's* promise of a people's community, by a new order of social justice. Both entered zealously into their training. Hans made the long field marches with heavy pack. He learned to read maps, camp in the open fields, and listen carefully to the eternal political indoctrination. He became a model for others, for young Germans on whom Hitler relied to make a new world.

The youngsters were delighted by their new role. Elder sister Inge described the milieu in a book she wrote later: "We were taken seriously—in a quite remarkable way—and that aroused our enthusiasm. We felt we belonged to a large, well-organized body which honored and embraced everyone from the ten-year-old to the grown man. We believed that there was a role for us in the historic process, in a movement that was transforming the masses into a *Volk*. . . . In our group there developed a sense of belonging that carried us safely through the difficulties and loneliness of adolescence, or at least gave us that illusion."

Tomboy Sophie, too, marched and sang with her fellow-students. She was entranced by the physical activity, climbing trees and doing her best to match the boys in racing, swimming, and wrestling. She became a leader of the *Bund Deutscher Mädel* (League of German Girls), the feminine counterpart of the Hitler Youth. She was proud of holding the same rank in her unit as Hans in his group.

Brother and sister, both quick-witted and intelligent, had one reservation at the time—they were disturbed by the anti-Semitic tone of the movement. Both had Jewish friends, and they could not see any justification for the intensifying campaign of vilification against Jews. Sophie was upset because one of her closest friends was not allowed to join her unit because she was

Jewish—yet the girl was blond and blue-eyed and seemed to be more "Aryan" than Sophie herself. It made no sense to Sophie. She dared to speak up about the matter.

Then came further disenchantment.

Hans was chosen to be flag-bearer for his troop at the flamboyant annual Party Rally held in Nuremberg in September 1936. It was an intoxicating jamboree of enormous size, with 200,000 Nazis of all ranks and blaring bands plus marching boots demonstrating the might and power of Nazism. The idea was to instill pride in all Germans because of their regeneration and to impress the world with the strength of the Hitler movement. Hans, at first caught in the delirium of the day, marched along with his enthusiastic comrades.

Hans had gone to the rally in an outburst of patriotic fervor. He returned to Ulm moody and depressed. Something had happened to the young man. Over and over again he had heard the words "blind obedience" and "absolute discipline." Bored with Nazi racialism, he was angered by obscenities hurled at Jews. He heard Hitler speak—and he did not like what the man said. "Force is the first law of nature. Only force rules. Conscience is a Jewish invention, a blemish, like circumcision."

And there had been an incident which caused trouble. To give his own unit a special distinction (he held the rank of *Fenleinfuehrer,* in charge of 150 boys), Hans proposed that they make a flag of their own to supplement the swastika banners which all other units carried. The boys agreed and made their own version of a homemade banner dedicated to the *Fuehrer* and to which they pledged their loyalty. At a parade before high officers of the Hitler Youth, a boy of twelve carried the new banner.

Seeing the unusual emblem, a Hitler Youth leader of superior rank demanded that it be surrendered. The twelve-year old, astonished by the order, stood firm. "Give it to me," said the Youth leader. "You have no right to a flag of your own." The order was repeated three times.

Standing by and noting the dilemma of his youngster, Hans intervened. Why in the world couldn't the Youth leader see what this banner meant to his boys? "Stop bullying him," he said. Then he stepped forward and slapped the Youth leader a sharp blow on the ear. Astonished reaction. That was never done in the Hitler Youth—it was an act of insubordination which could not be tolerated.

That was the end of Hans Scholl's career in the Hitler Youth.

The flag incident signalled an abrupt about-face for Hans. From then on he was convinced that he had made a mistake in pledging his allegiance to a movement which he now believed would lead to the destruction of his beloved country. Events tumbling over one another confirmed his skepticism. Something had to be done to rescue Germany from this compounding danger.

The First Leaflet

After much agonized deliberation, Hans Scholl decided that the only way to bring an end to the war was to write and circulate leaflets directed against the Nazi regime. He regarded German treatment of people in occupied territories as an abomination. "As a good citizen I could not remain indifferent to the fate of my people. I decided to assert my conviction in deeds, not merely in thought. In this way I was motivated by the idea of writing and producing leaflets." The thought came to him as early as the summer of 1941.

Hans needed only a typewriter, paper, and a duplicating machine. He managed to obtain the use of an empty studio in a basement at an isolated spot. There he would express his antagonism to the Hitler government. He would strike back against the dictatorship. From his underground shelter he wrote, mimeographed, and circulated the leaflets that were to cost him his life.

The first leaflet appeared in the summer of 1942. Like the succeeding five, this one had the heading:

Flugblätter der Weissen Rose (Leaflets of the White Rose)

The white rose was chosen as a symbol of purity and innocence. Use of the word "leaflets" in the plural gave notice that additional leaflets could be expected. For the first time in the existence of the Third Reich, opposition to Hitler and his policies appeared among angry students.

The text began on a highly moral, almost pedantic tone. Hans Scholl knew he was risking his life in a seditious act, but he was willing to take the chance:

> Nothing is more unworthy of a cultured nation than to allow itself, without opposition to be 'governed' by an irresponsible clique subject to dark instincts. It is certainly a fact that today every honest German is ashamed of his government. Who among us has any idea of the enormity of the shame that has befallen us and our children when one day the veil falls from our eyes and the most horrible of crimes—crimes that cannot even be measured—reach the light of day?

> If the German people are already so corrupted and decayed that they do not raise a hand and, unthinkingly, trusting in a questionable law of history, yield man's highest possession—which raises him as a human being above all other creatures, if they abandon free will, the freedom of mankind to grasp and turn the wheel of history in line with rational decisions, if they are so devoid of all individuality, have, indeed, gone so far on the road to becoming a spiritless and cowardly mass—then, indeed, they deserve their downfall.

Hans then went on to discuss a passage from Schiller's *"The Legislation of Lycurgus,"* in which the great poet revealed how the rigidity of the Spartan state inevitably led to its downfall. One passage obviously was intended to show a clear-cut contemporary relevance. The legislation of Lycurgus, Hans wrote, seemed to be a political and psychological masterpiece, unless one looked at it in human terms. Its very perfection and durability proved to be its weakness. The longer such a state existed, the more harm it caused. It sacrificed moral values. It not only accepted the idea of slavery, but called for cruelty in enforcing it. The Spartan republic could only endure "if the mental development of the people was arrested, and it could continue to maintain its existence only if it failed to fulfill the highest and only true purpose of political government.'' The passage was clearly meant to reveal the dangers of the Hitler regime.

The letter-writer then went on for a total of 800 words, seeking by reasoned logic to convince his readers of the tremendous danger of the Nazi regime. This was not a fiery tirade calling all Germans to the barricades, but an angry polemic seeking to awaken Germans to what was happening to them. Hans charged that ''by a slow, systematic, and treacherous process, the German people had been thrust into a spiritual prison.'' The times were desperate. Any German who felt himself to be a part of the Christian culture of the West must defend himself against Fascism and the system of totalitarianism. It was important to struggle against ''this atheistic war machine, before the last of our youth perishes for the hubris of a maniac.''

Heinrich Himmler's reaction when he saw the leaflet calling the *Fuehrer* a ''maniac'' may well be imagined. This was treason—and the perpetrator must be found and eliminated.

In his conclusion, Hans turned to Goethe, the greatest and most respected of German poets. In his *The Awakening of Epimenides*, Goethe offered hope that the beasts of the pit would not prevail:

> He who has risen courageously from the abyss,
> May conquer half the world
> Through cunning and ruthlessness,
> Yet to the abyss he must return.

Goethe urged solace in the voice of Hope. The ''beautiful word Freedom'' would be whispered and murmured until ''We, on the steps of our temple, sing out with fresh delight 'Freedom! Freedom!' ''

And at the bottom: ''COPY THIS PAGE AND PASS IT ON.''

Six More Leaflets

During the summer of 1942, four additional anti-Nazi leaflets of unknown origin were distributed anonymously and in deep secrecy. Most were posted in various cities to hide the fact that Munich was the center of the campaign. Several members of the White Rose group went by train to distribute the leaflets. Those who received copies by mail were assured that their names were simply taken from telephone books. The idea was to free them from fear of punishment.

Gestapo alert. For the secret police this was treason and the traitors had to be found. Those who wrote these leaflets, they said, were "hostile to the state in the highest degree." Ferret them out and throw them into *Gestapo* dungeons. It was absolutely necessary to eliminate these dangerous dissenters.

The second leaflet, again typewritten and produced on a duplicating machine, began in much the same way:

> It is impossible to discuss National Socialism rationally because there is nothing rational about it.

> It is false to speak of a National Socialist world view, Weltanschauung, because, if there is any such thing, one would have to try through analysis and discussion either to prove its validity or to fight it.

> In reality, however, there is an altogether different picture: from the time it first began this movement depended on the deception of one's fellow man. Even then it was rotten to the core and could save itself only by constant lies. Hitler wrote in his book (a book written in the worst German I have ever read, and still it has been elevated to the rank of a Bible in this nation of poets and thinkers): "It is unbelievable to what extent one must deceive a people in order to rule it."

The new leaflet then went on to denounce the German people for their silence in the face of the crimes being perpetrated in their name. At first, this cancerous growth was not noticeable because there were still enough forces at work operating for the good, so that the movement was kept at bay. But as it grew larger and finally won its way to power, "the tumor broke open and befouled the whole body." Most of the former opponents went into hiding and the German intelligentsia fled to a dark cellar, "like night shades away from light and sun, gradually to choke to death." It was the task of Germans to find one another again, to enlighten each other, never to rest until the last man was persuaded of the urgent need to struggle against the system.

The leaflet took on an optimistic tone. A wave of unrest would sweep the land, and in a mighty effort the system could be shaken off. "After all, better a terrible end than an endless terror."

The text then referred to the massacre of some 300,000 Jews in Poland. "We see here the most frightful crime against the dignity of man, a crime without parallel in human history." Every German should be aware of his own guilt in tolerating a regime which committed such crimes. "The apathetic behavior of the German people . . . made it possible for this government to come to power in the first place. Everyone wants to excuse himself from his share of blame and then go back to sleep with a good conscience. That cannot be done: everyone is guilty! guilty! guilty! *[Schuldig! Schuldig! Schuldig!]*."

For the first time the question of collective guilt, which would arise after the war, was projected inside Germany. "It is the first and highest duty—indeed, the sacred duty—of every German to exterminate these beasts."

Like the first leaflet, the second closed with a pertinent quotation. This time the words came from Chinese philosopher Lao-tze on the futility of violence and passion: "Whoever attempts to force the nation ruins it. And he who seeks to overpower it loses it."

Hans Scholl's judgment of the Nazi regime was very near to that of historians who after the fall of the Third Reich described the Hitler regime and its crimes. Here was a young German of the highest moral courage placing his life at stake in an attempt to warn his countrymen of the appalling danger they were facing.

The third leaflet discussed forms of governments and what the citizen had a right to expect from the state. The highest form was the City of God. The text denounced the Nazi regime as "a mechanical political contrivance operated by criminals and drunkards." This was a dictatorship of evil and something had to be done about it. It asked the questions: "Why do you not rise up? Why do you endure this? It is not only your right but your moral duty to overthrow this system." Cowardice must not hide behind a cloud of prudence. Germans will be scattered over the face of the earth like dust in the wind, if they could not summon up the courage that had thus far failed them.

The text went on to recommend resistance. It was not military victory over Bolshevism that must be the main concern of Germans, but, on the contrary, defeat of the Nazis. The leaflet recommended sabotage in armament and war-industry plants, in gatherings, meetings, festivals, organizations, anything which supported National Socialism. It urged citizens to refuse to give a *pfennig* to street collections or contribute to drives for scrap metal and clothing.

Again a final quotation, this time from Aristotle's *Politics,* a passage on tyranny. The reader was promised additional information.

The fourth leaflet, which appeared in mid-July 1942, had as its theme an appeal to Christians to strike back at the evil of Nazism. The struggle against Hitler was depicted as one against the devil. Monsters, symbolic of the anti-Christ, had emerged from the abyss. Germans must return to faith and religion. There was one quotation from *Ecclesiastes* and another from the German poet Novalis: "Only religion can reawaken Europe and restore Christianity to its earthly mission."

This new leaflet admitted that Hitler had won victories in Russia and Africa, but these triumphs were "illusory" and won at enormous cost. The *Fuehrer* had lied shamelessly: "Every word that comes out of his mouth is a lie. His mouth is the stinking pit of hell and his power corrupt to the core."

A postscript assured the reader that the White Rose was not in the pay of any foreign government. "We know that National

Socialist power must be destroyed by military means, but we seek a renewal from within. . . . We will not be silent."

There were two more leaflets, the final one a special appeal to students to win a new breakthrough to freedom and honor. There was good news—the Germans had had a staggering defeat at Stalingrad.

Prisoner of the *Gestapo*

As leaflets appeared one after the other in several cities, the *Gestapo* redoubled its efforts to find those guilty of "striking at the security of the State." After intense investigation, it was decided that the dangerous sheets were being produced in Munich and that elaborate steps had been taken to confuse the authorities by using false leads in other cities. The leaflets were being sent apparently only to important personages in the intellectual community, an indication that the treasonable work was that of students. In the lexicon of capital offenses drawn up by the *Gestapo,* this was the worst and most dangerous of all conspiracies. The traitors had to be found and exterminated.

Meanwhile, in Munich, Hans and Sophie Scholl and their comrades were redoubling their efforts. Both were encouraged by student reaction at the 470th anniversary celebration of the University of Munich. An audience of several thousand students was addressed by the Bavarian *Gauleiter* (district leader) Paul Giesler. He spoke glowingly of the celebration and the place of students in the national struggle. The enthusiastic speaker urged the women students present, even though they were at the university, to present the *Fuehrer* with a son for every year at the university. If they were not attractive enough to ensnare a man, then he, himself, would be glad to send an adjutant to each of them to give them "an enjoyable experience."

Pandemonium in the audience. Furious women who tried to leave were stopped by guards. Male students, many in uniform, began to boo Giesler. The angered speaker ordered the arrest of women protesters. Students turned on the police. The *Gauleiter* threatened to close the university if peace was not restored.

The Munich students had won a clear-cut, if temporary, victory. The Scholls were encouraged by the demonstration but certainly overestimated its importance. Yet, the incident at the auditorium showed them that students, indeed, could stand up to the Nazis. They became bolder. They now took to the streets of Munich to write graffiti on its walls. "Down with Nazis!" "Down with Hitler!" "Freedom!" They were armed and intended to fight their way out of any arrest.

February 18, 1943—a fateful day in the lives of brother and sister. At 10 o'clock on that morning, Hans and Sophie started out for the university, which was close to their living quarters. On that sunny day the two students seemed to be on their way to classes. But Hans was carrying a heavy suitcase. It was fully packed with leaflets.

Crossing the square, the two went through an arch leading to the university and entered the main hall. Hans was aware that the *Gestapo* was on his trail and might arrest him at any moment, but he was determined, nevertheless, to carry out his self-imposed mission. Friends later described his action on that day as "youthful recklessness." He was convinced, now that Nazism had received mortal blows at Stalingrad and North Africa, that the end of the Third Reich was fast approaching and that he must do what he could to facilitate it.

Sophie, at his side and fully agreeing with the intent of her brother, hoped with him to arouse the entire student body of the university into rebellion against the government. It was dangerous and risky, but they would chance it.

Moving cautiously, Hans and Sophie opened the suitcase and removed the leaflets, which numbered about 1,700. Lectures were in progress and the doors closed. The two moved up and down the corridors and deposited stacks of sheets at the closed doors. They placed other piles on stairs, window sills, and around the entrance hall.

There were some leaflets left several minutes before the morning lectures were to end. At this moment Hans and Sophie made a tragic mistake. On impulse they gathered the remaining leaflets and bounded up the steps to the high gallery running around the hall. Here they began to throw the sheets into the air and watched them flutter down to the floor below.

They were seen by university porter Jakob Schmid, Nazi and part-time Storm Trooper. Briefed by the *Gestapo* to watch for any suspicious activities among the students, he quickly locked the doors of the hall and rushed to a telephone to alert his boss. He grabbed Hans and Sophie, informed them that they were under arrest, and brought them to Dr. Walter Wüst, University Chancellor and a colonel in the *SS*. *Gestapo* agents soon arrived, handcuffed the two and took them off to headquarters.

Interrogation and Trial

At first, Hans and Sophie denied everything. They were at the university even though they had no classes because they had a date with a friend. They were carrying an empty suitcase because they were on their way to Ulm to get fresh laundry. The porter, with hundreds of students milling about, had become confused and took the wrong people into custody.

A likely story. *Gestapo* agents searched Hans's room and found incriminating evidence, including a large supply of postage stamps and the same kind of envelopes in which the leaflets had been mailed. In the nearby studio they discovered the typewriter, mimeograph machine, and special paper used for the leaflets. The police were efficient—by now it was clear that they had the guilty students.

Told about the new evidence against them, Hans and Sophie completely reversed their stand. They now admitted all the charges. What they had in mind was to divert suspicion from all their fellow-conspirators and to take the blame themselves. They were anxious to shield Professor Kurt Huber and their fellow-students from the fate they knew was in store for themselves.

There was much satisfaction among the higher echelons of the Nazi bureaucracy. To these officials, Hans and Sophie Scholl, as well as fellow-conspirator Christoph Hermann Probst, were guilty of the worst crime a German could commit.

They were calling for the overthrow of the government in the critical days of the war, and even worse, they had condemned the great *Fuehrer* as a mass murderer. Off with their heads!

Within three days, a formal indictment was drawn up by the Chief Prosecutor of the People's Court in Berlin. The three prisoners were charged with high treason, with the aim of seeking by force to change the Constitution of the Third Reich. They were accused of rendering the *Wehrmacht* incapable of fulfilling its duties, of distributing subversive literature, of helping foreign powers, and of trying to paralyze the will of the German people.

Found guilty, the three were sentenced to death.

In her last talk with her parents Sophie Scholl said with a wry smile: "We have taken everything upon ourselves." Hans added: "I have no hate." On February 22, 1943, Sophie told her fellow-prisoners that she thought "thousands will be stirred and awakened by what we have done." It was rumored that her leg had been broken by *Gestapo* interrogators and that she was forced to hobble on crutches to the scaffold. Eyewitnesses reported that both brother and sister went to their deaths with extraordinary courage and dignity. Sophie walked "as if she were looking into the sun." As the executioner was about to release the blade of the guillotine, Hans called out: "Long live freedom!"

Sophie Scholl had written in her diary:

My heart soon gets lost in petty anxieties and forgets that death is near. It is quite unprepared, quickly distracted by frivolous incidentals, it could easily be taken by surprise when the hour comes and miss the one great joy for the sake of little pleasures.

I realize this but not so my heart. It continues to dream, refuses to listen to reason, is lulled into safety by the consoling words of irritating warders and fluctuates between joy and sorrow. Sorrow is all that is left, paralysis, utter helplessness, and a faint hope.

Such was the lovely German maiden condemned to an ignominious death by a chimerical creature who saw himself as the
greatest German who ever lived.

"White Rose" for Freedom

What can one say about the tragic story of these two Resistance fighters found guilty and cut off in the prime of life?

Brother and sister Hans and Sophie Scholl would have been
the last to look upon themselves and their White Rose comrades
as heroes. There was nothing sensational in their background:
they came from a bourgeois-Christian family and like millions
of their generation believed originally in the national regeneration promised by the Austrian demagogue and his followers.

These two admirable young Germans learned more quickly
than other Germans that their country had fallen into the hands
of a criminal. They disdained the use of terror—they would not
place bombs in convenient spots. Instead, they opted for the
mimeographed word to plead for attention. In sarcastic prose
they "thanked" the *Fuehrer* for driving 330,000 Germans to
their deaths in Stalingrad. They warned that the day of settlement was coming. In the name of German youth they demanded
that Adolf Hitler's government restore freedom to the German
people.

For Hitler, Hans and Sophie Scholl were far too dangerous to
be allowed to live. These students who refused to be cowed had
to be wiped from the face of the earth. Vengeance was the Nazi
reply to calls for freedom.

The Scholls lost their battle. The same evening of the executions students at Munich, instead of rebelling as the Scholls had
hoped, held a demonstration at the university courtyard demonstrating their loyalty to Hitler.

Friedrich von Logau said it: "The mills of the gods grind
slowly." On July 13, 1958, fifteen years after the beheading of
Hans and Sophie Scholl, Munich University unveiled a memorial to the White Rose movement. The names of seven leaders
of the resistance group were engraved on a bronze plaque.

Both postwar German governments paid tribute to the brother and sister who had defied Hitler. In 1961 the German Democratic Republic issued a special postage stamp in honor of both Scholls. In 1964 another stamp dedicated to them was circulated by the Federal Republic of West Germany.

6*

PROFESSOR KURT HUBER:
Academician

―――――――

We must try to fan the spark of resistance that is in the heart of a million honorable Germans until it flares up boldly and brightly.

Irrepressible Academic

"THOSE WHO CAN, DO; THOSE WHO CAN'T, TEACH." THIS VERDICT BY iconoclast George Bernard Shaw satisfies those who worship the sound of money. There are many who ridicule the professoriate as composed of hopeless and helpless idiots who do not have sense enough to acquire material rewards for their labor. The theme: "If they are so smart, why don't they get rich?"

Not so in pre-Hitler Germany. By the end of the fifteenth century, Germany possessed a network of universities that served every large region or province of the Holy Roman Empire, including Switzerland (Basle) and the Low Countries (Louvain). Most of these great institutions, from Heidelberg to Cologne and Göttingen, played a significant role in the intellectual history of Europe. They enjoyed a widespread reputation and had the admiration of people everywhere.

The German public customarily placed their professors at the top level of society along with the military and industrialists. It was a normal spectacle in a university town to see the respected professor with books under arm and in top hat bicycling to his 8 A.M. morning lecture (he could not afford more expensive transportation). These were the men bringing honor and esteem to the German name throughout the world.

Though German historical development in the last several centuries tended toward the authoritarian, academics jealously guarded their idea of freedom of expression. Philosopher Johann Gottlieb Fichte, while teaching in Jena in 1793, published a short introduction to an essay in which God was defined as the moral order of the universe, the eternal law of right that is the foundation of all man's being. The electoral government of Saxony called for Fichte's expulsion from Jena as an atheist. The philosopher threatened to resign in case of a reprimand. Much to his distress this was taken as an offer to step down—and it was duly accepted.

There were other examples of conflict between independent professors and state authorities. When in August 1819 Prince Metternich drew up the Carlsbad Decrees designed to crush liberalism and nationalism in the Germanies he paid unusual attention to the universities. He appointed special officials "to observe carefully the spirit shown by the instructors in their lectures . . . and to give salutary direction to the teaching." Metternich's decrees, sanctioned by the Diet of the German Confederation, throttled opinion of the academics for a generation.

German professors seldom ceased to speak out in what they regarded as unjust situations. When in 1837 King William IV of England died, his brother in Hanover, Ernst August, in conjunction with the Salic Law, took over control of Hanover and lifted its constitution. Seven protesting Göttingen professors, the "Gottinger Seven" (Jakob and Wilhelm Grimm, Dahlmann, Gervinus, Ewald, Albrecht, and Weber), were removed from their posts on the faculty.

Though the spirit of independence persisted, most German professors at the outbreak of World War I came to the defense of the Fatherland. In the "Manifesto of the German University Professors and Men of Science," ninety-three of the country's most eminent intellectuals presented what was seen as an authoritative statement of the German case. "We hereby protest to the civilized world against the lies and calumnies with which our enemies are endeavoring to stain the honor of Germany in her hard struggle for existence—in a struggle that has been forced upon her." Among the signers were Emil von Behring, Professor of Medicine, Marburg; Professor Paul Ehrlich, Frankfurt am Main; Fritz Haber, Professor of Chemistry, Berlin; Professor Adolf von Harnack, General Director of the Royal Library, Berlin; Karl Lamprecht, Professor of History, Leipzig; Max Planck, Professor of Physics, Berlin; Max Reinhardt, Professor of the German Theater, Berlin; Wilhelm Roentgen, Professor of Physics, Munich; and Gustav von Schmoller, Professor of National Economy, Berlin. Distinguished scholars all.

As soon as he came to power, Hitler began his process of *Gleichschaltung,* or coördination of every institution in the nation to conform with Nazi ideology and doctrine. Among his first victims were Jewish academicians in many disciplines, who were forced to flee the country and later contributed mightily to the Allied power which eventually crushed the Third Reich. Other eminent professors were dismissed and replaced by Nazi Party stalwarts notable only for their ignorance and incompetency. The result was a cataclysmic drop in the reputation of German universities, once the envy of the entire world.

Among the academics who decided to stay in Germany and work from the inside in what they regarded as a catastrophic situation was a little, frail-looking, crippled professor with a will of iron. Let the others go—he would fight the tyrant with every ounce of his strength.

Toward a Brilliant Career

Kurt Huber was born on October 24, 1893, in Chur (Switzerland), where his father worked at the canton school. After 1897 the family lived in Stuttgart, where the young boy was a student at the *Gymnasium.* Born into a family of culture, with both parents as educators, the lad was taught the piano by his mother and harmony and counterpoint by his father. Unfortunately, young Kurt was physically handicapped by infantile paralysis, which left his right leg lame. When he walked the leg seemed to drag behind him. There may also have been some evidence of multiple sclerosis with head-shaking and trembling of hands. It was difficult for the young man to move about and it was impossible for him to take part in the usual games of his comrades. But those who knew him were impressed by the clarity of his mind and the logic of his expressions.

Kurt went on to an exceptionally fine university career. He enrolled at the University of Munich as a major in philosophy and psychology. His special interests were elementary motifs in music, Bavarian folk songs, and psychological problems of music theory, concerns that remained with him for the rest of his life. After study with distinguished musicologists, he took his doctorate in 1917 *summa cum laude*.

With this outstanding record as a student, Kurt decided on an academic career and soon was qualified as a university lecturer. His goal was to continue his studies at the University of Munich, where, along with his philosophical and psychological preferences, he hoped to devote his time to technical research on sound and acoustics.

In 1926 Huber applied for a permanent post at Munich, only to be told coldly by a university official that "only professors who are officer material" could be successful in an academic post there. The implication was clear—cripples were not wanted. More sensible heads prevailed. Huber's academic record was so superior that other university officials saw to it that he was appointed *Privatdozent,* or Assistant Professor. This was a special designation for a distinguished young graduate recognized as an effective teacher. The post was unsalaried and any income depended upon the number of students the *Dozent* could attract.

Huber was overjoyed. That was all he needed—appointment at the bottom rung of the academic ladder. He would take full advantage of the opportunity. Meanwhile, he began to acquire a reputation throughout Germany and abroad as an authority on folk songs and folk music. His name became known because of his special blend of scholar and technician and especially for his recordings of Bavarian folk songs.

Students began to talk about the young professor at Munich. They came from all over the country to attend his lectures. University officials were so impressed that they appointed Huber Professor Extraordinary of Musicology, a title which brought him enormous pleasure but little in the way of remuneration.

Students were excited by the little lame professor who seemed to have difficulty in mounting the platform. His voice was high-pitched and it was difficult for him to get the words out. Colleagues believed that his lectures would be sparsely attended because students would find it troublesome to understand him.

The concerned colleagues were wrong. Exactly the opposite occurred. Huber's lecture rooms were overcrowded by enthusiastic students. Fascinated by the brilliance of their teacher, they paid no attention to his physical handicaps and listened intently as he presented his logical, clear-cut expositions as if he were an intellectual architect. While the outside world seethed on the verge of madness, the crippled young professor brought some sense of decency to his eager students. He devoted special attention to theodicy, the justification of God's force to man and the vindication of divine justice as an alternative to evil.

As an admirer of Gottfried Wilhelm Leibniz and his theory of the pre-established harmony of the universe, Huber urged his students to accept the philosopher's conclusion that everything in life was working for an ultimate goal—the elimination of evil. It was a philosophy of optimism in pessimistic times. This universe is the best of all possible worlds. Faith and reason are essentially harmonious, and nothing can be received as an article of faith which contradicts the eternal truth. God is "the universal harmony." Admittedly, there is evil in this best of all possible worlds, but evil is a mere set-off to the good, which it increases by contrast. Evil, according to Leibniz, is a mere imperfection and would inevitably be conquered by the existing good in the world. All things are arranged from the time of creation for ultimate good, and this meant the final elimination of evil.

Huber's students listened intently as their teacher presented his optimistic philosophy. Many of them were embittered by the cruelty and brutality they saw in the world around them. In Huber's lectures they could find some explanation for the insanity of the world and some relief. They were grateful to the lame little professor and many rushed early to his lecture room to be sure to get a seat.

In 1936 Huber represented Germany at the International Congress of Folk Music in Barcelona. Already recognized as an expert in his field, he was invited in 1937 by the Prussian Ministry of Culture to come to Berlin to serve in the section dealing with German folk music.

Break with Nazism

By this time the Nazi regime was well under way and Hitler's policy of coördination had been inaugurated to bring every element of German society under the dictator's control. During these early years Huber, like many other Germans, was willing to give the frenzied politician the benefit of any doubt in the hope that he would be sobered by the responsibilities of his lofty position. But the professor and conscientious Germans were soon disenchanted. More and more they came to the conclusion that Germany's version of fascism was actually a descent into evil which had brought the entire country into a new form of slavery. Huber felt that this grotesque Nazi state was seeking to bring every German into its octopus-like claws, that its policy of aggression would eventually mean the destruction of the country. For the philosophic professor, Hitler was in reality the personification of evil.

Huber became even more convinced of his views during his year at Berlin. He came into conflict with leaders of the Hitler Youth as well as with students who accused him of being lukewarm in his enthusiasm for Nazism. Students attracted by the drum-beating and circuses of the Nazi movement demanded that Huber take a more active pro-Nazi role. The young professor, schooled in the struggle between good and evil, was not inclined to alter his views and support the Nazi procession. Far from joining the Hitler parade, he saw the dictator and his blinded followers as representing a new vulgarity and bestiality that had no place in a decent society. Far from retreating into silence, he cast his lot with dissenters who were willing to place their lives on the line to fight against what they regarded as a shameful situation for the Fatherland.

Sobered by his experience in Berlin, Huber resigned his post in 1938 and returned to Munich. There he hoped to find more of the students who had listened respectfully to his views on Leibniz and the conflict between good and evil. The unpolitical little professor now emerged as a "moral politician," as Kant had recommended. He would not sit back passively and see the reputation of his country destroyed. He would speak out and try to help stem the flood of evil.

Activist Dissenter

Nazi authorities were quick to recognize the danger. They would not allow this crippled little pedant to thwart the great work of the *Fuehrer*. The Nazi regime was making giant strides in its efforts to obtain living space for the German people and no one, least of all a loud-mouthed professor, would stand in the way. This recalcitrant academic must be silenced.

Among the students who sat transfixed in Professor Huber's classroom was a serious-minded young girl, Sophie Scholl, who made certain to come early to get a seat for the lectures. Sophie, among other students, felt that the evil of which the professor spoke had come to Germany in the form of National Socialism. A youthful idealist, she was certain that the more the rule of force was expanded, the less place there would be for all that gave meaning to the business of living. Barbarians had taken control of her country and were stamping out the goodness of German life. The professor was right; something had to be done to save the nation from impending disaster.

For Sophie Scholl, Professor Huber was a kindred spirit. As it turned out, his name was to be as closely connected with the White Rose society as her own. Other students, impressed by her enthusiasm, joined her in making a kind of cult of Professor Huber's classes.

In 1942, in the midst of the war, Sophie and her medical-student brother Hans founded the White Rose *(Weisse Rose)* to work for "the renewal of the morally wounded German spirit."

Encouraged by Professor Huber, they recruited students at Munich and other universities for their society. Their main weapon against a powerful state bureaucracy was a small duplicating machine. Their password "White Rose" was designed as a symbol of the Christian spirit which loved everything that was noble and beautiful and opposed the "evil" that had descended upon their country. Later, the group dropped the name of White Rose so that it could operate as much as possible outside the university and avoid the attention of the *Gestapo*.

Huber was delighted by the formation and activities of the White Rose. He made it a point to give advice and encouragement to the dissenting students. "Our task," he told them, "will be to send the truth as clearly and audibly as we can through the darkness of Germany. . . . Such a campaign will give those individuals who stand alone, isolated in their denial of Hitler, the sense of having at their side a great number of others who think as they do. That will strengthen their courage and endurance. We must also try to educate those Germans who do not yet clearly understand the sinister intentions of our Government and awaken in them too the spark of resistance and conscientious opposition. Together, perhaps, we may succeed in shaking off the tyranny at the eleventh hour and in using that wonderful moment to build up with the other peoples of Europe a new, more humane world, in which nations and states will regard each other as neighbors and not as enemies."

Considering Hitler's intention to apply force in stamping out all opposition, Huber and his students were showing enormous courage, perhaps foolhardy under the circumstances. The "Student Company" apparently did not care. Together with their professor they met in secret and discussed their plans for getting rid of the hated regime. They learned that medical students among them were to be posted to the Russian front to serve during their vacation period. The rumor was true: medical students received orders to leave for Russia within twenty-four hours.

Meanwhile, the students began their campaign of leaflets. From their duplicating machine came stirring words of protest. The name of Germany would remain forever disgraced unless

Dietrich Bonhoeffer

Carl Goerdeler

General Ludwig Beck

Ulrich von Hassell

Julius Leber

Sophie Scholl

Hans Scholl

Professor Kurt Huber

Hans von Dohnanyi

Helmuth von Moltke

Carl von Ossietsky

Adam von Trott zu Solz

Martin Niemoeller

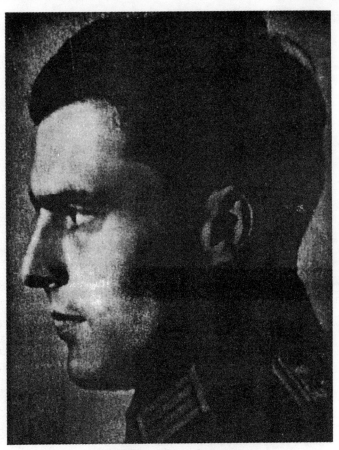
Bamberger Reiter Stauffenberg

Erwin Rommell

German youth rose up in anger, took revenge, smashed the torturers, and constructed a new spirit in Europe. The leaflets were sometimes thrown surreptitiously from a balcony at the university, where students passed them from hand to hand.

Professor Huber, immediately pleased by the leaflet campaign, joined by composing texts for sheets of his own. Typical was this one distributed in the courtyard of the university:

> In the name of German youth we demand that Adolf Hitler return to the German people their personal freedom, their valuable heritage, which he has taken from them in despicable form. We have grown up in a state which has ruthlessly muzzled free expression. The Hitler Youth, the SS, and the SA have tried to put us in uniforms, to revolutionize us, to narcotize us during the most fruitful years of our education.

> They call it "education for a world view" and use contemptible methods to cover independent thought in a fog of empty phrases. . . .

> We are motivated by genuine science and true freedom of spirit. . . .

> The German name has been eternally shamed, unless German youth stands up finally and smashes its tormenters and builds a new spiritual Europe. This is a battle of everyone of us for our future, our freedom and honor. . . .

When medical student Hans Scholl returned from the Eastern Front and reported atrocities by German troops there, Huber and his students redoubled their campaign against the regime. Despite their efforts, they remained amateur conspirators, no match for the efficient *Gestapo*. They tried hard. They investigated thoroughly the background of new members. Each one was given a small task to perform. They had no idea of the hopelessness of their work, but they did not stop. They spoke brave words: "We must dare to deny a despotism which not only tries to annihilate us all who would not agree with it, but

sets itself in arrogance above the deepest and holiest things in
life. We must risk the denial in defense of life itself—none can
relieve us of that responsibility.''

Huber and his students refused to remain silent. They
"thanked" the *Fuehrer* for "Tunisgrad and the coming of the
R.A.F." They denounced "the Hitler bandits" and called for a
free, democratic Germany. At a time when German troops were
being killed on many fronts, student rebels demanded an end to
both the Hitler regime and the unwanted war.

Prisoner of the *Gestapo*

The energetic professor and his amateur conspirators became
prime targets of *Gestapo* agents. Angered Nazi authorities intent upon implementing the orders of their *Fuehrer,* would not
tolerate "traitors" at the university, those misguided students
and professors who were speaking out against the "senseless"
continuation of the war. They had to be silenced. Enough was
enough. The student movement of dissent was spreading from
Munich to Karlsruhe, Freiburg, Leipzig, Königsberg, and
Berlin.

Word came from on high—arrest the lot of them.

On February 27, 1943, grim *Gestapo* agents appeared at Huber's home and took him into custody. The result of his trial
before the People's Court was expected. Huber knew well that
he would be condemned but he faced his destiny calmly and
with raw courage. He had no intention of submitting to Nazi
slavery and he made that clear by his demeanor before the court.

Huber spoke boldly in his defense. He had wanted only order,
security, and trust in the state apparatus, and he had tried to
instill those ideas in his students. He warned about the consequences of placing naked power above simple justice. He urged
his judges to recognize the clear voice of conscience of his
students, their idealistic search for justice and truth. It was
necessary to call a halt to any further assaults on the German
spirit. "I have done only what my conscience orders me to do
and I am willing to take the consequences."

Huber was speaking to deaf ears. He was condemned to death on April 19, 1943, together with his students Willi Graf and Alexander Schmorell.

Final Statement

In prison Huber did what he could to occupy his mind by continuing his professional work as much as possible. Among the notes he kept in his cell was a draft he titled "Final Statement by the Accused." It is not certain but this is probably the statement he made in his defense, or at least the sense of it, before the People's Court. In any event it reveals the character of the man and explains the goal of his teaching career:

> As a German citizen, a German university teacher and a man of political conviction, I regard it not only as a right, but as a moral duty to help shape the destiny of my country, to uncover and to oppose manifest evils. . . .

> What I aimed to do was to rouse my students, not by means of an organization but by the simple word, not to an act of violence, but to an ethical understanding of the grave evils in our present political life. A return to definite ethical principles, to the rule of law, to mutual trust between man and man—that is not illegal, rather in it is the re-establishment of legality. In accordance with Kant's categorical imperative, I have asked myself what would happen if these subjective maxims which govern my own actions become a general rule. To that question there is only one answer—the result would be the restoration of order, security, confidence in our political organization.

> Everyone with any sense of moral responsibility should raise his voice with us against the menacing tyranny of naked power over law, of naked despotism over the will to do what is morally right. The demand for free self-determination, even of the smallest sections, has been violated throughout Europe equally with the demand for the preser-

vation of racial and national traits. The basic condition of the national community has been destroyed because faith between man and man has been systematically undermined. There is no more terrible indictment of a nation than to have to admit—as we all must—that no one can trust his neighbor, that a father cannot even trust his son. . . .

I demand that freedom be restored to the German people. We will not spend our short lives as fettered slaves, even though they be the golden fetters of material abundance.

They have taken from me my title and rights of a professor, my doctorate, bestowed with the highest distinction, and have reduced me to the level of the lowest criminal. But no trial for high treason can rob me of the inner worth of a university teacher, of one who openly and courageously proclaims his philosophy of politics and life. The implacable march of history will justify my aims and actions, of that I am firmly convinced.

I pray to God that the spiritual energies which Germany possesses may be released in time among my countrymen. I have acted in accordance with an inner compulsion. I accept the consequences of the fine words of Johann Gottlieb Fichte:

> And thus you are to act,
> As though the destiny of German life
> Hung solely from your deeds and you,
> And you alone were accountable.*

Postscript

Huber was beheaded on July 13, 1943.

By an ironic twist of fate the adamant professor was enrolled as Member No. 8–282–981 of the National Socialist Party. Huber, who had only contempt for Hitler and the Nazi way of

*From Inge Scholl, *Six Against Tyranny* (London: Murray, 1955), pp. 67-69.

life, was never aware of the fact. In the days when his university income was far too low to support wife Clara, daughter Birgit, and son Wolfgang, with only a few marks available to buy food, wife Clara, without telling her husband, went to the nearest National Socialist headquarters and enrolled her husband as a member of the Party. Huber was astonished when his income suddenly rose to 600 marks a month. He had no explanation for his sudden good fortune.

Party leaders believed that they had now bought the services of the professor and that he would spout Nazi philosophy in his classroom. It was one among many mistakes they made.

For psychohistorians the story of Kurt Huber remains a fascinating case in human motivation. What combination of psychological causes drove the crippled little professor to thrust his entire weight against the Nazi colossus, a little flawed David against a giant Goliath? Perhaps able researchers may one day clarify the mystery of why men of principle willingly sacrifice themselves for a just cause.

7 *

HELMUTH VON MOLTKE:
Kreisau Circle

> *The greatest person morally . . . that I met on either side of
> the battle lines in the Second World War.*
> —*George Kennan*

The Military Heritage

SIX-AND-A-HALF-FEET TALL, LEAN AND STRONG, HE WAS A MAN OF
striking appearance and intellect. He seldom drank and never
smoked. He was known for his exuberant sense of humor. He
loved the simple pleasures of home and countryside and had no
use for the sin spots of Berlin. Throughout his short life of
thirty-eight years he remained a steadfast admirer of Christian
principles. Again, a decent man.

During the war Helmuth James Count von Moltke served his
country as legal adviser to the German High Command. But so
nauseated was he by the tyranny and terror of the Hitler regime
that he became a leading figure of the Resistance. Good Germans, he said, simply had to realize that they were working in
"unnatural surroundings" and had to do what they could to
oppose an inhuman dictator. But he stopped short of tyrannicide: despite his personal courage, he was opposed to any plans
for assassinating Hitler. Opposition and resistance—yes. Murder—no—!

This man of peace bore the famous name of a family known
for its military tradition. The von Moltke surname was one of
the most famous in German history. Helmuth Karl Bernhard
von Moltke (1800–1891), Prussian Field Marshal, was for thirty
years Chief of Staff of the Prussian Army. He had a reputation
as the greatest strategist of the 19th century and creator of the
art of directing armies in the field. Honored by his fellow-coun-

trymen as the architect of victories over Denmark (1864), Austria (1866), and France (1870–71), he was the trustworthy military leader who paved the way for German unification under Otto von Bismarck.

In 1866 Count von Moltke, as a reward for his service in the war against Austria, was awarded a grant of 200,000 thalers by King Wilhelm I of Prussia. When stationed as a young officer at Frankfurt on Oder, he had developed a warm affection for the Silesian countryside. Two years later he bought three neighboring estates of Kreisau, Nieder-Gräditz, and Querilschau. All were relatively modest in size. At Kreisau, Moltke improved the home already existing there. Situated along foothills facing the mountains, the estate became the cherished residence of the Moltkes. Run as a farm, Kreisau produced grain and summer barley for brewers. Provisions were made to pass the estate on to members of the family.

The great name of the original Field Marshal was carried on by Helmuth Johannes Ludwig von Moltke (1848–1916), nephew of his famous namesake. This Moltke was Chief of the General Staff at the outbreak of the Great War in 1914. But the magic of decisive victory was now gone. The new Moltke modified the German attack in the west but was unable to maintain control of his rapidly advancing army, which contributed to the halted German offensive on the Marne in September 1914. Efforts for a quick, decisive victory were frustrated. On September 14, 1940, Kaiser William II replaced Moltke, though the general retained nominal command until the end of the year. He died on June 16, 1918, a broken man.

Helmuth James Count von Moltke, great-grandnephew of the famous Field Marshal, was born at Kreisau, the family estate, on March 11, 1907, the son of a German father and an English–South African mother. His mother, Dorothy Rose James, who had been staying at the Kreisau estate, met Helmuth's father when she was only eighteen, and became engaged within a week. Through his mother young Helmuth learned to speak English fluently, visited England often, and made many friends there. He became a fervent admirer of English liberalism. During his early years his entire family, including eight children, were ardent Christian Scientists.

Helmuth's father, lacking foresight or thrift, turned out to be improvident and had difficulties in managing the Kreisau estate. Young Moltke, who was just twenty-three in 1930 and was studying law, was forced to take over management of the landed property, then in the hands of creditors. Without training in farming or business management, he drove himself to the point of a nervous breakdown, but managed to straighten out the legal problems and keep the estate in the family. He was pleased with his accomplishment, which he had not expected. "People here," he said, "that is to say my family and fellow-workers, keep on being astounded that I am so relaxed and content and unperturbed when everything seems to be going wrong." The young man turned out to be an enlightened landlord.

With control of the estate established, Helmuth resumed his studies in international law at Basle, Berne, Geneva, Paris, The Hague, and especially London and Oxford. So great was his admiration for English law and institutions that in 1938, while in London, he applied for admission to the Inner Temple and started reading English law. At that time he was seriously considering the possibility of earning his living in Britain. Moreover, because his studies required him to eat a number of dinners at the Temple, he had a legitimate excuse for his many trips to London, some seventeen in all.

In London Moltke met such important people as Geoffrey Dawson, editor of *The Times*; Lord Halifax, Foreign Secretary from 1938–40; and Sir John Simon, Home Secretary from 1931–33. Through friends he had access to the Round Table of All Souls College, Oxford. From them he learned much of what he later presented to his own Kreisau Circle. In November 1937 he wrote home: "I now have more friends in London than I have in Berlin."

Formation of the Kreisau Circle

The outbreak of the war in September 1939 depressed Moltke, who deemed it a tragedy that his country was at war with a people he admired and respected. Despite his famous name, he had little use for the military life and had no intention of following in the footsteps of his illustrious forbears. Nevertheless, he offered his services for the duration. Because of his legal training he was attached to the Supreme Command of the German Armed Forces as adviser in law and economic affairs. As an expert in international law, he took up his work in the *Amt/Ausland* (Foreign Office) of the *OKW* (German High Command).

It is not known exactly when Moltke began his opposition to the Hitler regime. Uncomfortable during the Nazi drive to power in the 1930s, he gradually came to the conclusion that this government was not for his beloved country. He was sure that Hitler would lead the nation to destruction. He turned to a close friend for support in organizing a Resistance movement.

That friend, Peter Count Yorck von Wartenburg, also bore a famous name in German military history, a name which brought to mind the Napoleonic wars. Gen. Hans David Ludwig von Yorck (1759–1830) was Prussian Field Marshal and successful commander during the War of Liberation (1813–15). Direct descendant Peter von Yorck, born in 1904, served in the Polish campaign in 1939, but soon turned against Hitler and decided to join the Resistance movement. Working in the War Office in the Bendlerstrasse, he was in an important position to help dissenters. He could make good contacts for the German opposition both in his office and during the many trips he had to make in the course of his duties.

Close friends Helmuth Moltke and Peter Yorck founded the Kreisau Circle, named after the Moltke estate, which dedicated itself to the task of planning for the reorganization of the state after the expected fall of Hitler. Moltke invited a small but trusted group of friends to spend week-ends at Kreisau. Here they could devote themselves to conferences broken by walks in the attractive countryside. They discussed the proper relationship between state and church, the school system and university reform. There were lively debates about the role of both Catholics and Protestants under the Hitler regime.

The Kreisau Circle agreed that the damage done by Hitler to German moral values was deplorable and had to be repaired. They insisted that religion be brought back into German life, as a unifying and not as a divisive factor. There were discussions on actions that had to be taken to punish those who had been guilty of crimes against the law. There were endless talks on how to get rid of the *Fuehrer* and his henchmen, with Moltke invariably speaking against assassination.

The Kreisau group gradually widened its activities. By 1943 in the midst of the war, there were more than twenty members, including representatives of both Catholic and Protestant Churches. All were pledged to secrecy. It was inevitable that word would leak out about existence of the Kreisau Circle. Hitler's security police learned about it and began to seek out the "traitors." Had Hitler realized what his legal adviser was doing he would undoubtedly have ordered his arrest. For the touchy *Fuehrer* anyone working for a "New Order" to replace Nazism was automatically a candidate for extinction. Moltke was willing to take chances in his crusade to restore the image of man in the minds of his fellow-countrymen.

The dedicated dissenter was troubled by the fact that some of his close British friends supported a policy of appeasing Hitler. They had come to the naïve conclusion that concessions would modify Hitler's behavior and that some of his wilder ideas might disappear. Moltke did his best to disabuse them. He urged them to throw support to Catholics and Protestants inside Germany in their opposition to Hitler's new "Positive Christianity." He was especially careful to warn them against the belief that Hitler genuinely desired peace. He contradicted his English friends who cynically believed that relations between nations were anarchic and insisted that there were important unwritten international laws. The man Hitler, he said, was a calamity. Appeasement was dangerous, even stupid.

Moltke wrote to an English friend, even before the war:

> I fear Hitler's policy will be successful in England. I fear that it will prove to be misleading for Germany; it will induce our government to believe that we can count on

English neutrality while in truth should a European war break out, England would fight on the side of France; the possibility of misleading others is what I fear most about the English policy of keeping the balance; England is not an arbiter but a party to struggle, but its lack of rigid policy is what induces Germans to believe she is an arbiter.

Discouraged by the silence of the British Government, Moltke on June 1, 1942, wrote a letter to his close friend, Lionel Curtis, at All Souls College, Oxford. The message, signed "James," was carried back to England by George Bell, Bishop of Chichester, who had traveled to Sweden at the request of the Ministry of Information, ostensibly to maintain contacts with the Swedish Church. Moltke's letter described conditions in Germany in mid-1942:

I hope to get this letter through to you and tell you about the state of affairs on our side. Things are both better and worse than anybody outside Germany can believe. They are worse because the tyranny, the terror, the loss of values of all kinds are greater than I could have believed a short time ago.

Those good people who try to stem the tide are isolated in working in such unnatural surroundings. They cannot trust their comrades, and they are in danger. . . . Thousands of Germans who will survive will be dead mentally, and useless for normal work. . . .

But things are also better in many ways. Most important is the spiritual awakening combined with the preparedness to be found in both Christian confessions, Protestant as well as Catholic. . . . We are trying to build on this foundation, and I hope there will be more tangible proof of this to the outside. Many hundreds of our people will have to die before this is strong enough, but today they are prepared to do so.

It is beginning to dawn on many that they have been misled and are in for a hard time. Not that they might lose the war, that what is done is sinful and that they are person-

ally responsible for every savage act, not in a moral way but
as Christians. . . .

You know that I have fought the Nazis from the first
day. . . . The success of our struggle may probably mean
total collapse as a national unit. But we are ready to face
this. . . .

We can only expect to get our people to overthrow this
reign of terror and horror if we are able to show a picture
beyond the terrifying and hopeless immediate future. . . .

Meanwhile, although he was no longer a Christian Scientist,
Moltke remained dedicated to Christian principles. He did what
he could to help many Jews escape from Germany. Don't kill
the tyrant, but work for his overthrow.

The Kreisau Document

Moltke and his comrades in the Kreisau Circle rejected both
National Socialism and Communism as ways of life for the
future Germany they hoped to see succeed the Third Reich.
They also felt that Western democratic forms, such as that tried
in the Weimar Republic between 1919 and 1933, were not
satisfactory either. They admitted that the kind of traditions that
enabled parliamentary democracy to succeed in the West did
not exist in their Fatherland. What they wanted was a new
political and social form that might bring to Germany—and also
to all Europe—peace, justice, and individual freedom. They
would set up the "German way," a system of law which gave
each individual citizen not only his rights and liberties but also
set the limits of those rights and duties. The idea was "duty of
each to all."

This idea was expressed in the opening "General Principles":

The Government shall look upon Christianity for the basis
of the moral and spiritual renewal of our people, for the

overcoming of hatred and lies, for the rebuilding of the European community of nations.

The point of departure lies in man's obligation to recognize the divine order of things on which human existence is founded both inwardly and outwardly. Only when the divine order has made the test of relations between states can the disorders of the age be overcome and a just and lasting peace created.

The internal reordering of the Reich is the basis on which a just and lasting peace can be built. . . .

The Government of the Reich is determined to fulfill by every means the following essential demands:

1. The principle of legality, which has been trampled under foot, must be made supreme again over all human affairs. Under conscientious, independent, and courageous judges, the foundations of a future peaceful world can be built.

2. Freedom of belief and conscience will be guaranteed. All laws and ordinances which contradict these principles will be repealed immediately.

3. Totalitarian interference with the moral conscience will be broken. The inviolable dignity of human life will be the foundation on which a peaceful and just order will be created. Each citizen will bear his full measure of responsibility in his own social, political, and international activities. The right to work and the right to property will be assured without regard to race, nationality, or religion.

4. The family will be the basic unit of the peaceful life of the community. The family will be assured education and such external necessities of life as food, clothing, housing, garden, and health.

5. Work will be organized so that it encourages rather than restricts the taking of responsibility. . . .

6. The personal political responsibility requires that each person should make his voice heard in small, face-to-face communities. Every individual will have a voice in the State and in the national community, with representatives of his own choice. He will have a living awareness of his personal responsibility for the general course of events.

7. The special responsibility and loyalty which each man owes to his national origin, language, and spiritual heritage and historic heritage of his people must be respected and protected. . . . With the free consent of all participating nations guaranteed, the representatives of this order must be given the right to demand of each individual obedience and respect, and, if it be necessary, even the sacrifice of life and property in the service of the highest political authority of the Community of Nations.

The document went on at length to describe the new political structure, religion and education, industry and economics, foreign affairs, and punishment of crimes. Moltke and his comrades were nauseated by the Nazi regime and its totalitarian character. They wanted to get rid of this charlatan and his gang of cutthroats who, they were convinced, were dragging the name of Germany into the dustbin of history. But at the same time they were anxious to see a successor government established that would merit the respect of all nations. Beyond the simple overthrow of Nazis they saw it as important to halt the spread of religious apathy. They rejected dictatorship and all its values and denounced the idea of power and responsibility concentrated in one hand.

Despite the high-sounding text of the Kreisau document, there were those who criticized it. Helmuth and his comrades belonged to the upper and middle classes, whereas the majority of the lower bourgeoisie turned out to be pro-Nazi. Critics complained that the Kreisau plan was geared to the restoration and privileges of a limited group at the higher level of society, and that its goal was to restore the rights of those who had been subjected to the National Socialist revolution. Other critics complained of the religious intensity displayed in the document. The most important objection was that a portion of German society which had been demoted by the Nazis was trying to recover for itself the rights and privileges which had been denied.

In the long run the document had little effect. It was completed in 1943 at a time when resistance to Hitler, although persistent, was comparatively weak. There would be little freedom—then downfall—imprisonment and death for members of the Kreisau Circle.

Solf Tea Party to Prison Cell

It was almost certain that Hitler's bloodhounds would catch up with Moltke and his colleagues of the Kreisau Circle. Sooner or later one misstep would be made. It happened at the tragic Solf tea party.

The Solf *Kreis* (Circle) was a peripheral group to the Kreisau Circle in the conspiracy against Hitler. It was led by the widow of Wilhelm Solf, for years Colonial Minister under Kaiser William II. Solf also served the Weimar Republic after abdication of the last Hohenzollern and had long warned against the dangers of National Socialism. After his death, Frau Solf and daughter, the Countess Ballestren, and Elizabeth von Thadden, former mistress of a well-known girls' school near Heidelberg, joined in a small group of Anglophile intellectuals. Disgusted by the excesses of Nazism, the Solf circle worked in opposition to Hitler, especially in helping Jews escape the wrath of the *Fuehrer*.

On September 10, 1943, a tea party was held for the conspirators at Fräulein von Thadden's home. Among the guests was Helmuth von Moltke. But, unfortunately for him, there was another guest, a Dr. Reckze, a young physician from the Charité Hospital, who posed as a Swiss national but who was actually a spy for the *Gestapo*. When Frau Solf mentioned that she had a letter which she wanted to send to Switzerland, Reckze graciously offered to take it there for her. He immediately informed the *Gestapo*.

Fatal mistake by Frau Solf. The secret police waited four months and then struck at its quarry.

All the guests at that tea party were to be executed with the exception of Frau Solf and her daughter. They were being tried later before the People's Court on February 3, 1945, when an American bomb fell on the courtroom, killing Judge Roland Freisler and destroying the entire dossier of the Solf case. Through a bureaucratic oversight, mother and daughter were released from Moabit Prison on April 23, 1945.

Moltke was not to be so fortunate. He was brought before the People's Court on January 10, 1945, in a commandeered building in the Bellevue Strasse between the Wilhelmstrasse and the Tiergarten in the very center of Berlin.

The trial was a farce. The prisoner had to face "Hanging Judge" Freisler, the infamous jurist who had presided over the court since 1942. Seldom in the history of jurisprudence has there been anyone to compare with Roland Freisler. As a young man he had been a prisoner during World War I. A Communist after the war, he was chairman of a local Workers' and Soldiers' Council. Joining the Nazis in 1925, he was appointed undersecretary in the Prussian State Ministry of Justice. When the *Volksgericht* (People's Court) was revived in 1942, he was designated its president.

Because of his Communist background Freisler was determined to show his National Socialist zeal. With his eye on the post of Minister of Justice, he sought to win Hitler's attention by becoming more Nazi than the Nazis themselves. He would eliminate all dissenters, just as Stalin had slaughtered the Old Bolsheviks. Shrewd, sharp-witted, cold-blooded, he was unmerciful in the courtroom. He screamed imprecations at the prisoners brought before him and denounced them as miserable traitors. His loud voice reverberated through the courtroom. He was supposed to be an objective judge, but, instead, he conducted proceedings as if he were the prosecuting attorney. One moment he spoke softly but sarcastically, the next his voice rose as he turned on his calculated screams.

The indictment accused Moltke of defeatism of the blackest sort as well as open preparation for treason. It charged that he had revealed an anti-German attitude in a dangerous "assent to tyrannicide." He was being tried because "the People's Court regards as being tantamount to treason any failure to report defeatist utterances such as Moltke's, especially when emanating from a man of consequence and position."

The prosecution brought up Moltke's conversation with conspirator Carl Friedrich Goerdeler. Moltke objected that the police and the security authorities had known all about this talk. Freisler could not control himself. His face went the color of his red robe. He banged on the table and roared: "I cannot stand that. I won't listen to that sort of thing." He went on to denounce the entire Kreisau Circle. He shouted that all of Hitler's officials set about their work in the full belief that victory was at hand. He would not listen to the defense. "It is clearly the duty of every single man for his own part to promote confidence in victory."

"And who was present at Kreisau?" cried the judge. "A Jesuit father! Of all people, a Jesuit father! And a Protestant minister, as well as three others who were condemned for complicity in the July 20th plot! And not a single National Socialist! No, not one! Well, all I can say is now the cat is out of the bag! A Jesuit father, and with him, of all people, you discuss the question of civil disobedience! And the provincial head of the Jesuits, you know him, too! He even came to Kreisau once! Provincial of the Jesuits, one of the highest officials of Germany's most dangerous enemies, he visits Graf Moltke in Kreisau! And you are not ashamed of it, even though no decent German would touch the Jesuits with a barge-pole!"

Irony of ironies! "Judge" Freisler speaking of decent Germans!

At one point in his tirade Freisler shouted at the prisoner: "Now do you appreciate that you are guilty?" Moltke replied that he did not think so. Freisler cried out: "Look here, if you still can't see it, if it still has to be drummed into you, then that shows that you are living in a world of your own, and by your own act have cut yourself off from the fighting community of our people."

The lecture went on: "Only in one respect does National Socialism resemble Christianity: We demand the whole man."

Moltke felt isolated. He regarded himself as a knight representing the spirit of Christianity in a struggle with the Devil incarnate. He described his feelings to his wife: "Finally, I am selected as a Protestant, and attacked and condemned primarily because of my friendship with Catholics, which means that I stood before Freisler as a Protestant, not as a great landowner, not as a nobleman, but as a Prussian, not even as a German. No, I stood as a Christian and nothing else."

Demand for the death penalty. Announcement of the sentence was postponed for twenty-four hours. Then came the verdict: guilty and condemnation to death. No one was surprised. Witnesses reported that Moltke smiled when he heard the words.

Freisler was content. He had eliminated "another archtraitor," another "rank defeatist," and he was doing exactly what the *Fuehrer* wanted him to do. Most of all, he had delivered the death blow to the Kreisau Circle.

Letters from Tegel Prison

For the next eleven days Moltke remained in a death cell at Tegel Prison. His last letters, smuggled from prison, have survived. He wrote to his family in hourly expectation of death. These letters presented his belief that his loved ones, his wife and children, would be protected in the troublesome times ahead through the power of their faith. Moltke saw himself as overwhelmed by the presence of God. The final hours of his life he regarded as no different from any others. He confessed that he was not worried about his last sunset, that the clock would only go around twice more, and that he was really a little intoxicated. "I certainly cannot deny that at present I am in the best of spirits. Only I beg our Heavenly Father that He will keep me in them, for so to die is easier for the flesh. How good God has been to me."

To the very end he maintained his principle of objection to violence. To him that was a manifestation of "the beast in man." Violence, in his view, bred violence. The man facing death did not change his views.

In a farewell letter to his son, Moltke wrote that throughout his life from his schoolboy days on he had fought against a spirit of narrowness and subservience, against arrogance and intolerance, "against the absolute merciless consistency which is deeply engrained in the Germans and has formed its expression in the National Socialist state." He had made it his aim to get that spirit overcome with its evil accomplishments, such as the wrong kind of nationalism, racial persecution, lack of faith, and materialism. And then an amazing admission: "In this case and seen from their own standpoint the National Socialists are right in putting me to death." Thus, a father's last words, stripped of sentiment, to his son.

Even more striking and indicative of the man's character was Moltke's final letter to his wife written on January 11, 1945:

> I think with serene joy about you and our little sons at Kreisau and all the people there. Just now I do not find the departure hard at all. It is possible that this attitude may change. But right now it poses no problem to me. I do not feel at all that I am leaving this earth. . . .
>
> My inner self tells (a) God can bring me back today even as yesterday; and (b) if He calls me to Himself, then I accept it. . . . As I live today I must cling to Him. He does not want more. Is that pharisaical? I do not know. But I believe that I am now living in His grace and mercy. . . .
>
> I am speaking, my heart, the thoughts that come to mind. Something quite different comes now. In the final analysis, what was dramatic at the trial was this: No tangible accusations could be borne out and all of them were dropped. They were forgotten. What the Third Reich fears is that it has to send five men—later it will be seven—to death is in the end only this: your husband, a private individual, of whom they learned that he had talked with two clergymen of both con-

fessions, a Jesuit and a few bishops. They talked, without any intention of doing anything concrete, about things "which belong exclusively to the competence of the Fuehrer." What they discussed was by no means any questions of organization of the Reich, . . . but only the ethical and practical claims of Christianity. Nothing more. For that alone we are being convicted.

Freisler said to me in one of his tirades: "Only in one respect are we and Christianity alike; We demand 'the whole man.' " I do not know whether the audience got all that—it was a kind of dialogue between Freisler and myself It was mental, for I could scarcely get in any words. . . . We talked with each other in a vacuum. . . . "From whom do you have your orders. From the other world or from Adolf Hitler?"

My heart, I have just received your dear letter. The first letter, my heart, in which you have not understood my mood and my situation. No, I am not occupying myself with God or with my death. He has the overwhelming grace to come to me and to concern Himself with me. Is this vainglorious of me? Perhaps. . . .

My heart, my life is completed. I can say of myself that he died old and satiated with life. This does not alter the fact that I should really like to live a little longer, that I should like to accompany you more for a time on this earth. But a new order from God would be necessary for that. The order for which God made me has been fulfilled. If, perhaps, he wants to give me a new order we shall learn about it. Accordingly, you can without hesitating make an effort to save my life in the event that I survive today. Perhaps there may, indeed, be a new order.

Now I stop, for there is nothing more to say. . . . All our dear sayings are in my heart and in your heart. But, at the end I say to you, by virtue of the treasure which has been placed in me, and which fills this modest earthen vessel.

May the grace of our Lord Jesus Christ and the love of God
and the community of the Holy Spirit be with you all.
　　Amen.*

On January 23, 1945, thirteen days after the sentence of death
had been passed, upon him, Moltke was hanged at Plötzensee
Prison. Pastor Harald Poelschau, chaplain at Tegel Prison who
had himself been a member of the Kreisau Circle but was unsus-
pected by the Nazis, was with him at eleven o'clock on that final
day. Poelschau smuggled Moltke's final letters from the prison.
At one o'clock, in common with his usual practice, he glanced
in the cell again and found no one there. Later he telephoned a
Catholic colleague at Plötzensee, who volunteered to go over at
once to the death cell and who reported: ''Helmuth went on his
way steadfast and calm.''

Integrity or Naïveté?

The man who bore a famous military name rejected the old
tradition and emerged as a man of peace. Those who honor him
are divided in their estimates. Some see him as a Christian
martyr, keeper of the flame, the soul of integrity, who refused
to compromise his principles. He had consistently opposed the
assassination even of an inhuman monster.

Others, while expressing reverence for the Moltke name and
lauding courage against hopeless odds, speak sadly of his
naîveté. They point to his stubborn opposition to tyrannicide
under all circumstances. They ask how it was possible to remove an intrenched dictator without taking the extreme step of
killing him? All Germans at the time were faced with an iron-
clad apparatus of oppression and the apolitical public was held
in slavery by the Nazi *Gestapo*. The *Fuehrer* had brought death
to millions of innocent victims. To expect him to listen to the
voice of the ballot box was the height of absurdity. Even such
clerics as Pastor Dietrich Bonhoeffer, as spiritually Christian as

*From *Helmuth J. Graf Moltke, 1907–1945: Last Letters from Prison* (Berlin: Karl H. Henssel Verlag, 1951), pp. 48 *ff*.

Moltke, had seen the necessity for action and had willingly joined the conspiracy.

Whatever the judgment of fair-minded people, Moltke remained the man of principle and spokesman for that other Germany. He deserves a place in the pantheon of German heroes.

8

HANS VON DOHNANYI:
Legalist

Sometimes I have faith that I will win through, even if the world is full of devils.

To the Hangman on a Stretcher

IT WAS PLAINLY AN EXERCISE IN SADISM, A DESCENT INTO VULGAR barbarism. They were members of Hitler's "honorable" order of *Gestapo*—extensions of his own personality. The victim this time was Hans von Dohnanyi, brother-in-law of Pastor Dietrich Bonhoeffer, legal expert, and decent German. *Gestapo* goons damned him as "the instigator and guiding spirit of the movement to destroy the *Fuehrer*."

Caught in the *Gestapo* net, Dohnanyi was handed over to experts in torture. He endured excruciating physical and mental pain inflicted by uneducated boors who tore into him in frustrated rage.

An eyewitness was there to tell the grim story. From 1942 on, fellow-prisoner Max Geisler worked continuously as assistant medical orderly in the sick ward of Sachsenhausen concentration camp. In this capacity he had a better opportunity than most other inmates to observe what went on in his special department. By the summer of 1944 he was a trusty and a senior block warden in the special department handling Dohnanyi.

Geisler told about it in testimony after the war. On an evening at the end of July 1944, at a time when prisoners in the camp were asleep for the night, he was awakened by physician and *Obersturmfuehrer* (*SS* First Lieutenant) Dr. Gabler, who ordered him to get a room ready immediately for a special patient.

An ambulance then drove up. Dohnanyi was brought in on a stretcher by several *SS* men and *Gestapo* officials. Dr. Gabler ordered Geisler that, aside from himself, no one, unless accompanied by security police, was to enter the room where Dohnanyi was lying. Nor was he allowed to talk to the patient.

Geisler reported that as a result of much ill-treatment, Dohnanyi was so weakened and paralyzed that he was unable especially to feed himself, or even to turn over in bed. The prisoner was in terrible shape. There seemed to be no prospect that he could ever recover. Dohnanyi, himself, told the orderly that he was finished. The Norwegian prisoner-physician who examined the patient, told Geisler that Dohnanyi had received internal injuries, including heavy damage to his spine, all due entirely to ill-treatment by his captors.

"Throughout the whole time," Geisler testified, "Dohnanyi suffered great pain. In spite of that he was interested in all happenings in the camp and outside it. During the weeks he was lying in R-II-b, I had to report to him daily about everything I could learn. The night he was admitted, he could not sleep at all, and I sat at his bedside until the early hours of the morning, answering hundreds of questions, all with reference to treatment in the camp. Later he was transformed to the so-called recreation department R-V, where the possibilities of good care were far less than at R-II-b. They took him away from there, too, during 1945; I cannot recall the exact date. Once more he was moved by ambulance on a stretcher. There was not the least doubt in our minds that his trip was to end in his liquidation."

Geisler testified that Dohnanyi told him little about his anti-Nazi activities. "He only remarked that his religious convictions made him an enemy of Hitler, and that they accused him of having taken part in the preparations for July 20."

Geisler further reported that the first *Gestapo* interrogation on the day after Dohnanyi's admission to the camp lasted more than eight hours. The questioning took place in the office of the security service, while all other interrogations were in the sickroom. "The *Gestapo* always took security measures so that I could not overhear anything, as I could in many other cases.

But, of course, the abuse by the *Gestapo* could be heard through the walls.''

Geisler concluded his macabre testimony: "It can be said without any doubt that Dohnanyi was carried to the gallows on a stretcher, for he could not walk a single step by himself.''

There was another eyewitness—Prison Chaplain Harald Poelschau. In his memoirs the chaplain told that in late July or August 1944, after he had taken over temporary duties at the nearby Military Prison at Buch, he inquired which of the prisoners of the *Gestapo* had registered for visits by the chaplain of the garrison. He was told that several names were mentioned, including a "Colonel Z." When he asked the identity of Colonel Z, he was told that no one knew. When he was alone with Colonel Z, the chaplain introduced himself. The prisoner said: "I am Dohnanyi. I know about you." "Physically, he was suffering, but he was quite composed, a man of strength and personality, for whom I could do very little."

Career of the "Instigator"

Hans von Dohnanyi was born on January 1, 1902, in Vienna, the son of Hungarian composer and pianist Ernst von Dohnanyi. After the separation of his parents, he went along with his mother and sister to Berlin. Here he spent his early years and attended the Grünewald *Gymnasium*. Brother and sister Dohnanyi formed close friendships with the Bonhoeffer, von Harnack, and Delbrück children, offsprings who represented the best cultured traditions of Germany. Invited often to the family circle of psychiatrist Karl Bonhoeffer, Hans became the best friend of Dietrich Bonhoeffer, later the distinguished pastor and colleague in the struggle against Hitler. Dohnanyi later married Dietrich Bonhoeffer's sister.

Young Dohnanyi also was a chum of Justus Delbrück, son of the historian Hans Delbrück, a youngster who saw him as a member of the family. At the home of famous theologian Adolf von Harnack, Dohnanyi met many of the outstanding personalities of the day. In this atmosphere the young man absorbed the spiritual qualities that were to distinguish his short life in the struggle against Nazism.

After his *Abiturium* (leaving-certificate from secondary school entitling the holder to matriculation at a university) Dohnanyi registered at the University of Berlin as a student of jurisprudence. A gifted and hard worker, even at that time he turned his attention to additional duties in the Foreign Office as a research assistant. Here he worked on two important publications, including the governmental edition of *Die grosse Politik der europäischen Kabinette, 1871–1914*, a monumental publication of the most secret papers from the archives of the German Foreign Office, and *Die gesammelten Werke Otto von Bismarcks*, the so-called *Friedrichsruhe Ausgabe*, a 15-volume study presenting a full and critical collection of the Chancellor's private and official correspondence, speeches, conversations, and memoirs, (1924–35). In June 1924 Dohnanyi passed his examination as *Referender*, junior barrister, before the Supreme Court of Judicature at Berlin.

Meanwhile, Dohnanyi was appointed to the post of assistant at the Institute for Foreign Policy at the University of Hamburg. In February 1925 he married Christine Bonhoeffer and settled in Hamburg. He also served without pay as a teacher at the university in order to qualify for his second professional examination for the post of *Assessor*. He took the degree *Dr. jur.* in 1926 and in July 1928 passed the *Assessor* examination.

In the fall of 1928 Dohnanyi was appointed by the mayor of Hamburg to serve on the Commission of the Hamburg Senate for Foreign Affairs. In 1929 he was brought to the Reich Ministry of Justice, where he worked in the Departments of International Constitutional, and Administrative Law, with special attention to matters of high treason. At the same time he worked as private secretary to several Ministers of Justice.

His legal career thus far gave Dohnanyi early insight into the true nature of the rising National Socialist movement. Under the regime of Chancellor Heinrich Brüning, which began in 1930, Dohnanyi attended cabinet meetings as legal adviser. A devoted follower of the Reich Chancellor, Dohnanyi again and again issued warnings against rightist nationalists who were fighting to win the battle of the streets. He argued that these nationalists were a danger to the state and should be forbidden to wear uniforms. He saw the ideology of the up-and-coming Nazis as presenting a clear and present danger to the German state. The government, he warned, was not taking strong enough steps to counter the danger of Nazism. When on May 10, 1932, the virtually senile President Paul von Hindenburg called for Brüning's resignation, the distressed Dohnanyi sadly called it the *"finis Germaniae."*

Older colleagues listened to Dohnanyi's warnings but did not follow him. By this time too many higher officials in the ministries and the high courts were infected with the Hitler virus.

In January 1933, a few weeks before Hitler took power, Dohnanyi took a temporary assignment to the attorney-general's office in Hamburg. He was uncomfortable in the realization that the Nazis were continuing to gain strength and were well on the way to political success.

Dohnanyi was able to continue his work after the advent of the Nazi regime. Although he was partly of Jewish descent, he was "Aryanized" according to a special order by Hitler, who was anxious to retain some experts in office pending future developments. After the *Reichstag* fire on the night of February 27, 1933, Dohnanyi tried to start a public inquiry by German judges into the growing rate of terrorism in German society. He appealed to the President of the Supreme Court of the Reich only to be turned down. At this time Franz Gürtner, the Reich Minister of Justice, who later was made responsible for coördinating justice in the Third Reich, appointed Dohnanyi head of the Minister's private office. In this capacity he was to see even more about the nature of the new National Socialist state. Again and again he attempted to rescue victims of Hitler's vengeance, but he found it most difficult to foil the powerful new regime. Too many of his colleagues had succumbed to Hitler's mass psychology and reckoned it best not to oppose the dictator.

Nevertheless, Dohnanyi did what he could for the victims of persecution despite the futility of legal protests. Without regard for his own safety or that of his family, he did what he could for those who were oppressed on religious or ethnic grounds. His office in the Ministry of Justice was for endangered Germans the last refuge for rescue. In one way or another he used his influence to ease the way of strangers out of the Third Reich. He worked closely with brother-in-law Dietrich Bonhoeffer and Pastor Martin Niemoeller in winning sanctuary for terrified victims of the Nazi regime.

In the summer of 1933 Dohnanyi was called to Obersalzberg, where he was given the honor of being introduced to the *Fuehrer*. During this visit he managed to have a short talk with Propaganda Minister Dr. Joseph Goebbels, to whom he protested as "a guardian of justice" against the injustice of the concentration-camp system. Goebbels told him: "Dear Doctor, you don't make me hot!" Dohnanyi left Obersalzberg even more convinced of his anti-Nazi sentiment.

Thoroughly disgusted and certain that a political solution to the problem of National Socialism was futile, Dohnanyi decided on active resistance.

Crossing the Threshold

Extraordinary psychological reaction. How does one explain the transformation of decent human beings into advocates of the ultimate weapon of assassination? Hans von Dohnanyi and Dietrich Bonhoeffer, among other dissenting Germans, were men of conscience who abhorred the very existence of violence. They were at first apolitical intellectuals who saw the best of the German spirit in the works of Goethe, Schiller, and Kant.

But these men who dared to resist tyranny in a closed society also possessed great courage. They refused to submit to the dictator. For them Hitler and his cronies were more than just simple liars representing a hideous regime. They could not close their eyes to the slaughter of innocents. It was impossible to stand by and see the name of Germany shamed before all the world.

Men of the Resistance knew well that they had neither the resources nor the opportunity of inflicting real damage on the authoritarian state. For them it was no longer a matter of practicality. What they had to do was to demonstrate to the world and before history that they were willing to take the decisive gamble. Everything else became a matter of indifference. The motivation was strong but to act in a state where police power was overwhelming took more than ordinary resolve.

Dohnanyi and his colleagues knew that they were placing their lives in jeopardy. So great was their love for their country, so profound was their pride in its good name, that they were willing to sacrifice themselves for a higher cause. For Dohnanyi especially it was a long and painful road to oblivion.

In the early years of the Hitler regime Dohnanyi began to keep a secret record of Nazi crimes and notes on the men who committed them. Buried away in the office of the Prussian Ministry of Justice, these records could be used after the end of the Nazi dictatorship. Because of his post in the Ministry of Justice he knew exactly what was going on in governmental circles. He was careful to watch the machinations of Roland Freisler, head of the personnel department of the Prussian Ministry of Justice and later permanent Secretary of the Ministry in charge of sabotage, and still later the "Hanging Judge" of the notorious People's Court. For five years Dohnanyi managed to counter the intrigues of Freisler in the office of the Ministry. He did this despite the fact that he did not become a member of the *Rechtswahrbund*, "The Association of the Guardians of Justice," a Nazi organization to which all members of the legal profession were expected to belong.

By the summer of 1934 Dohnanyi had become the pivot of various civilian Resistance groups. He worked closely with Carl Friedrich Goerdeler, the Lord Mayor of Leipzig, leader of the German civilian Resistance. At this time Dohnanyi was not in close touch with the military clique which opposed Hitler. Only later did he become the right-hand man of Gen. Ludwig Beck, the professional soldier, the only German general who consistently tried to thwart or delay Hitler's plans for war and who later became the acknowledged leader of the conspiracy against Hitler.

Dohnanyi's work in the Prussian Ministry of Justice was endangered by the enmity of two colleagues there—Roland Freisler and Martin Bormann. Freisler, becoming increasingly mistrustful, denounced Dohnanyi again and again for "suspicious activities," especially for his "non–National Socialist attitude" and for his "non-Aryan background." Freisler was supported by Martin Bormann, at that time slowly working his way to the fulcrum of the Party apparatus. Dohnanyi presented documentary proof that he had been officially "Aryanized" by legal decree, but Freisler and Bormann persisted and finally had their way. In November 1938 Dohnanyi was transferred to the post of liaison officer in the Imperial High Court of Justice in Leipzig.

Because of his legal duties, Dohnanyi managed to make frequent trips to Berlin and continue his secret work against the government. By this time he was closely associated with Gen. Beck. At the outbreak of war in 1939, Beck saw to it that Dohnanyi, although he had no military experience, was posted to the staff of the High Command of the Armed Forces under Maj. Gen. Hans Oster as a political specialist. This section of the *Abwehr* (Counterintelligence), headed by Adm. Wilhelm Canaris, became a center for the conspiracy against Hitler.

Dohnanyi worked with a close friend, Josef Müller, a giant man of inexhaustible courage and raw energy, who reveled in his nickname of *"Ochsensupp"* ("Joe the Ox"). Müller, a devout Catholic and secretly contemptuous of Hitler and his ilk, was posted by the *Abwehr* for duty in Rome. With Dohnanyi's encouragement he managed to obtain from the papacy an unambiguous offer of peace, which was passed on to leading generals. Hitler was not interested—he was triumphant on the battlefields. His offensive and victory over France meant oblivion for the papal action.

Conspiracy

Dohnanyi was adamant—he would play an active role in the succession of conspiracies against Hitler, all of which were unsuccessful. He worked in close harmony with the men behind the Smolensk attentat when the *Fuehrer* was at his headquarters on the Russian Front. His task was to prepare the political background in Berlin and he even flew to eastern headquarters of Army Group *Mitte* (Center) on behalf of the conspirators.

It was called "Operation Flash" and was meant to obliterate Hitler on his private airplane. Maj. Gen. Henning von Tresckow, who had served with distinction in Poland and France, was descended from a long line of Prussian officers. At first he embraced National Socialism, but he was soon disillusioned and turned first to opposition, then resistance, and finally conspiracy. Together with his staff officer, 1st Lieut. Fabian von Schlabrendorff, Treschkow acted as agent on the Eastern Front for the Resistance circle in Berlin.

Tresckow and Schlabrendorff had a plan. They would kill Hitler with a delayed-action bomb concealed in his airplane during a return flight from Smolensk to his headquarters in Rastenburg in East Prussia. On March 13, 1943, the *Fuehrer's* private air cavalcade arrived at Smolensk and a planned conference took place without incident. At lunch Tresckow asked one of the officers accompanying Hitler, Col. Heinz Brandt, who in 1936 had been a leading contender at the Olympic Games in Berlin, to take a bottle of brandy to an old friend, Col. Helmuth Stieff. Brandt, unsuspecting, agreed. As Hitler boarded the plane, Schlabrendorff secretly started the time fuse to go off in half an hour and handed the parcel to Brandt. The two conspirators then went off to inform their colleagues in Berlin that the main part of the plan had succeeded.

Premature judgment. After two and a half hours word came from Rastenburg that Hitler had arrived safely. Schlabrendorff now faced the critical task of retrieving the faulty bomb. Tresckow telephoned to hold the gift—the date was wrong. He arrived at Rastenburg bringing two bottles of real brandy and took back the original bomb package. That night he dismantled the device in a railway car and reported to the conspirators in Berlin that the detonator had been defective. Once again the fortunate *Fuehrer* had escaped assassination as if by a miracle.

Meanwhile, *Gestapo* agents had become suspicious of Dohnanyi. Friends in the Reich Research Office, the telephone-tapping agency, warned him that his telephone was being

tapped, whereupon he advised his fellow-plotters not to telephone him under any circumstances.

Dohnanyi was denounced to the *Gestapo* by a Dr. Wilhelm
Schmidhuber, a prosperous Munich businessman who had done
some work for the *Abwehr* and who knew of Dohnanyi's underground work in its office. Schmidhuber became involved in
some illegal business in Italy and was brought back to Germany
in handcuffs. He expected that Dohnanyi would arrange his
release through the *Abwehr*, but because his arrest did not involve any political background and was due completely to his
unscrupulous business dealings, Dohnanyi did nothing.

Schmidhuber was enraged. Soon his charges moved up the
line all the way to Hermann Goering about Dohnanyi's under-
cover activities in the *Abwehr*. Schmidhuber claimed that
Dohnanyi was involved in some "murky business" with the
Vatican, that he had helped Jews cross into Switzerland by
awarding them commissions for the *Abwehr* involving huge
sums, and that he had used brother-in-law Dietrich Bonhoeffer
for contacts with the enemy by sending him on missions to
Rome and Stockholm. Goering demanded that Dohnanyi be
dismissed from the *Wehrmacht* immediately and handed over to
the *Gestapo*.

On April 5, 1943, *Gestapo* officials arrested Dohnanyi, his
wife, his secretary, Josef Müller and wife, and Dietrich Bonhoeffer. Taking Dohnanyi into custody was illegal because
Hitler's order exempting *Wehrmacht* officers from *Gestapo* ju-
risdiction was still in force, but suspicious *Gestapo* agents were
determined to "bring Dohnanyi to the gallows."

The wives were released at the end of April, but Dohnanyi
was kept in the military prison at Tegel. Otto John, a fellow
conspirator, described Dohnanyi's treatment by the *Gestapo*:
First he was not allowed to smoke. Then he was forbidden to
read, write, or draw. Finally, all the notes made about his interrogations to assist in his defense were confiscated. Dohnanyi's
wife was allowed to take food to him twice a week. She hid
secret notes under a jam-jar cover and he did the same. Dietrich
Bonhoeffer's family regularly received letters from Dohnanyi
smuggled out of the prison: they were frequently accompanied

by poems and theological treatises. The prisoner used his arrest to think and write as if in voluntary retreat. Warders were so impressed by his personality that they granted him many privileges. Some even smuggled out letters for him.

Gestapo interrogators did their best to break Dohnanyi. Delicate and sensitive, but at the same time possessing an iron will, the prisoner used his superior brain as an expert on criminal law to outwit his captors. Interrogator Dr. Manfred Roeder, senior *Luftwaffe* judge-advocate, was annoyed by Dohnanyi's tactics: again and again the prisoner insisted that incriminating papers found in his files were there because of his work as counter-intelligence agent of the *Abwehr*. Roeder warned Dohnanyi: "I shall not stop attacking you personally until I have destroyed you."

The *Gestapo* softening process had an effect on Dohnanyi, who developed phlebitis in both legs. During an Allied heavy air raid on the night of December 23, 1943, Dohnanyi's cell was set on fire and he was found with partial paralysis of his speech and loss of sight. The record of his case was burned during the air raid. The *Gestapo* tried to reconstitute the file on the basis of other material, but the effort failed. Dohnanyi was eventually freed for "lack of evidence."

July 20, 1944

Dohnanyi's arrest and interrogation damaged the political structure of the conspiracy against Hitler. Many members of the Resistance were disillusioned and discouraged. Not Dohnanyi. Despite his ordeal in Tegel prison, he was more determined than ever to go ahead with the conspiracy. There is little doubt that the *Gestapo* was correct in its suspicion that Dohnanyi had helped in the preparations for July 20, the Stauffenberg attempt on the life of Hitler at Rastenburg. At any rate he was arrested again shortly before the July 20 plot and this time sent to Sachsenhausen concentration camp.

At Sachsenhausen Dohnanyi was subjected to especially brutal treatment, which left him paralyzed and so weakened that he was unable to wash himself. Ill-treatment by the *Gestapo* resulted in serious internal injuries and damage to his spine. At the end of January 1945, after months of persecution, he was taken in an ambulance back to the *Gestapo* prison in Berlin. Here he lay in a cell in the midst of winter, with no water, light, or heat.

The Allied air raid on Berlin on February 3, 1945, was one of the heaviest of the war and the most terrible the Berliners had experienced. One of the bombs struck the building where Roland Freisler was conducing his People's Court. The Hanging Judge had hurried to the cellar only to have his skull fractured by a falling beam. *Gestapo* headquarters also received a direct hit. In his cell Dohnanyi lay with his legs paralyzed with diptheria bacilli, with which he had infected himself. The germs had been smuggled into the prison by his wife. This was Dohnanyi's method of passive resistance—he would remain permanently ill and outwit his tormenters. He survived the Allied air attack.

During the final weeks of his captivity, Dohnanyi kept in touch with his wife through messages placed inside the false bottom of a paper drinking cup. In early March he wrote to her: "The interrogations are going on, and it is obvious what I have to reckon with, unless a miracle happens. This misery all around me is so great that I would willingly throw away this bit of life if it were not for you. But the thought of you all, of your great love and mine for you, makes my will to live so strong that I sometimes have faith that I will win through, even if the world were full of devils. I must get out of this place into a hospital, but in such a state as to make further interrogations impossible. Fainting, heart attacks, make no impression, and if they take me to a hospital without another illness, that might even be more dangerous, as they would cure me more quickly there."

Dohnanyi was moved to Potsdam Isolation Hospital, where he lay seriously ill with diptheria and scarlet fever. Legally, his prospects had improved. Because of his dangerous condition, authorities postponed proceedings against him to the end of the war and orders were sent out that he was to be interned in a sanatorium.

Meanwhile, in the closing days of the war. Heinrich Himmler, who had become master of Berlin, ordered that Dohnanyi be moved back to Sachsenhausen. On April 5, 1945, the prisoner was brought to the concentration camp again. Three days later, on the charge that he had masterminded the conspiracy against Hitler, he was put to death at the camp.

The circumstances surrounding Dohnanyi's execution have never been clarified.

9

ADAM VON TROTT ZU SOLZ:
Esthete, Patriot

―――――――

I die in profound trust and faith.

Patriot as Hero

HE WAS AN EXTRAORDINARILY HANDSOME MAN, PRUSSIAN GENTLE-
man, Rhodes scholar, lawyer, unofficial diplomat, and interme-
diary between the Allies and the conspirators. He regarded
Nazis as criminals not because he felt that they wanted to overthrow the Treaty of Versailles, but because the methods they
used in pursuing this goal were a disgrace to German honor. He
was devoted to the ecumenical concept of Christianity. Like
other dissenters he went the route from opposition to resistance
to conspiracy.

The outstanding feature of Adam von Trott zu Solz's life
was his stubborn determination to remain in Germany to the
end, even though he had many opportunities to escape the
vengeance of Hitler. Germany, he said, was where a German
belonged. He devoted his final efforts to convince the Allies
that they should scrap ''unconditional surrender'' in the event
that Hitler was overthrown and a new German government installed—a task in which he was altogether unsuccessful.

Trott zu Solz was one of those courageous Germans who was
prepared to risk his life because he refused to remain silent in
the face of tyranny and brutality. Those who knew him spoke of
his charming personality combined with a streak of recklessness
and an engrained sense of national duty. He was, indeed, an
ambiguous character who remained an enigma to the end of his
short life.

He was hanged in Berlin on August 26, 1944, seventeen days after his 35th birthday.

Heritage Aristocratic

Adam von Trott zu Solz was born in Potsdam on August 9, 1909, to an aristocratic Hessian family noted for its line of distinguished diplomats and officials. His father was Prussian Minister of Culture and Education from 1909 to 1917. His mother was half-Silesian aristocrat and half-American, descended from John Jay, Chief Justice of the United States. A woman of strong personality, proud of her Calvinist-Huguenot background, she instilled in her son a sense of religious devotion and Christian behavior. As a small child he received much affection from his English nurse and as a youth developed a sense of admiration for English customs and traditions. He remained an Anglophile for the rest of his life. At the same time he was thoroughly German. His love affair with the English, both in public and private life, was often disturbed by a sense of injury on both sides.

Young Adam's pro-English sentiment was strengthened in 1929 when he was awarded a Rhodes Scholarship at Oxford to study philosophy, political science, and economics. Reading "Modern Greats," he later spent the years 1931–32 at Oxford, where he made many close friends. He was a steady visitor at the dinner table of All Souls' College. In temperament he remained deeply German. He was steeped in Hegelianism with its dialectic—the endless veering between utter despair and divine joy, typical of many Germans. He saw his own fellow-countrymen as never satisfied, always searching for something beyond them. But ah! the English! These people seemed happy with cottage and garden, with tennis and cricket, with pubs and warm beer, self-satisfied and content with life as it was. At the same time he remained a Hegelian nationalist with strong territorial roots and imperialist ideas.

The young German student charmed his friends at Oxford with his mixture of Teutonic seriousness and swaggering frivolity. Actually, Trott zu Solz was in a serious predicament.

He was a patriot who loved his country but who was ashamed of the Hitler movement. Although he spoke strongly against Nazism, he at the same time made it plain that he was a German nationalist sympathetic with some of Hitler's aims. Several of his Oxford friends came to the conclusion that he was an accomplice, if not an agent, of Nazism. They were suspicious because of his denunciation of the Weimar Republic as a hollow shell. Such acquaintances never dreamed that this happy-go-lucky German would become one of the conspirators dedicated to the task of assassinating Hitler.

On his return to Germany in 1933, Trott zu Solz went on to study law, although his esthetic instinct rebelled against the boredom of it all. Nevertheless, he pursued his studies at Munich, Berlin, and Göttingen. Still intrigued by Hegel, he wrote his dissertation on ''Hegel's Philosophy of State and International Law.'' Admirer of poet Heinrich von Kleist, in 1935 he published an edition of Kleist's political and journalistic works. He included a commentary on Kleist as a rebel against tyranny, an indication of his dissatisfaction with the trends of the new National Socialist regime.

For a time he kept his feelings to himself, but more and more he began to see himself as a representative of that ''other Germany,'' the decent Germans who had won the admiration of his English friends. He had the uncomfortable feeling that Hitler was leading his people to catastrophe. Troubled by the question as to whether he should abandon Germany and emigrate until the Nazi regime might no longer exist, he returned to London to talk about his predicament with Lord Lothian, secretary of the Rhodes Trust. It was agreed to send him to China for a year to give him time to think about his decision.

During his year in Peking, (1937–38), Trott zu Solz tried to absorb the wisdom of Confucian China but simultaneously to consider his future as a German citizen. He came to the conclusion that it was his duty to return home and join the fight against Hitler. British officials at the embassy in Peking watched him closely and came to the erroneous conclusion that he was a Nazi sympathizer. Far from it. On his return he threw himself into the task of opposing the oncoming war, which he felt was Hitler's work. At the same time he supported the policy of appeasement and found some comfort in the Munich Pact.

The Rowse Connection

The erstwhile Rhodes scholar was careful to retain his friendship with his Oxford friends. Among them was A. L. Rowse, later to be known as historian of the Elizabethan Age, poet, and devotee of Shakespearean scholarship. In one volume of his autobiography, *A Man of the Thirties* (London: Weidenfeld—Nicholson, 1979), Rowse devoted an entire chapter, "Adam von Trott: Portrait of a German," to his German friend.

Briton and German met as students and there was an immediate attraction between them. On the one side there was the brash young Cornishman full of eccentricities, of working-class origin though not a Communist. On the other side the young German aristocrat, pious ecumenical Christian, conservative in outlook. There were also differences of psychological complexity. Rowse was admittedly homosexual, Trott zu Solz heterosexual.

In his autobiography Rowse described the attraction from his point of view: "We had made a profound impact on each other in that short space of time. It *was* love at first sight. But what kind of love? And what could be made of it? On my side, there was a residual defeatism from the first. . . . I accepted beforehand the fact that Adam was dominantly heterosexual, as I was not; on the other hand, the thought of physical relations was strongly repressed in me." Rowse saw the relationship as "intensely pure, not in the ordinary physical sense which it was, but esthetically, almost spiritually, since the world of beauty was the life of the spirit to me."

Truly an extraordinary friendship. Rowse was obsessed with the handsome young German. He felt a high degree of sympathy, even of telepathy, which he believed bound the two together. "He intuits exactly what is in my mind. I have never met anything like it."

Trott zu Solz felt much the same way about Rowse, though he cast his friendship on a platonic basis. For the German esthete it was love on a higher basis. On one occasion he wrote to Rowse: ''After all, haven't you some positive hopes about the future of our friendship. Our friendship and, let me say, love, has a kind of exquisite craft, the main point of which is that nothing right can be done by one alone, but together.''

If anything, the German was a dedicated womanizer. According to biographer Christopher Sykes (*Troubled Loyalty* London: Collins, 1968), Trott zu Solz always enjoyed the society of women, for whom he found that he was unusually attractive, far more than ordinarily the case with a handsome young man. He often surrendered to temptation. Two women, one German and one British, were so taken by Adam that they later wrote books about him. Christobel Bielenberg, an Englishwoman who had married a German, made him the pivot of her story (*The Past Is Myself* London: Chatto, 1968). To her he was all charm and virtue, a human god. Diana Hopkinson, in *The Incense Tree* (London: Routledge & Kegan, 1968) wrote of him as her lover during seven years of her youth. She remembered that he had said: ''Our friendship will outlive the moon and the stars and something of each of us will outlive the other.'' Trott zu Solz later married ''my beloved Charitchen'' in Germany and became the father of two sons.

Rowse in Oxford and Trott zu Solz in Berlin maintained a long correspondence. The Englishman sent poems to Adam and received in turn long pages of pseudo-Hegelian profundities. The two esthetes considered themselves above the trauma of war.

Togetherness became the theme of this friendship. ''I didn't want to possess him, body or soul,'' Rowse wrote. ''He may have feared that I did. To be frank, proselytizer as I was, I think I wanted him as a disciple, someone who would take on my ideas.'' He spoke of ''the Wonderful, which two men can make together.'' He tried to understand his German friend, who, zigzagging from confidence to despair, hopelessly insecure, filled with self-doubt, sought solace from his English friend.

The German's admiration and respect for Rowse and for all things British served to make him all the more contemptuous of Nazism. He could not help contrast what he believed to be the decencies of British life with the brutalities and horrors of Hitlerism.

Rowse later confessed to guilt feelings about the tragic death of his German friend: "To put it on the lowest practical plane, beneath our high-minded exchanges—he wanted to learn English and England, I wanted to learn German and Germany (or was I in part responsible for his terrible end?). I have sometimes reproached myself."

Peace Negotiator

Largely because of his connections in Britain, Trott zu Solz was regarded in his post at the Foreign Office as a man who had important contacts in London and who could assist the *Fuehrer* in his diplomacy. In June 1939 he was sent on a fact-finding mission to London. Actually, he was hoping to gain time, not only to prevent the oncoming war but also to convince the British that there were forces working in Germany against Hitler, especially in the Army, and that there might be a chance of overthrowing the Nazi government without a war.

Before Trott zu Solz went off to London, he was instructed by conspirator Gen. Ludwig Beck that on no account must the British agree to Hitler's demands. As a friend of the Astor family, Trott zu Solz was received on a week end at Cliveden, then a hotbed of appeasement. He met Prime Minister Chamberlain, Foreign Secretary Lord Halifax, and renewed his acquaintance with Lord Lothian. He was careful to avoid contacting Winston Churchill, in his view a warmonger. Nor did Churchill want to see the German—the hard British politician had been told the visitor had a formidable dossier against him.

Trott zu Solz hoped to help maintain peace by reporting back to Berlin, in contradiction to the opinions delivered there by Joachim von Ribbentrop, Hitler's Minister for Foreign Affairs. Trott zu Solz said that influential Britons supported a war if Hitler made any further territorial annexations, and that Germanophiles in Britain would be on Hitler's side if he avoided war.

Trott zu Solz also hoped to convince British statesmen to resist further German annexations, by war if necessary, and also to help any potential German opposition to Hitler. During his talk with Lord Halifax, he warned that there were rumors in Berlin that the Nazis "were up to something" although he did not know what (it proved to be the Hitler-Stalin Pact). Trott zu Solz was discouraged by his visit to Prime Minister Chamberlain, whom he judged to be "nice but a man already half-dead." Chamberlain was not anxious to encourage potentially disaffected Germans to oppose their regime.

On his return to Berlin, Trott zu Solz submitted an official report in which he made it a point deliberately to flatter Hitler. The *Fuehrer*, he wrote, could appease British public opinion and "paralyze his enemies" if only he would withdraw from Bohemia and Moravia. There was much sympathy in London for Germany. Trott zu Solz reported especially on the "Cliveden set" named for Viscountess Nancy Astor's home in Buckinghamshire, where British architects of appeasement toward Nazi Germany met. Although Hitler had no intention of relinquishing Bohemia and Moravia, he may well have regarded "sympathy in London" as paving the way for his intended invasion of Poland.

In 1940, after the outbreak of war, Trott zu Solz was invited to the neutral United States to attend a conference. His real purpose was to judge American public opinion and its reaction to a Germany without Hitler. He hoped to win President Roosevelt's support for the German opposition to Nazism, but his mission was torpedoed by the British Embassy in Washington. Behind it was a strange set of circumstances. The British public had been outraged by the Munich Pact and there was hostility against everything German. This was expressed dramatically by Sir Robert (later Lord) Vansittart, former head of the British Foreign Office. "Vansittartism" existed in the British Foreign Office even without Vansittart. Word sped from London to the British Embassy in Washington that Whitehall had a "formidable" dossier on Trott zu Solz and that he was a German spy. Moreover, it was charged that he and his comrades-in-dissent were not in favor of restoring any territory gained by Hitler.

Mission unaccomplished. In the United States, the German was sabotaged from London.

Trott zu Solz's visits to London and Washington were disasters and achieved nothing. He had made a serious mistake. He was acting on the premise that Hitler could be used, unaware that the *Fuehrer* could not be controlled this way, especially by an amateur diplomat. Hitler was not a temporary despot but a dictator firmly entrenched in power. Trott zu Solz saw the man as destroying not only Germany but all of Europe. Something drastic had to be done to prevent a terrible catastrophe. The dictator must be eliminated.

A disgusted German was to devote the last four years of his life to that goal.

To the Kreisau Circle

In 1940 Trott zu Solz returned via Japan to Germany. By now he was Legations Secretary in the Foreign Office. He would use this post to work from the inside against Hitler and to continue his efforts to win support abroad.

As soon as he learned about the work of Helmuth James Count von Moltke and his Kreisau Circle, Trott zu Solz decided to join the group and take part in his underground activities against the Nazis. He was attracted by the high ideals of its members and especially by the variety of its membership— army officers, academics, theologians, trade unionists, and lawyers. Some 32 members of the circle met at Kreisau, at Count Yorck von Wartenburg's home in Berlin, and elsewhere to plan a post-Hitlerian Germany based on liberal Christian principles. They would rehumanize a stricken Germany and revive its Christian morality.

From 1940 to 1944 Trott zu Solz attended some 62 meetings of the Kreisau Circle. In his post at the Foreign Office he served as a link between the group and Gen. Ludwig Beck, Chief of Staff of the Armed Forces, and leader of the active conspirators.

Many members of the circle agreed with Moltke that they were not concerned with the assassination of Hitler but chose to support the idea of a new German Order after the political fall of Hitler.

Not Trott zu Solz. He judged Hitler to be the prime source of evil and dedicated himself to the task of bringing an end to the life of the dictator.

There were differences between Trott zu Solz and Moltke, founder of the Kreisau Circle. On the surface they seemed to have much in common. Both had Anglo-Saxon traditions on their mothers' side and both were zealous Anglophiles. They were handsome men, tall and impressive. Both came from a landowning family and loved the soil of their heritage. Both had legal training and were united in their contempt for Hitler and his court.

But these were different personalities. Moltke was withdrawn and esthetic. Social-minded, he was unimpressed by conventional patriotism. He condemned idealization of the state, to him an anachronism. Trott zu Solz, the Hegelian, identified community with state and believed firmly in its complete sovereignty. On October 12–13, 1941, Moltke recorded in his diary that at Kreisau he and Trott zu Solz engaged in a debating duel "about the prescription for thinking how the state should be set up." For Trott zu Solz it was a matter of urgency to reconcile what he believed to be true German principles with his anger at Hitler's flaunting of Christian morality. Moltke recorded in his diary on November 5, 1941: "He was very obstinate. He is astoundingly intelligent but handicapped as a result. It keeps on being funny. Besides he has for some inexplicable reason an inferiority complex toward me which results in his adopting very aggressive attitudes and expressions."

Nevertheless, despite such differences, the two agreed that the Nazi menace must be ended. But each continued to hold his own view on the matter of assassination, which Moltke opposed. Important for both were plans for a postwar Germany purged of Nazi authoritarianism and paranoia.

Sabotage

Throughout the war Trott zu Solz continued his personal campaign against the Nazis. At the same time he hoped to bolster the position of his country *vis-à-vis* the Allies. In January 1943, using his *Abwehr* contacts in Switzerland, he met several British and American agents. He warned Allan Dulles, American counterintelligence chief, that if the Allies did not offer "a decent peace" and did not retreat from the policy of unconditional surrender, Germany might be forced to turn to the Soviet Union.

Trott zu Solz made similar efforts in Stockholm. Here he met with Dr. Harry Johannson, director of the Nordic Ecumenical Institute, who had formed a group of Swedes to act as a link with the German opposition, especially the Kreisau Circle. Both Trott zu Solz and Johannson hoped to negotiate with the Allies for lenient terms after the overthrow of Hitler.

All this work as peace negotiator was totally unsuccessful. Allied intelligence agents were quite willing to open discussions with Trott zu Solz and his Swedish friends. These were important contacts and had to be used, especially for military information. But from their viewpoint his insistence on scrapping the demand for unconditional surrender was naïve and altogether unacceptable. Nor were the Russians inclined to give in on that demand.

Despite one setback after another, Trott zu Solz persisted in his efforts as peace negotiator. In June 1943 he went to Istanbul in the belief that even better connections with the West could be made there than in either Switzerland or Sweden, both of which could be reached only by crossing German-held territory. He continued his contacts with Allied agents in Switzerland and Sweden. At the end of November 1943 he again talked with British officials, always with the hope of easing peace terms for a defeated Germany.

One of the documents with which Trott zu Solz was concerned was titled "Conditions of Collaboration with the Allies." It was forwarded from Istanbul to the United States by agents of the Office of Strategic Services. The report was said to have been submitted to President Franklin D. Roosevelt, who asked his friend Felix Frankfurter, Associate Justice of the U.S. Supreme Court, for his advice. Frankfurter, who had already reported adversely on Trott zu Solz, told the President that in his view the document was a decoy drawn up by insincere people.

Faithful Conspirator

By the summer of 1944 Trott zu Solz accepted the bankruptcy of his efforts on behalf of a negotiated peace. He was now convinced that there was nothing left but tyrannicide, assassination of the monster. He, therefore, cast his lot with the Stauffenberg conspiracy, which led to the attentat of July 1944.

The War Office at the Bendlerstrasse in Berlin was a beehive of activity on the evening of July 20th. Claus von Stauffenberg returned there absolutely convinced that Hitler was dead. How in the world could the man have survived in that tremendous blast—a really deadly explosion? Stauffenberg denounced messages from Rastenburg that the *Fuehrer* was alive as damnable lies. The Nazis, he charged, were merely trying to gain time. "Start Operation Valkyrie! Hitler is dead, victim of an attempted coup by the *SS!* Goebbels, the only top Nazi remaining in Berlin, will be arrested!"

There was trouble for the conspirators. Goebbels had actually spoken to Hitler. Major Otto Remer, battalion commander of the guards, at first obeyed orders of the conspirators, but changed his mind when Goebbels had him speak directly to Hitler and then reminded him of his oath of loyalty. Loyal *SS* units led by Otto Skorzeny, who had rescued Mussolini at the Gran Sasso d'Italia in July 1943, led the attack on the bewildered plotters. One by one they were arrested.

For the next several days the *Gestapo* and the *SS* roamed through Berlin arresting anyone they suspected of complicity in the assassination attempt. Trott zu Solz was among those caught in the net. He made no effort to escape. He urged Otto John, one of the conspirators present at the Bendlerstrasse, to leave Berlin while there was time to do so. "Tell the world what it was we wanted to achieve and why we had failed."

On August 15, 1944, Trott zu Solz was brought before "Hanging Judge" Roland Freisler, the jurist who screamed abuse at the prisoners appearing before him. His defense was simple. He believed that he could help his country through contacts with friends in the Allied countries. What pained him most was that he would no longer be able to use his special experience in foreign policy for the benefit of his fellow-countrymen. He would have been happy to direct all his thoughts for the advantage of his country.

The measure of the man was shown at his trial when he pretended to have given military intelligence to his British friends, with the deliberate aim of drawing attention away from German civilian colleagues who were not yet incriminated in anti-Nazi activities. It was characteristically courageous and generous of a man who was realistic about his own plight. He had gambled and lost and he was prepared to pay the price for what he believed.

The sentence, as everyone in the court expected, was death.

Prison and Execution

Only eleven more days of life were allotted to Adam Trott zu Solz. He faced death stoically. On August 26, 1944, he wrote a final letter to his wife:

Beloved Claritchen:

This is almost certainly the last of my letters. I hope that you got my previous long one.

Before all else, forgive me for the deep sorrow that I have had to cause you.

Rest assured that I am still with you in thought and that I die in profound trust and faith.

To-day there is a clear "Peking sky" and the trees are rustling. Teach our dear sweet little ones to be grateful for the signs from God, and for the deeper ones, but in an active and valiant spirit.

I love you very much. There is still so much to write to you—but there is no more time.

May God keep you—I know that you will not let yourself be defeated and will struggle through to a life where I shall be standing by your side in spirit, even when you seem to be all alone. I pray for strength for you—and do the same for me, I beg. . . .

In my former letter I asked you to give my greetings to all our many friends. I have this at heart. You know just who they are and will give the messages correctly without my help.

I embrace you with all my soul and know that you are with me.

God bless you and the little ones.

In steadfast love

Give Werner and Heini the same trust that they gave me in love and loyalty. Greet Immshausen and its hills from me
Your Adam*

Adam also sent a farewell letter to his mother, to whom he was deeply attached. He had never forgotten the Christian training she had given him. It was a sad farewell:

Dearest Mother:

Thank God I have the opportunity to write you a short note: You have always been very near to me, and you are

*Christopher Sykes, *Troubled Loyalty: A Biography of Adam von Trott zu Solz* (London: Collins, 1968), p. 448.

now. In gratitude I cling hard to the bond which has bound us together forever. God has been merciful to me in these weeks and has sent me joyous, clear strength for everything, or almost everything—and he has taught me where and how I failed. I ask your forgiveness above all for imposing on you this great sorrow, and that I must not be there to support you in your old age.

Tell Werner that he, too, has become very close to me in these last weeks that had we seen each other again I would have gone back on every step that led to our estrangement and would have had a deep fruitful reconciliation with him. To him and to his chivalrous care I commend my beloved Clarita and the sweet little ones, of whom I saw so little, and I ask him to extend his protection to their individuality and then freedom to find their own way of life. Stand by them in all their need!

I ask that of Heinz too—in love and gratitude.

To you last a grateful kiss from the heart until we meet again.

A greeting to all who can remember me without rancour.

Your son who loves you very much.
Adam*

Hitler's vengeance on the men of July 20th was terrible. The wounded dictator, angered to the point of hysteria, vowed to tarnish the memory of those who had dared to plot against him by subjecting them to utter degradation. He ordered a massive blood purge. Some of the conspirators were strangled with piano wire and their bodies hung like animal carcasses on large meat-hooks. The Fuehrer had the scenes photographed and watched movies of them being replayed over and over again. Young cadets, forced to view the gruesome films, fainted.

*Ibid., p. 449.

Further executions began again on August 8th in a chamber at Berlin's Plötzensee Prison. Trott zu Solz was brought to his death cell on August 26th. It is not known whether his execution took place in the brutal, agonizing fashion of the others. The executioners were coarsened men, but it is possible that even they could not bring themselves down to the level of Hitler's prescribed cruelty. They may have enacted their orders in token fashion.

Third Man as Hero

Intimate friend A. L. Rowse at Oxford later described the execution as too terrible, even if inevitable, for a man of his German friend's upbringing and given the hopelessness of it all. The British scholar pointed out that many Communists had died in Hitler's hands. "Why didn't one of the idiots, who was going to lose his life anyway, get him? It would have saved the lives of millions, for Nazism stood or fell, lived or died, with Hitler."

In Germany today Trott zu Solz is regarded as a genuine hero, a courageous patriot who tried first to use Hitler and then to kill him. Curiously, however, there is a diversity of opinion in Britain among the friends the German knew at Oxford and later as a friend of British statesmen. Many praised his personality, his integrity, his charm of companionship. Richard Crossman, treasurer of the German Club at Oxford and later Oxford City Councillor, wrote that he felt a rather Germanic spiritual kinship with him. "It was one of the very few who never for a moment doubted his integrity and when his Anglo-Saxon friends called him turncoat I thought they were the turncoats. This was not because I was wiser than the others but because I was emotionally tuned to his appalling predicament."

David Astor, of the Astor family and the Cliveden set, knew von Trott zu Solz as a personal friend from his student days at Oxford. Astor later complained that at no time did any British officials inquire of him what he knew of Trott zu Solz's activities. "They were content to compile an incorrect dossier. The effect was that his repeated wartime contacts with British diplomatic missions in neutral countries, made on behalf of the most valuable elements in Germany, and at repeated risk of his life, were always futile. He was never willing to become the secret agent of another country, which was the only role in which London might have recognized him, because his intention was to play a part in the political life of Germany after the war.''

Oxford historian Hugh Trevor-Roper, though he recognized courage and conviction, was not too favorably impressed. Trevor-Roper, who worked in British Intelligence during the war, saw the German's actions as sometimes ambiguous. ''Although he had spoken against Nazism, he had also spoken for it. His Western sympathies had been exclusively with the 'appeasers.' He had even been thought to be a Nazi spy.''

Trevor-Roper wrote that even after Trott zu Solz's death, such suspicions lingered on:

> In 1956, among the captured German documents, there was published a long report by Trott of a week-end at Clive-den followed by a private interview with Neville Chamberlain. This report was written by Trott for Hitler himself, and was phrased in language appropriate for such a reader. To us, after 1945, it does not make pleasant reading.

> An even more distasteful document—Trott's report from America in 1940—mercifully escaped publication. But how, people asked, was Trott able to go to America from wartime Germany? Surely he must have been a Nazi agent. Undoubtedly he uttered many anti-Nazi sentiments; but for every anti-Nazi utterance, there had been a disturbing pro-Nazi utterance which had lost him an English or American friendship. As one of his English friends wrote in 1960, ''Though I am ashamed to say so, I was not sure he was not reporting back to Berlin what our opinion and attitudes were.''*

Trevor-Roper tempered his criticism with a mild compliment: ''Even those who did not know him must surely admire a German nationalist who could win the real friendship not only of his contemporaries and of the pro-German British Establish-

*Hugh Trevor-Roper, in *The Sunday Times* (London), November 24, 1968.

ment but also of the Romantic Christian Socialist R. H. Tawney and that austere doctrinaire of the Left, Sir Stafford Cripps.''

One can, indeed, recognize the ambiguous nature of Trott zu Solz's personality and character. On the one side, the brilliant, unpredictable esthete, imbued with his neo-Hegelian philosophy, Pan-German mysticism, patriot and imperialist. On the other side, the pious Christian dedicated to decency and morality, the representative of that other Germany, the man of action who rejected an unworkable pacifism at the time and who became the trusted mentor of Stauffenberg, the convinced tyrannicide. On balance, von Trott zu Solz deserves a place among the heroes in Naziland who refused to remain passive in the face of Nazi barbarism.

10*

ULRICH VON HASSELL:
Diplomat

―――――――

*Even if we do win, it will necessarily be a Pyrrhic victory,
even leaving out of account the internal destruction and
inconceivable atrocities in Poland, which are covering the
German name with disgrace, and for which the army shares
the responsibility.*

Diplomat against Hitler

HE WAS A VETERAN DIPLOMAT AND FOREIGN AFFAIRS EXPERT, WHO
like the others in this pantheon of decent human beings, refused
to accept the Hitler regime. Eventually, he emerged as one of
the most important leaders of the German Resistance. In the
best sense of the word he was a patriot, a man of the right but
emphatically no reactionary. He was noted for his trenchant
sense of humor, his diplomatic ability, and above all, for his
unshakeable political principles.

Close to the fulcrum of power, he regarded the Third Reich
as an immoral and criminal regime which smeared the best and
most valuable traditions of German *Kultur*. He was alienated by
a government which he saw as holding the entire nation in
chains. In his view it was simply *"bodenlosen Schweinereien
der SS"* ("bottomless filthiness of the *SS*"), which threatened
to bring "hatred and disgust" by all the world for Germans.
This regime, he charged, represented nothing more than "the
liquidation of morality." A decent man could not accept it.

Christian Albrecht Ulrich von Hassell was born on November 12, 1881, in Anklam, Pomerania, to a well-known aristocratic North German family. The original home of his ancestors
was in Hanover. As a student of law in Lausanne, he worked
actively for international economic and cultural coöperation on

the basis of free agreement. Early in his career he felt that
smaller European nations should be guaranteed full independence and equality of rights. Because his instincts were all for
the underdog, he could not accept the chains of dictatorship.

Turning to a diplomatic career, Hassell entered the Foreign
Office, where he hoped to serve his country to the best of his
ability. After 1911 he held several posts abroad, beginning as
Vice-Consul in Genoa. Immediately after the outbreak of war in
1914, he enlisted and was sent to the front as a combat officer.
On September 8, 1914, at the Battle of the Marne, he was badly
wounded by a French bullet which lodged near his heart. In
1916 he became councillor to the local government in Stettin.

After the end of the war Hassell returned to Berlin, where he
played an active role in the formation of the new Weimar Republic. In 1918 he founded the State Political Workers' Society,
which he hoped would wield influence in the republican state.

Hassell decided to continue with his diplomatic career,
which, at first, consisted of posts at lower levels. Although
highly gifted in his profession, he was considered to be too
young to serve as an ambassador. He was embassy Councillor
in Rome in 1919 and Consul-General in Barcelona from 1921
to 1926. In 1926, at the age of 45, he was appointed German
Ambassador in Copenhagen, where he remained for four years.
He served as Ambassador in Belgrade from 1930 to 1932, and
in Rome between 1932 and his recall in 1938. Meanwhile, he
married the daughter of Grand Admiral Alfred von Tirpitz, who
had exerted a dominant influence on German foreign policy
before World War I and who had created the formidable German High Seas Fleet.

In his work Hassell became known as a distinguished representative of the German nobility and as a man proud of his
Prussian heritage. His sense of militarism was tempered by a
Christian outlook and belief in European solidarity. He was
always a man of independence. As Ambassador in Rome, he
opposed Italo-German rapprochement and warned that war
against Britain and France would be disastrous for Germany.
On June 7, 1933, in common with representatives of England,
France, and Italy, Hassell prepared the so-called Four-Power

Pact, which proposed to regulate relations between the Western Great Powers. Although the agreement was signed on July 15, it was not ratified. Hitler and Mussolini were in the process of drawing closer together and to Hassell this seemed to mean possible aggression. He was also worried about the Anti-Comintern Pact of November 25, 1936, between Germany and Japan, which he regarded as dangerous. He wrote to Foreign Minister Constantin Neurath: "This means a new orientation of German foreign policy, due to the support of the Ambassador in London [*Joachim von Ribbentrop*] and obviously directed against England, and it may well lead to a world of conflict."

When Ribbentrop became Foreign Minister in 1938, he decided that he was dissatisfied with Hassell's behavior in Rome and decided to recall him from the Quirinal. He would have no dissenter in this important post, especially one who was issuing protests and warnings against his own foreign policy. He dismissed Hassell.

Meanwhile, Hassell was becoming more and more disillusioned with the Nazi regime. In the early days of the National Socialist drive for power, he was mildly sympathetic to Hitler and Nazism and tolerant of what he believed to be its temporary excesses. True, for a patrician and representative of the old nobility, the Austrian politician was somewhat vulgar, an uncouth personality, but Hitler had the right idea about the iniquitous Treaty of Versailles and perhaps should be given a chance to lift the country out of its doldrums.

Scorn for Hitler

"This wanton and megalomaniac corporal."

"This irresponsible gambler, who can himself hardly be accounted mentally normal, and who is surrounded by rabble."

"Did ever any man in history assume with such wantonness such a terrific responsibility?"

Like others of the Resistance who were ashamed of their country's descent into vulgarity, Hassell had contempt for Adolf Hitler as a human being. In his memoirs he wrote again and again of "this half-demented *Fuehrer*," "this demoniac

Spartacus with his destructive effect,'' ''this man with a hybris-like immoderation coupled with a complete ignorance of the world.'' Hassell denounced Hitler for his ''criminal wantonness'' in launching a war against Poland. Hitler, he wrote, would address his generals with wild, lawyer-like eloquence for three full hours: ''This impressed the harmless soldiers, but the more intelligent among them gained the impression of 'a raging Genghis Khan.' '' The self-proclaimed hero said in so many words that humanity was an invention of the 19th century, that neutrality was nothing, ''and if he were to meet his ruin in the enterprise, all Germans would have to accompany him into the abyss.'' The denunciation was classic in its intensity.

An entry in Hassell's diary, dated Berlin, May 24 to 27, 1940, foresaw catastrophe for Germany if Hitler was allowed to have his way:

> A reshaping of the face of Europe according to Hitler's ideas now seems inevitable. In outward manifestation it will be a peace that coincides with its broad objectives. The annulment of the Peace of Westphalia is already being prepared in Münster and Osnabrück. It is as yet open whether the reduction of France's power to nil combined, as it now seems, with a certain tolerance of England overseas, is to remain the order of the day, or the complete destruction of the British Empire is to form the main emphasis. The inner manifestation will be the rise to power of Socialism as Hitler sees it, the breaking up of the upper classes, the reduction of the churches to insignificant sects, and so on. Since National Socialism, as it has developed, lacks any semblance of a soul and has force as its only ideal, we shall have a Nature without God, a Germany with neither soul nor culture and perhaps also a Europe raw and without conscience.

Hassell was perplexed and saddened by what he believed to be the mass acceptance of this dangerous Austrian by the German public. He could not understand how a people with a magnificent cultural heritage could allow themselves to fall into bondage to Hitler, his henchmen, and his terror regime. They had been led down a dangerous path by irresponsible leadership. Hassell saw the Germany he loved transformed into a moral and bankrupt society rolling toward a bottomless pit.

What had happened to his countrymen? Hassell was wounded and disappointed: "Has any people yielded with such apathy?" It was unbelievable: "Among the people, stupendous, obtuse indifference holds sway, as a result of their having been subjected for several years to a barrage of loudspeaker orations." Hassell's reaction was gloomy: "The tragic burden of not being able to rejoice at [*Hitler's*] successes is enough to drive one to despair."

One might expect that a man so grievously disappointed in his people would desert his troubled homeland. But not Hassell. A patriot who loved his country, he would stay and fight the battle from inside. In the process he took no special precautions to save his life in a critical time. He would not desert the Fatherland. It was a decision that cost him his life.

Contempt for the Generals

Hassell's scorn for Hitler was matched by his utter contempt for the generals. His work in the higher echelons of power in the state brought him into close contact with leaders of the military. For years he carried on a desperate and hopeless campaign for the souls of those in military service. He directed his personal campaign not only at lowly brigade leaders and division commanders, but also against top military figures of the Third Reich. These included Generals Walther von Brauchitsch, Gerd von Rundstedt, Ewald von Kleist, and Erich von Manstein, all close to the center of power.

Hassell himself, the son of a Prussian officer and holder of a commission in an old and respected guard regiment, carried a French bullet near his heart. He saw himself as a member of a respected fraternity. But he found it incomprehensible that responsible military leaders could subjugate themselves so completely to a lance corporal who had risen to a post of exalted power.

Oath of loyalty? How could any intelligent general take seriously an oath that was forced upon him? On August 2, 1934, the day on which President Paul von Hindenburg died, Hitler required every member of the armed forces, from general to private, to take a solemn oath: "I swear by God this sacred oath that I shall render unconditional obedience to Adolf Hitler, the *Fuehrer* of the German Reich, Supreme Commander of the Armed Forces, and that I shall at all times be prepared, as a brave soldier, to give my life for this oath." The allegiance was to Hitler—not to the German Constitution.

For Hassell this was *"Gehorsambegriff mit den Hand an der Hosennaht"*—a military term meaning "idea of obedience with the middle finger touching the seam of the trousers." In other words, it was forced obedience. For Hassell this was not a true oath, but a pledge which Hitler, himself, had lost through innumerable violations of his own words. Men of conscience, according to Hassell, need not feel it necessary to hold to a pledge forced upon them. Instead, they should have understood that a regime of violence could be broken only by violent means and should have been ended by the decisive role played by leaders of the *Wehrmacht*. By submitting to Hitler they had failed in their duty to defend and maintain the honor of the army.

In his war diary* Hassell wrote disdainfully about the generals and their submission to Hitler. Brauchitsch and the others were under Hitler's spell. Most of them gave "stupid reasons" for supporting a criminal they knew well was precipitating Germany into disaster. Hassell acidly referred to them as "the Josephs," who believed that "when one is face to face with the enemy, one cannot revolt." The generals, Hassell wrote, held lamely that "the time was just not ripe to overthrow Hitler." And again: "They are not sure of the young officers." And again, with sarcasm: "After all, they have taken an oath."

Always the generals:

Ebenhausen, November 26, 1942

. . . There is absolutely no help to be expected from the alleged temper of the people (fury against Hitler). We are the

*Ulrich von Hassell, *Von andern Deutschland*, (Zürich und Freiburg i. Br.: Atlanta Verlag, 1946).

oddest mixture of heroes and slaves. The latter applies particularly to the generals, who have succeeded absolutely brilliantly in reducing their own authority to nil, particularly towards Hitler. After the failures in the East he raged like a madman, for, of course, when things go wrong, it is not "the greatest strategical genius of all time" that is in command, but "the generals." Sauberbruch, who visited him recently, thought him old and wasted. He apparently interspersed the conversation with strange unconnected mutterings (as: "I must go to India," or, "For every dead German, ten of the enemy must die."). Sauerbruch was convinced that he is now undoubtedly insane.

Berlin, January 22, 1943

If the *Josephs* (generals) have been holding back their intervention until it should become obvious that the "corporal" is leading us into the abyss, he has now complied with their wishes. The worst of it is that our confident predictions have proved true: that it will come too late and that any new regime will have to be a liquidation commission. It is probably not possible to say with certainty that the war is lost, but it is certain that it can no longer be won, and there is precious little hope of inducing the other side to make an acceptable peace now. The result is that the recognition that something must be done has gained ground among the *Josephs*, while at the same time so has the weakness of the external and internal front.

Ebenhausen, April 20, 1943

The longer the war lasts, the lower my esteem for the generals sinks. Admittedly, they have professional ability and physical courage, but little moral courage, absolutely no over-all or international view. Nor have they the least spiritual or intellectual independence or resistance based on true culture. They are accordingly unable to deal with a man like Hitler and absolutely at his mercy. In addition, the majority regard career in the worst sense, money and the field marshal's baton, as more important than the great principles and moral values that are at stake. All those on whom hopes had been set have proved worthless. And in the most miserable fashion: They agree to everything one says to them and join in the wildest plans, but cannot summon up the courage to act.

Ebenhausen, December 27, 1943

The *Josephs* would never make up their minds, but would first let things come to a full catastrophe.

In his relations with the generals, Hassell hoped in vain for a thunderstorm to clear the air. In his view only a change of regime could bring at least the possibility of a tolerable peace, internal recovery, and a return to health of Germany and all Europe. "Failure has crowned every attempt to put a bit of backbone into men who, with their instrument of power, are lending support to a half-insane, half-criminal policy." The *Josephs*, he said sadly, were guilty of irresponsible leadership and had brought disgrace to the Fatherland.

The Noble Conspirator

Hassell was a man of principle. At the beginning of World War I his father-in-law, Grand Admiral von Tirpitz, had told him that it would not be difficult for him to find a safe and well-paying job in heavy industry. The old man was surprised when his son-in-law, with reddened face, said sharply: "No, under no circumstances! The Hassells have always been poor, but respectable."

After his forced recall, Hassell refused to sink into passive retirement. His country was in danger with this new regime and he could not as a matter of principle sit back and witness its degeneration. The events of the year 1938 increased his sense of disillusionment. "There is nothing more bitter in life," he said, "than to see foreign attacks on one's own country as fully justified." In early 1939 he did his best to help avoid what he saw was a coming world war. For this goal he worked closely with Nevile Henderson, British Ambassador to Germany in the crucial prewar years 1937–39, who believed implicitly in "Germany's honor and good sense." Both Henderson and Hassell found it impossible to deter the rampaging *Fuehrer*.

The disillusioned diplomat decided to join the opposition to Hitler. Where Gen. Ludwig Beck represented the military and Carl Goerdeler the civilian factions, Hassell became head of the diplomatic activists against Nazism. The goal was to bring together as many dissenters as possible, including the Kreisau Circle. Hassell traveled widely throughout Europe on behalf of the Resistance. He was disgusted with the behavior of German troops in Poland. The diplomat of the old school could not tolerate such behavior: "Disgraceful—the waging of war in Poland, partly through the brutal activities of the flyers, partly through the dreadful bestialities of the *SS*, above all against the Jews—all this has stained the German name." He worked, with little success, to attract top generals for a negotiated peace. In June 1943: "Hitler has made Germans appear before the entire world as abominable wild animals!"

As the war went on, Hassell continued his work—travels inside and outside Germany, conferences with military leaders, efforts to bring together various groups of the Resistance, and negotiations with the political left. He drew up plans for a postwar Germany, which would retain almost all of Hitler's conquests, and was puzzled to find no response from the British. As a monarchist he favored the restoration of the Hohenzollern dynasty, which he believed would act as a bulwark against the Bolshevization of Europe.

Again and again Hassell was warned by friends that he was being watched by the *Gestapo*, but he paid little attention. He had no fear. He would allow no danger to force him from what he regarded as a duty of conscience.

When the July 20, 1944, plot on Hitler's life failed, Hassell knew that the secret police would come to arrest him. He received them calmly on July 28 as they burst into his home and found him working at his desk. He was brought before the People's Court, which he had already denounced for "its brutal comedy, its murder of justice." He heard the sentence of death on September 8, 1944.

Exactly thirty years had elapsed since Hassell had received his almost mortal wound at the Battle of the Marne and he still carried the French bullet near his heart. In a farewell letter to his wife he wrote: "Do not become embittered! May God protect you and bless Germany!" He was hanged at Plötzensee Prison.

Hassell's diaries, titled *The Other Germany*, were hidden in a tea chest in the garden of his home in Ebenhausen, Bavaria. Published posthumously, the book became a main source of information about the Resistance movement. It gives a fascinating picture of the daily activities and dangers of those who served in the attempt to remove Hitler.

Here was, in fact, additional evidence of the existence of that other Germany.

Inner Motivation

Again our minds turn to the psychological implications of resistance. Hassell and others of his persuasion acted from more than an elemental spirit of rebellion. They represented not only political opposition but revolt against evil itself, against the mockery of simple concepts of justice. They prove that human beings can measure their conscience and integrity against their own lives and strike back at soul-killing tyranny.

They remain honored human beings in civilized society.

11*

For such a good and just cause, the proper price is the risking of one's own life.

What Comes Tomorrow

"WHEN IT IS A MATTER OF FIGHTING FOR FREEDOM, ONE DOES NOT ask what comes tomorrow."

Like other heroes of the Resistance, Julius Leber was aware of the risks he was taking. He was no ordinary politician seeking access to the reins of power. Those who knew the man, with the exception of his Nazi enemies, spoke admiringly of him as an extraordinary human being, as a statesman by instinct and wealth of qualifications. During the late days of the Weimar Republic his colleagues respected him as a powerful personality, a man of spirit and vitality, of integrity and honor. He was the kind of human being who refused to turn away in the presence of injustice.

Others surrendered ignominiously to Nazi barbarism. Not Julius Leber. His courage was legendary. The judges of the notorious People's Court who expected him to collapse when he heard the sentence of death must have been amazed by his bearing. A journalist who was present reported that never in his life had he observed such deep earnestness and nobility of character as shown by Leber at the moment when the verdict was pronounced. To his Party friends the condemned man directed a last greeting: "We have done what was in our power. It is not our fault that everything has ended this way and not otherwise."

179

There was much in the character and demeanor of Julius Leber to bring honor to the German people. Throughout the life of the Nazi regime, people all over the world realized that inside Germany there were men like Julius Leber who refused to accept the barbarities of a depraved government. They recognized and admired those who spoke out fearlessly against the evil and yet knew that the struggle was virtually hopeless.

Julius Leber takes place among Germans of Honor along with Pastor Dietrich Bonhoeffer, Professor Curt Huber, Hans and Sophie Scholl, and those others who asserted their conscience over the demands of the State. These Germans were to die along with those who had no choice in the matter—Jews, Gypsies, and Poles. They were the courageous idealists who did much to rescue the German name from the blight of Nazism.

Road to Politics

Julius Leber was born on November 16, 1891, in Biesheim, Alsace, in modest circumstances, more proletarian than bourgeois in origin. His father was a mason and his mother a farm worker. During his poverty-stricken youth he had money neither for books nor for shoes. The pastor of his village school was so impressed by the boy that he recommended him for *Realschule* (six-year non-classical secondary school). But the lad's family was so poor that he had to go to work as an apprentice in a rug factory. From 1910 to 1912 he attended the *Oberrealschule* (upper secondary school) on a scholarship and at the same time managed to earn a living by tutoring other students and writing short articles for local newspapers.

With such additional work, Leber was able to study political economy and history at Freiburg and Strassburg Universities. When war broke out in 1914, he volunteered for service and as a reward for his courage in combat was promoted to officer rank and awarded several decorations.

After the war Leber returned to Berlin. In March 1920 a group of rightist officers and civilians tried to overthrow the government in the so-called Kapp *Putsch*. On this occasion

Leber played an important role by leading workers in a universal strike. The attempted *coup d'état* failed.

That same year Leber continued his studies at Freiburg and was awarded the doctorate there. For a time he considered joining the *Freikorps* (Free Corps), freebooters whose sense of nationalism appealed to him because they seemed to be working for the regeneration of the country. But he soon learned that he had little in common with these gangster-minded advocates of terror. In disgust he turned his back on them. Granted, the war was lost but Leber was convinced that Germany must go the way of a real democracy, not that of paramilitary units anxious to set up a "force of being." He wanted nothing to do with military adventurers or anti-Semitic nationalists.

With his working-class origin, Leber was attracted to the Social Democratic Party, whose goals he felt to be similar to his own. He served that party for the rest of his life. In 1921 his political activities took him to Lübeck, where he became editor of the *Volksbote (People's Messenger)*, a post he held until his imprisonment in 1933. Meanwhile, he took a leading role in local politics. In 1924 he was a successful candidate of the Social Democratic Party for the *Reichstag* and became a member of the SPD parliamentary faction there. With this step he transferred his political interests from a communal to a national basis. He served until the *Reichstag* Fire on February 27, 1933.

In *Reichstag* debates Leber represented the left wing of his party and was regarded by the right wing as "a lost son." Because of his army service he was interested especially in problems of the military. Although opposed to any attempt to change the provisions of the Treaty of Versailles by force, he, nevertheless, emerged as an advocate of funds to be voted for the construction of new German cruisers allowed by the treaty. The cruisers were so strongly built that they could carry big guns normally used only on battleships of greater tonnage. His support of the cruiser bill cost Leber the good will of many liberal members of his party who opposed remilitarization of any kind.

Reaction to National Socialism

Determined to support a working democracy in the Weimar Republic, Leber fought against those on both right and left who wanted to undermine it. He was concerned about the rising Nazi movement and its ideology, which he saw as a dangerous threat to the new republic. When Nazi strategists attempted to arrange a speech by Hitler in Lübeck, they were thwarted by Leber, who did not want the wild man and his followers in Leber's home territory. It was an insult Hitler never forgot.

It was inevitable that the SPD delegate from Lübeck should become one of the first victims of Nazi revenge. The day after President Paul von Hindenburg appointed Hitler Chancellor (January 30, 1933), Leber was the target of an assassination attempt. He was wounded in the fray, but was rescued by a young member of the *Reichsbanner Schwarz-Rot-Gold* (Reich Banner Black-Red-Gold), a uniformed but unarmed Social Democratic ex-serviceman, who came to his aid and killed one of the attackers. The next day Leber was arrested by the *Gestapo*. He remained a prisoner for the next four-and-a-half years.

With courage and patience, Leber endured the humiliation of life in prison and concentration camp. He defied the refined tortures of guards who tried to break his spirit by every conceivable means. All to no avail. For twelve months he was kept in a dark cell and subjected to inhuman punishment. His reaction: "I made it my business not to give in. But when they tried to force me to eat my own excrement, I knew that I could not overcome such a humiliation because then I would have lost all respect for myself. For that denial I had to undergo terrible punishment which I accepted as better than the intended punishment."

When Leber was confined in Marstall Prison in Lübeck, his wife Annedore and two young children were left without means of support. Frau Leber learned the trade of a seamstress and after passing the necessary examinations opened an atelier. For years she worked for the release of her husband, but met refusal after refusal. Meanwhile, he endured the tortures while confined as "a danger to the state."

While in custody Leber wrote notes to his friends about love as a prerequisite for humanity and justice. "Without love there is no Fatherland. At times I doubt myself whether I shall ever again see a Fatherland of justice. For my generation August 1, 1914, was the greatest curse from which it could be healed." He called for a modern, democratic state which should be protected from the tragic circumstances of chance. He had been disappointed by the leaders of the Weimar Republic, all of whom in his view were infected with bloodless idealism. "Our highest goal, amidst all the nerve-wracking tensions and burdens, through all political troubles, is to build a better future for the working man on the firm grounds of justice and freedom."

Released finally from his imprisonment in 1937, Leber tried to make a living as a coal merchant in Berlin. But he was by no means satisfied with an inactive role in political affairs. He soon became deeply involved in resistance to Hitler and made close contacts with those dissidents who were resolved to put an end to the National Socialist regime. He found it impossible to adjust to the nightmare of Nazi terror. He had already seen it in a *Gestapo* prison and in Hitler's concentration camps. He could not forget the unforgivable results of State-sponsored evil. He could scarcely believe his eyes—this half-demented Austrian was trying to turn the future of Germany and all Europe over to a racially selected élite, a thrust of primitivism that tainted the good German name. To him it was just senseless to accept this grotesque future for his people. He would not and could not stand idly by—he would do his best to help put an end to the Nazi regime.

After his release Leber joined the Kreisau Circle, then a small group of some twenty members, including army officers, academicians, conservatives, Liberals, Socialists, Catholics, and Protestants. Led by Helmuth James Count von Moltke and Peter Count Yorck von Wartenburg, the Kreisau members considered themselves to be planners for the future of Germany. They would strike down this dictator, overthrow his evil regime, and substitute for it a decent political and social ethic with the country returned to Christianity.

Leber used his small coal business as a cover for his work against the Nazi regime. His office at the Bruno Meyer Company in Berlin-Schönberg, of which he was co-owner, served as a meeting-place for friends opposed to the National Socialist regime. Here enthusiastic discussions were held on preparing the rebellion. At clandestine meetings Leber demonstrated again and again that he was more qualified for political leadership than others. His coconspirators admired him for his calm outward bearing, depth of feeling, and sense of responsibility. Dedicated to the cause of democracy and outraged by what was happening in his homeland, he devoted all his energy to the task at hand. For him no plan was too dangerous, no goal too high.

Colleagues were so impressed with Leber's qualities of leadership that they proposed him for various posts in a new government—from Minister of the Interior to even higher positions. He was politically close to Claus Count von Stauffenberg, the General Staff officer who became the driving force behind the Resistance movement. Leber was Stauffenberg's candidate for Reich Chancellor if the plot against Hitler succeeded. Moreover, as a leading Social Democrat, Leber worked closely with Carl Goerdeler, former Lord Mayor of Leipzig and acknowledged civilian leader of the conspiracy.

Leber's comrades in the Resistance respected his qualities of leadership and were impressed by his insistence on building a workable democracy with a strong government free from narrow political doctrine. Gustav Dahrendorf, one of his colleagues, summarized what most of his co-workers thought of Leber: "His whole life was action. Inspired by his great moral strength and his own strong will, he was at all stages of his life a soldier, a politician, and a human being."

Leber was absorbed not merely by the negative goal of getting rid of Hitler. He always thought in terms of the future for his beloved countrymen: "If we wish to achieve more than the collapse of the Nazi regime, then we must set up a positive goal, a goal to which the misled German masses can reorient themselves.'' This was no dogmatic politician speaking parrot-like words, but an intense human being anxious to improve the lot of his countrymen. Germans, he said, were faced with the critical task of rejecting a dangerous regime and setting up in its place a government representing basic human, social, and democratic rights. He called for a new *Volksfront* (People's Front), which would stand in direct opposition to National Socialism and would work for its downfall. He admitted that Hitler could not be overthrown in one night and a working democracy immediately installed, but that a gradual revival of a multi-party system would be instituted while the German people were being trained in democracy.

To words, Leber added an active participation in the plot against Hitler. As the war went on and millions of German lives were being sacrificed in a vain cause, he joined Stauffenberg and Goerdeler in October 1943 in what was to be a military *coup d'état* after the assassination of Hitler. Convinced that the war was lost after the Allied invasion at Normandy of June 6, 1944, these three worked energetically to promote a final attempt on Hitler's life. Leber had predicted the Allied invasion long before the German General Staff did and felt that the time for action against the dictator was at hand.

At this moment Leber made a critical mistake, one which would cost him his life. With his own leftist leanings and his belief that Social Democrats must work with Communists to break the Nazi regime, he made contact with the highest leadership of the KPD, the banned Communist Party. Although he took precautions, he did not know that he would become the victim of an informer who had found his way into the KPD leadership. On July 5, 1944, he was arrested by the *Gestapo*. The Nazi terror apparatus was working efficiently.

As soon as he heard of Leber's arrest, Stauffenberg was moved to proceed as quickly as possible with his plan to kill Hitler. At the same time, he hoped to rescue close-associate Leber. The hurried developments helped result in a fiasco with the *Fuehrer* surviving the bomb thrown in the barracks room at Rastenburg, East Prussia, Hilter's field headquarters.

Before the "Hanging Judge"

In the entire history of jurisprudence there was no one to compare with Roland Freisler, President of the *Volksgericht*, (People's Court), a special tribunal set up to provide speedy justice in cases of presumed treason. We have met him before in these minibiographies. His task was to defend the Nazi state against those who would seek to overthrow it.

Spectators in the courtroom were astonished by Leber's demeanor before the Hanging Judge. Where others were bewildered, dismayed, or crushed by Freisler's hysterical outbursts, Leber stood calmly in the dock and refused to be cowed. He made no secret of the fact that he had tried to overthrow the Nazi government. He knew well what his fate would be before this maniacal judge but he did not flinch. A spectator in the courtroom described it: "He was not at all overwrought, but calm and patient. He listened attentively to the enemy and then answered in a low voice, but distinctly and steadily ... His voice remained clear and he did not tremble. I could see from behind him, from where the spectators were sitting, the heels of his shoes moving up and down (they were slightly worn down—we are in the fifth year of the war and Leber is not a rich man), but he remained absolutely cool and controlled."

Looking furiously down at the prisoner, Freisler in his red robe was not satisfied merely to convict him of treason. He wanted much more. He would humiliate the man, break his spirit, make him collapse in fear. Shouting at the top of his voice, he accused Leber of being a coward. This to a man who had been decorated for valor on the battlefields of World War I. Freisler expected to goad Leber into fury so that he could once again interrupt him and insult him anew. But the prisoner listened quietly and replied calmly: "That is an error."

The courtroom spectator: "As the duel went on, one had the impression that the roles were reversed, that the judge in the red robe up there was losing his nerve. At the end he seemed disappointed, exhausted, and angry. He decided to end the trial. He was still the man in power. He was the one to command. But the prisoner was the victor in this duel. Virtually alone in that courtroom, helpless, faced with malicious opponents, with his death already determined, yet in the final analysis he had out-maneuvered his opponent.''

Leber's counsel, appointed by the State, did little to defend him, not even pleading extenuating circumstances. The lawyer merely stated that his client was fully aware of what he had done and that he knew what to expect.

The prisoner remained calm and patient as the sentence was read. He walked erectly from Freisler's court of justice.

On October 20, 1944, Leber was hanged at Plötzensee Prison in Berlin on charges of high treason, aid to the enemy, and sedition.

"This Great Fighter"

Friend Gustav Dahrendorf, who shared Leber's imprisonment in Ravensbrück concentration camp, paid tribute to his fellow-inmate:

"We see a piece of the sky. Julius Leber looks at me penetratingly as we pass at a distance. His body is taut, he expresses a message both friendly and defiant: "Don't let yourself go; hold yourself together!" "

"He was a great human being, a powerful personality."

"He was completely dedicated to the 'cause' of democracy and Socialism and 'to the God or demon who fosters them.' "

"We miss his presence among us! Our memory of this great fighter and human being constitutes an obligation for active service in the spirit of democracy."

12*

ERWIN ROMMEL:
Desert Fox

─────────

To die by the hand of one's people is hard.

To a Military Career

ERWIN JOHANNES EUGEN ROMMEL WAS BORN ON NOVEMBER 15, 1891, at Heidenheim, a small town in Württemberg, northeast of Ulm, which remained his home base for the rest of his life. Both father and grandfather were schoolmasters, mathematicians highly regarded in their home town. His mother, Helene Luz, was the daughter of the President of the Government of Württemberg.

Although his later career demanded a core of toughness, Rommel was a gentle and docile child, small for his age, and set apart from other boys by his slow manner of speaking. He always showed his courage while playing childhood games in surrounding fields and woods. He was often sickly. He was a dreamy little boy, indifferent to his studies in his early years, and showing little signs of the kind of physical prowess he later developed.

There was a sudden change in his early teens, when it appeared that he had inherited the mathematical bent of his father and grandfather. He cast aside his air of distraction and began to take an interest in his school work, his bicycle in summer, and his skis in winter. He also turned to mechanical things and spoke of a career in mechanical engineering. At the age of fourteen, together with a friend, he built a full-scale, box-type glider in a field near his home. The two made many unsuccessful attempts to leave the ground in their strange contraption. When his friend mentioned a career at the Zeppelin works

189

at Friedrichshafen, Erwin was determined to go along with him.

Father Rommel was not intrigued by the idea. Although the family had no military tradition, he decided that it would be fine to have a son in the armed forces. Accordingly, he recommended Erwin to the military authorities in Württemberg as "thrifty, reliable, and a good gymnast." The young man was accepted without too much enthusiasm by recruiting officers. In July 1910, at the age of eighteen, Erwin joined the 124th Infantry Regiment at Weingarten as an aspirant, or officer cadet, a post which required him to serve in the ranks before becoming eligible for officer training. Within a few months he was promoted to corporal and then sergeant. In March 1911 he was sent to the War Academy at Danzig. Although the young Swabian was far removed from the material considered to be essential for the Prussian officer class, he was well on his way in his army career. His superiors at the War Academy judged him to be good at rifle and drill work, adequate in gymnastics, fencing, and riding, but physically "somewhat awkward and delicate." He could become "a useful soldier," for he was "intelligent, conscientious, and guided by a strict sense of duty."

After passing his examinations, Rommel received his commission as a 2nd Lieutenant in January 1912. For the next two years he was engaged in the training of recruits. Though still undersized, he had a strong body, and even in these early days always managed to win the confidence of men serving under him. He was a quiet and serious young officer who went about his duties methodically in a small garrison town.

Rommel was attached to a Field Artillery regiment in Ulm when in August 1914 the 124th went off to war. From the beginning the neophyte officer turned out to be a perfect fighting animal, cool, courageous, quick to make important decisions in the heat of battle. For the next two years he was in the thick of combat on the Western Front. In September 1914 he was wounded by a ricocheting bullet in his left thigh, and was awarded the Iron Cross, Second Class. Returning to action in January 1915, he was engaged in deadly trench warfare in the

Argonne Forest. He led his riflemen through barbed wire into the main French positions and then shrewdly withdrew before the inevitable counterattack. This time his courage won him the Iron Cross, First Class, the first time a lieutenant in his regiment received that honor. There were new injuries, but Rommel shrugged off the pain of shrapnel in one shin.

One of his platoon leaders described Rommel in action: "He was slightly built, almost schoolboyish, but he was inspired by a holy zeal always eager and anxious to act. Everyone was inspired by his initiative, his courage, his dazzling acts of gallantry. Anyone who came under the spell of his personality turned into a real soldier. No matter how tough the strain, he seemed to be inexhaustible. He seemed instinctively to know exactly what the enemy was like. His plans were often startling, spontaneous, and sometimes obscure. He had an extraordinary imagination, which enabled him to come to altogether unexpected solutions for even the toughest situations. When there was danger, he was always out in front calling on us to follow him. He knew no fear. His men idolized him and had complete faith in him."

This estimate of Rommel in action was remarkable for its accuracy. His conduct in World War II could be described in exactly the same terms—the same courage, the same reactions in combat, the same leadership qualities which won the respect and confidence of men serving under him.

In the latter part of World War I, Rommel won attention for his feats in Rumania and Italy. An advocate of speedy attack, he led his men on forays behind enemy lines, always attacking and then withdrawing at precisely the right moment. He was only twenty-five, but he was already causing comment in high quarters. His bold operations in Italy won him the *Pour le Mérite*, and he was promoted to Captain. At this time, together with half a dozen men roped together, he swam the icy waters of the Piave at night and captured an Italian village with its entire garrison. He was then ordered on leave, to his disgust, and given a staff appointment until the end of the war.

Reluctant Hero

Though he fought hard for his country, Rommel took no satisfaction in the bloody business of war. It was beyond his understanding why civilized men took periodic descents into this kind of barbarism. It was an old story—from cave man to modern man it was always the same—human beings devoted their supreme energy to the task of destroying one another. Like many others, Rommel was profoundly pessimistic about the progress of mankind. To explain the puzzle it was necessary to turn to minds greater than his own.

Perhaps English rationalist Thomas Robert Malthus had the answer. Malthusian doctrine claimed simply that it was a law of Nature: population when unchecked increases in geometrical ration while subsistence increases only along arithmetical lines: population always increases up to the limits of subsistence. The number of people is prevented from going beyond these limits by the "positive" aspects of war, famine, pestilence, and the influence of misery and vice. Thus, warfare among humans is to be expected as a force of Nature.

"Positive aspects." It was hard to find any in the savage cruelty and harsh inhumanity of war. Rommel, like other generals, saw the existence of war as a fact of life. Wars had to be fought and there was a profession of arms. The professional soldier dedicated himself to the task of defending his country in time of crisis. He had no say in the origin of hostilities. Once the conflict began, however, it was his duty to use his energy and skill to bring about a triumphant conclusion. One must plan with intelligence, strike swiftly, and seek an end to the carnage with as little loss as possible on both sides.

Rommel was, indeed, a great general among the strategists and tacticians of warfare. Small in stature, with a disarming grin on his face, he was a superb field commander, bold and dashing in combat, devoted to his troops, always considerate of his conquered enemy. Expert at confounding his opponents, he won victory after victory under unfavorable circumstances. He was a master in the process of confusing and demoralizing his enemies. Again and again he was able to snatch victory from defeat. Skilled in the game of bluffing, his greatest joy was to trick an enemy into unnecessary surrender.

This general was adored by his troops. He had no intention of being a rear-tent commander safe from danger. He preferred going into battle while in a lead tank. He had little concern for his own safety, as if he were immortal in combat. His courage and consideration for his men made him a living legend. Other German officers at a high level were envious. Even Field Marshall Gerd von Rundstedt judged him to be ''just a good division commander, no more than that.'' It is possible that this kind of jealousy of Rommel played a role in his tragic end.

In a war brutalized by Nazi savagery, Rommel ordered his men to fight honorably. He would return to the long-forgotten days of chivalry, when the enemy was accorded respect and consideration. He treated his prisoners well, and ignored orders from above to execute captured commandos or to shoot hostages. He expected his officers to forbid looting of any kind. In his mind such behavior was outside the ken of the decent fighting man. It was imperative to maintain the discipline of and respect for the German armed forces.

Inevitably, Rommel's exploits on the battlefield made him the darling of the German public. Here was an authentic hero in whom the people could take pride. He was catapulted to the plane of national hero. The legend and magic of his name grew as his exploits were described in glowing terms to an audience hungry for news of war victories. For most of World War II he was Hitler's favorite general, although the dictator was annoyed by Rommel's great popularity.

The Rommel myth also captivated his British and American opponents. To them doing something right in combat meant ''doing a Rommel.'' By the very nature of conflict, few professional soldiers manage to win the admiration of their enemies. The opposing leader is there to destroy you—scorn him, revile him, hate him. But not Rommel. Word got around among Allied troops about the character and personality of ''the Desert Fox.'' To them he was a man to be admired.

British Field Marshal Sir Claude J. E. Auchinleck saw Rommel as a respected soldier misused by Hitler. The Allied commander said that he never could translate his intense dislike of the Nazi regime he fought into personal hatred for Rommel. He described the German commander as a stout-hearted adversary, one to be admired as a brave, able, and scrupulous opponent. "Rommel remained pre-eminent as a leader on the battlefield. I can testify myself to his resilience, resourcefulness, and mental agility, and so long as we are still unhappily obliged to train our youth to arms and our officers to lead them into battle, there is much that one can learn from a study of his methods."

Rommel's exploits in North Africa made a strong impression on Winston Churchill. "Rommel! Rommel! Rommel! What else matters but beating him?" In late January 1942, when Rommel led his tanks straight for Benghazi, Churchill rose to his feet before an angry Parliament to answer questions about the crisis in North Africa. Rommel, with his everpresent goggles, had by this time become a hero of the world's press. The British Prime Minister paid tribute to his dashing opponent: "I cannot tell you what the position at the present moment is on the western front in Cyrenaica. We have a very daring and skillful opponent against us, and may I say across the havoc of war a great general."

It was a smashing tribute from the grizzled lion of Britain. The Rommel legend persisted even after the war. The exploits of the great man were recounted with joy. Throughout Germany there were new Rommel Streets. Americans, too, were entranced by the man. Hollywood produced a fulsomely flattering portrait, *The Desert Fox,* which became enormously popular.

Historians were kind to the dashing German field commander. Almost without exception they paid tribute to his soldierly skill and human attributes. They were impressed by the fact that he was worshipped by his fighting men and concluded that what he got out of them was far beyond any rational calculation. They saw him as a master of the art of warfare. "Rommel," wrote B. H. Liddell Hart, "grasped the super-mobile style of warfare with armored and motorized force, the element of *Blitzkrieg,* lighting war, and developed it with freshmindedness and innate ability. He had the power to sense what was going on behind enemy lines as well as in the enemy mind. He had extraordinary psychological understanding. Like Napoleon and Bedford Forrest before him, he was a master of suprise and speed. Here was an enemy commander to be respected.''

For most of World War II, Rommel was a supporter of Hitler and the Third Reich. The *Fuehrer* represented the political force in the state, while he, Rommel, among other commanders, was the powerful arm. He was Hitler's favorite, and as a loyal subordinate he would do all in his power to help the new Germany.

Slowly but surely, however, there arose doubts in Rommel's mind as he began to understand the real nature of the regime to which he had pledged his loyalty. There was something wrong about the emotional eccentric of Berchtesgaden. As battlefield commander, Rommel was perplexed and angered by Hitler's bizarre military blunders. More, he was appalled and ashamed by brutal Nazi excesses. This was a way of life utterly repugnant to his sense of decency. He did not enter into the formal conspiracy against Hitler—he refused an active role. But he could not help but be sympathetic with its aim to overthrow this sullied leader.

There was an unfortunate incident that was to cost him his life. His name had been mentioned among the plotters as excellent material for high office in a post-Hitler government. That was enough to damn him forever in the eyes of the suspicious *Fuehrer*. It was a no-win situation—dangerous enough to lead to his premature death.

Road to Fame and Misfortune

The story of Rommel's career as a fighting man reads like a novel portraying the life of a German hero. Following his country's defeat in 1918, he elected to stay in the army, although many fellow-officers were discharged. In the early days of the Weimar Republic he was posted to Stuttgart to command a rifle company of an infantry regiment in the drastically reduced army allowed to Germany by the Treaty of Versailles. He served in this capacity for the next nine years. His superiors praised his "great military gifts" and his work as an exemplary combat commander. In early 1929 he was assigned to the School of Infantry in Dresden as a junior instructor. A popular teacher, he lectured to his men on the art of small-scale warfare in difficult terrain. His colleagues described him as a towering personality, a genuine leader, "respected by his colleagues, worshipped by the cadets."

Rommel met Hitler for the first time in 1934. He was impressed at first by the *Fuehrer's* strong leadership qualities and especially by the esteem Hitler showed for the army. In these early days Rommel spoke of Hitler's "military genius," a judgment that was to undergo a drastic change late in his career. In 1937 he published a book, *Infantry greift an (The Infantry Attacks),* which soon became a best-seller and brought him what he believed to be an embarrassing amount of riches.

In late August 1939 Rommel left the Reich Chancellery as a brand new general and as commandant of the *Fuehrer's* headquarters. On Hitler's orders he led his escort battalion toward the Polish frontier. When war broke out on September 1, Rommel was convinced that the whole thing would peter out within a few days and that Britain and France would not move. On September 19 he accompanied the *Fuehrer* on his ceremonial entrance into Danzig.

Hitler had expected a peaceful settlement with Britain and France. It was a thoroughly wrong estimate of the situation.

During this dangerous period, Hitler and Rommel developed what seemed to be a kind of mutual admiration. Anxious to lead a *Panzer* tank division, Rommel asked for such an assignment, but was turned down by the army personnel chief. Rommel, said the chief, was only an infantry officer and he knew nothing about tanks. But in early February 1940 Rommel was ordered to report to Bad Godesberg on the Rhine to take over command of the Seventh *Panzer* Division. Apparently, Hitler had intervened on his behalf. The *Fuehrer* presented him with a copy of *Mein Kampf,* inscribed "To General Rommel with pleasant memories."

The infantry officer then went ahead with the serious business of making himself a master of tank warfare. First, he made himself known to every officer and man in his division. Then, within the next two months, he worked out his own special tactics, adding ideas to those of British and French military writers on the subject. On May 13, 1940, he led his division on its first assignment—to cross the Meuse. Under heavy fire, he worked with his men in water up to his waist to help build a bridge across the river. When the French counterattacked with tanks and infantry, Rommel was in the lead German tank to blunt their drive. In the process he was hit in the face. Several nights later, he launched a tank attack by moonlight, with the mass of his men following him. Within a few days he broke through the French fortified zone and made secure several vital crossings of the Sambre.

Word soon spread about the personal courage of tank commander Rommel. He was awarded the Knighthood Cross. On May 21 he met the British for the first time at Arras and claimed the destruction of 45 enemy tanks. Between May 29 and June 4 some 300,000 British troops managed to escape the Continent at Dunkirk. Rommel led his tanks on St. Valéry, headquarters of the British 51st Division. Here the Germans took 12,000 prisoners, of whom 8,000 were British. The surrender took place on June 12. Five days later Marshal Henri Pétain asked for an armistice.

Rommel had moved far and fast with his division. The German triumph was achieved with relatively light casualties—men were killed and wounded, but Rommel was given the credit for being parsimonious with the lives of those who served under him. The Rommel legend was already in process of formation. Here was truly an effective fighting machine. The name of Rommel sped through German ranks with touches of praise and pride. He was a rough and tough commander, but he was credited with saving lives on both sides.

The British were annoyed by having to surrender to so youthful a general. The French were astonished. One captured elderly French general told Rommel: "You are far too fast, young man." Another French officer spoke in puzzled tones: "The

Ghost Division again! First in Belgium, then at Arras, and then the Somme. Now here again. We will call you the Ghost Division!''

Six days later Rommel moved on Cherbourg, with orders from Hitler to take the important French seaport. Although outnumbered at least twenty times, and the fortress guns were still intact, Rommel captured the city after his tanks had covered more than 200 miles on that single day. The Germans took more than 20,000 prisoners in and around Cherbourg. In its *Blitzkrieg* against France, Rommel's Ghost Division took 97,000 prisoners with the loss of only 42 tanks.

Joy in Germany. The Nazi propaganda machine went into action. "He is like one of the Horsemen of the Apocalypse. His magic word is speed, boldness is his stock in trade. He shocks the enemy, outflanks them, suddenly appears far in their rear. His tanks carve long bloody trails across the map of Europe, like the scalpel of a surgeon."

Nazi Germany had a new national hero.

Rommel's reputation as the darling of the German public was already established when in early February 1941 he was ordered to report to the *Fuehrer*. Hitler gave him a detailed account of the situation in Africa and informed him that he had been recommended as the man who could most quickly adapt himself to the altogether different conditions of the new theater of war. He would be given command of the new *Afrika Korps* with the task of pushing the British back into Egypt. Here, on the shifting sands of North Africa, he would be responsible for implementing Hitler's grand design for victory over the Allies.

Aware of the tenseness of the situation and the sluggishness of the Italian command, Rommel went to work to get his troops ready for an offensive toward Tripoli. He soon demonstrated a mastery of a new kind of warfare and earned the title of "The Desert Fox." What he accomplished there was done in the face of serious difficulties with the High Command at home, which, apparently, did not take the North African campaign seriously. Although he enjoyed the confidence of the *Fuehrer,* while he was a German hero worshipped by his troops, Rommel had to face the envy of other officers and an unwillingness to give him the support he needed.

The first round started successfully when Rommel defeated the British under Gen. Archibald Wavell at El Agheila and advanced to Tobruk. In late 1941 the British counterattacked. He moved back to Benghazi. This was the beginning of a series of ups-and-downs. Driven back to the borders of Cyrenaica, Rommel again turned to the attack at the end of the year.

It was a difficult situation for the tank commander. He had to face an enemy vastly superior in men and equipment. He found it difficult to get along with his Italian allies. He was at odds with his own supreme command. Although Hitler spoke eloquently about the necessity for victory in North Africa, it became obvious that the *Fuehrer* regarded the area as only a side show. There were increasing difficulties of supply. Moreover, to add to Rommel's worries, his troops were exhausted.

In May 1942 Hitler ordered an attack on Cairo and the Suez Canal. Despite his combination of problems, Rommel struck swiftly in a renewed offensive and drove the British back toward the Egyptian frontier. On June 21 he captured Tobruk, key to the British defenses. With his spectacular suprise attacks, Rommel led his *Afrika Korps* past Tobruk, Morsa Matruh, and El Daba to El Alamein, 60 miles from Alexandria.

Outburst of joy inside Germany. The "People's Marshal" had done it again! The British would be pushed into the sands of North Africa. The *Fuehrer's* grand strategy was working to perfection. On to Cairo and the Suez Canal! It was a dark moment of the war for the Allies.

Then came the decisive battle of El Alamein—and a drastic turn in the fortunes of the Desert Fox. El Alamein was a stony, waterless desert spot. Here Gen. Bernard Law Montgomery, who turned out to be Rommel's nemesis, had gathered reinforcements—jeeps, trucks, Sherman tanks, planes, and ammunition, for the special purpose of meeting the Desert Fox head on. Montgomery shrewdly waited to strike until he had superiority on ground and in the air. Using deception on a vast scale, he convinced the Germans that he would strike in the south instead of the north of the area. "Kill Germans," he told his troops, "even the *padres*—one per weekday and two on Sundays!"

Montgomery hurled his full strength at Rommel and the *Afrika Korps* on October 23, 1942. First came a violent artillery attack as the whole horizon burst into flame. Then Montgomery sent 41,000 men, 9,000 vehicles of all kinds, and 1,000 tanks against the Germans. Rommel, who had drawn up defensive plans, had returned to Germany for medical attention. At Hitler's urgent request he rushed back to North Africa, only to find that the Battle of El Alamein was lost. When his counterattack failed, Rommel was forced to withdraw to the German bridgehead in Tunis. He fell back 700 miles with the remnants of his African army.

It was a disheartening defeat for both Rommel and Hitler. "It may almost be said," commented Churchill, "before Alamein we never had a victory, after Alamein we never had a defeat."

Rommel was recalled from Tunis on March 9, 1943. Several months later he was given command of Army Group B in northern Italy with the assignment of preventing Italian defection and a possible Allied invasion of southern Europe. In early 1944 he was transferred to command of an army group in northern France.

On two occasions, on June 17 and 29, 1944, Rommel, together with Gen. Gerd von Rundstedt, Commander-in-Chief of Army West, reported to Hitler and tried to convince him that he should end the war while considerable German forces still existed. Pale and shaken, the *Fuehrer* excoriated his two Field Marshals with angry diatribes, denouncing their "defeatism" and ordering them to fight to the last man.

Rommel, in charge of the defense of the French Channel coast, went back to his work of preparing for a possible invasion. He was depressed—he knew that his recommendation for a strong force to be held in reserve to counterattack after bridgeheads had been established would be disregarded. He predicted that the issue would be decided on the very first day of the invasion, a prophecy which turned out to be highly accurate.

On July 17, 1944, after the Allied invasion of June 6, Rommel was severely injured when his automobile was strafed by a British plane. Flying at great speed only a few feet above the road, the British pilot opened fire on several of the thousands of German vehicles shot up on the roads of Normandy that month. Rommel's car was hit by the first burst. He was wounded in the face by broken glass and received a blow on the left temple and cheekbone, apparently from the pillar of the windshield, which caused triple fracture of the skull and made him lose consciousness immediately. He was sent back to Ulm to recover.

Conspiracy against Hitler

Like millions of other Germans, Rommel was at first fooled by Hitler. From the accession of the Nazis to power in 1933 through the decade, Rommel, again like many other Germans, was impressed by the former Austrian who seemed to have found the answer to Germany's problems. Hitler was eccentric, to be sure, but he seemed to be a man of action and perhaps he could be relied upon to do something about that detested Treaty of Versailles.

In these early days, Rommel drew a distinction between Hitler and his Nazi hierarchy. In his mind the *Fuehrer* was a man of political talent who apparently knew what he was doing. Unfortunately, however, the man was surrounded by a band of scoundrels, a legacy of the past. But he was a great man, an idealist, one who could be served well by professional soldiers. Rommel was grateful at first for the fact that Hitler seemed to favor the army. Here was a strong leader, just what the country needed at the moment. And certainly he seemed to have military genius, something of prime importance to an officer in the upper echelon of command.

By 1938 Rommel's regard for Hitler was at a high point. As a professional soldier he was not attracted by political ideology, but he gave little thought to Nazi philosophy. In private postcards to friends, he used the then popular expression when signing off: "*Heil Hitler!* Yours, E. Rommel."

Rommel's friendly attitude continued during the early days of World War II. In fact, he became even more drawn to the *Fuehrer* when he was appointed to Hitler's personal bodyguard. On the invasion of Poland, Rommel wrote excitedly to wife Lucie: "What do you make of the events of September 1— Hitler's speech? Isn't that wonderful that we have such a man?" The quick victory in Poland convinced Rommel that the whole war would soon peter out. "I think I shall be home before winter. The war's going just the way we planned. In fact it's exceeding even our boldest expectations. . . . Every evening there's a long war conference here. I'm allowed to attend it and even chip in from time to time. It's wonderful to see the way [Hitler] deals with problems. . . . The *Fuehrer's* in the best possible mood. I have had frequent chats with him, we are on quite close terms."

The *Fuehrer* returned the good will shown by Rommel. It was a mutual admiration relationship—for a limited time.

The next two years were to see an about-face on the part of Rommel, now a combat general known inside Germany and throughout the world as The Desert Fox. By this time Rommel had come to some troublesome conclusions: (1) far from being a military genius Hitler was a bumbling amateur with grotesque notions of military strategy; (2) the war could no longer be won and Hitler was not able to face the reality of that fact; and (3) something had to be done to make peace with the Western powers.

More than that—Rommel, once the loyal paladin, as a decent German, began to be troubled by the real nature of the Nazi regime he had supported. The man had turned out to be a hideous misfit, a charlatan who was leading the country to ruin. The *Fuehrer* was responsible for appalling human losses, the legless, the armless, the sightless, the jawless—and the twisted minds of battlefield veterans. As a strategist, the master of Berchtesgaden knew only one rule—stay and fight to the death. His orders to his generals at Stalingrad were simply stupid.

Something had to be done before this madman led the country to utter destruction.

By early 1945 several determined Germans were involved in a conspiracy to eliminate the half-demented *Fuehrer*. Concerned by what the *Fuehrer* had done to the German name before all the world, they would place their lives in jeopardy in an effort to remove him and halt the damage. Among these clandestine plotters were high army officers, governmental administrators, and theologians, all seeking to put an end to the Nazi regime.

Among the conspirators was Admiral Wilhelm Canaris, Hitler's intelligence chief, who was leading a double life and who had been plotting Hitler's downfall for several years. Canaris and others who worked with him at first looked upon Rommel as a convinced Nazi and made no efforts to contact him. Rommel was still the *Fuehrer*'s favorite Field Marshal.

In late February 1943, Dr. Karl Strölin, Mayor of Stuttgart, who had served in the same unit as Rommel in World War I, visited him at his home in Herrlingen. The Field Marshal was on leave of ten days for a well-deserved rest. He did not know it, but the mayor was an important member of the Hitler conspiracy. Suddenly, the visitor drew out a sheaf of papers and in dramatic tones began to speak about the ''criminality'' of the Nazi regime. One of the papers described the abominable crimes being committed against Jews in extermination camps in Poland. Rommel, said Strölin, must join in an effort to ''save the Reich.''

Rommel rose to his feet and shouted: ''Herr Strölin, I would be pleased if you would stop saying such things in the presence of my young son.''

In mid-April 1944, Rommel appointed Gen. Hans Speidel as his new chief of staff. Again, he did not know that Speidel had been involved since Stalingrad in plans of the plotters against Hitler. Meanwhile, the conspirators gave Speidel authorization to enlist the Field Marshal in the plot. They needed Rommel's name to attract the broad mass of the army after the assassination of Hitler. They looked to Speidel to convert Rommel. At this time Rommel was unaware of these activities. He trusted Speidel implicitly.

Speidel proceeded cautiously in his plan to prepare Rommel for the possibility of a revolt. Until the Normandy invasion of June 6, 1944, the Field Marshal kept closely to his oath of allegiance to Hitler. On June 11, Speidel, driving back with Rommel to the front from Paris, told Rommel about Nazi mass-extermination atrocities in Poland. By now Rommel was beginning to think that a unilaterial surrender in the West was probably the best solution to the grave military situation. He was appalled by what the Nazis were doing.

On July 10, 1944, came a fateful interview. The conspirators sent an emissary, Lt. Col. Caesar von Hofacker, in *Luftwaffe* uniform, to Rommel to enlist his support in the plot. It is not known exactly what was said at the meeting. Hofacker apparently spoke for about a half an hour, informing Rommel that the situation called for swift action, and that if the *Fuehrer* refused to act, he must be coerced. There was no talk about killing Hitler. The plotters knew that Rommel was opposed to assassination.

Hofacker seemed to be delighted by his mission. He reported excitedly back to Paris that he was more successful than he had hoped. "Rommel can scarcely be restrained, He wants to lash out at once, even if the plot in the Reich fails. Rommel has placed himself completely at our disposal." "Furthermore," Hofacker said, "Rommel was willing to lead the Armistice talks with the Western powers."

Exaggeration by an incurable romantic. What had happened was that the conspirators suggested that it was Rommel's duty to take over as head of state after Hitler had been overthrown. Rommel did not reject the suggestion—and thereby signed his own death warrant.

The Tragic End

Rommel's ordeal began when he heard of the arrest of close friend Speidel. On April 15, 1944, while Chief of Staff of the Eighth Army in the East, Speidel was called by Rommel, a fellow Württemberger and old frontline comrade, to France as his Chief of Staff for Army Group B. From then on, Rommel's headquarters in France became a nerve center for the plot against Hitler. Speidel and Gen. Karl Heinrich von Stuelpnagel, tried to draw Rommel into the conspiracy, but Rommel, though sympathetic, avoided a direct role in the cabal.

Speidel was arrested on September 7, 1944, and removed from his post. Interrogated by the *Gestapo,* he admitted nothing and betrayed no one. Rommel was much concerned about Speidel's fate. On October 1, anxious to save the life of his assistant and friend, he wrote his final letter to Hitler. He described Speidel as an outstandingly efficient and diligent Chief of Staff, with understanding for the troops and a loyal aide in completing the defenses of the Atlantic Wall as quickly as possible with the available means. Rommel's words: ''When the Battle of Normandy started, Speidel did not spare himself to bring success in the struggle with the enemy, who set us in a heavy task, especially with his superiority in the air, his heavy naval guns, and his other superiority in materials. Up to that day when I was wounded, Speidel was loyally at my side. Field Marshal von Kluge also seems to have been satisfied with him. I cannot imagine what can have led to Lt. Gen. Speidel's removal and arrest.''

Rommel then went on to describe the situation at the front. He hoped that it would be reported to the *Fuehrer* quite openly ''and not to conceal unpleasant facts, for only by such service could you, *mein Fuehrer,* be enabled to see clearly and arrive at the right decisions.'' Rommel closed the letter with words designed to allay suspicions of the *Fuehrer:* ''You, *mein Fuehrer,* know how I have exerted my whole strength and capacity, in the Western campaign in 1940 or in Africa in 1941-43, or in Italy 1943, or again in the West 1944. One thought only possesses me all the time, to fight and win for your new Germany. *Heil, mein Fuehrer!*—E. Rommel.''

Rommel sent this mild letter of protest, which he addressed to Hitler personally, via Sepp Dietrich, butcher by trade, high military figure in the Third Reich and close to the *Fuehrer,* and asked that it be forwarded to Hitler. It is not known whether or not Dietrich passed the letter on. In any event, there was no reply.

Speidel, still protesting his innocence, was brought before a Court of Honor. He was acquitted, though Field Marshal Wilhelm Keitel informed the court that Hitler believed him guilty.

Meanwhile, Rommel was in serious trouble. There was an unfortunate stroke of bad luck. Col. Hofacker, one of the conspirators, blurted out Rommel's name to his torturers before he died in agony. It amounted to a death sentence.

Then came a cascading series of events which gave Rommel his life for only a few more days.

On October 7, 1944, word was sent to Rommel ordering him to come to Berlin for an important conference three days later. A special train would be sent to Ulm to fetch him. Rommel was suspicious. "I'm not that much of a fool," he told his son Manfred. "We know these people now. I would never get to Berlin alive." The Field Marshal was still suffering from his war wounds, including a triple fracture of the skull. He spoke to Professor Albrecht, brain specialist at Tübingen University, who was taking care of him. The physician immediately insisted that he was unfit to travel.

At noon on October 14, two emissaries from Hitler came to Rommel's home at Herrlingen. Both were generals. Gen. Wilhelm Burgdorf, a large, ruddy-faced man, who was detested by most of his fellow-officers for his brutality, was accompanied by Gen. Ernst Maisel, attached to the Personnel branch. Maisel was a short, bantam cock of a man, with a large, pointed nose, who had been assigned the task of interrogating officers suspected of taking part in the July 20th plot against Hitler. Both men acted with the utmost courtesy. Rommel assumed that the two had come to talk with him about a new post.

Rommel was mistaken. The two generals were on a deadly mission. Far from offering Rommel a new command in the East, they brought shattering news. Hitler was charging Rommel with high treason. His name had been found on Carl Goerdeler's list to be President of the Reich. In view of his services in Africa, he was to have the chance of dying by poison, which the two generals had brought with them, poison which would act within three seconds. If he accepted, none of the "usual steps" would be taken against his family. His staff would also be let alone. He would be given a State funeral, and a monument would be erected in his memory. Otherwise, he would be brought before the People's Court.

Rommel went upstairs to his wife. There was a terrible expression on his pale face. "I have come to say good-bye. In a quarter of an hour I shall be dead." Appalled, Frau Rommel urged her husband to go before the People's Court because he had never been a party to the plot on Hitler's life. His adjutant, Capt. Hermann Aldinger, urged him at least to make an attempt to escape, even to the extent of shooting the two generals. "No," Rommel said, "they have their orders. Besides, I have my wife and Manfred to think of." It was no good: all the streets were blocked by *SS* cars and *Gestapo* agents surrounded the house.

By this time Rommel had recovered his poise. It was a fine autumn day. He was helped into his great coat, put on his military cap, and grasped his Field Marshal's baton. He shook hands with members of his staff and left his home for the last time. He entered the back of the waiting car with Burgdorf and Maisel.

A half hour later the telephone bell rang in the Rommel home. "There is terrible news. The Field Marshal has had a hemorrhage, a brainstorm in the car. He is dead."

It is not altogether clear what happened in the Opel as it left the Rommel house. The car stopped a few hundred yards from the house. Burgdorf ordered Maisel and the driver to get out because he wished to be alone with Rommel. Five minutes later he left the car and walked up and down the road alongside it. In another five minutes the three approached the auto and found the Field Marshal lifeless on the back seat. The area was surrounded by *Gestapo* agents ready to shoot Rommel if he tried to escape. The body was unloaded at the hospital, where efforts made to revive the Field Marshal were unsuccessful.

On orders from Berlin there was no post-mortem. "When I saw my husband," said Frau Rommel, "I immediately noted an expression of deep contempt on his face. It was an expression we had never seen on it in life."

The public announcement of Rommel's death brought a flood of telegrams and letters of condolence to the stricken family. Among them were three extraordinary messages from the Big Three of Nazidom. Only a colloquialism—ironically—from a Yiddish dictionary can explain adequately the tenor of their reaction—the most glaring example of *chutzpah* in the 20th century. *Chutzpah* means crust, effrontery, brazen nerve, incredible guts, presumptuous arrogance. Few other languages do justice to that word.

Adolf Hitler: "Please accept my sincerest sympathy on the loss of your husband. The name of Field Marshal Rommel will be linked forever with the heroic fighting in North Africa."

Hermann Goering: "The fact that your husband, Field Marshal Rommel, has died a hero's death due to his wounds, after we had all hoped that he would have remained with the German people, has touched me deeply. I send you, dear Frau Rommel, the heartfelt sympathy of myself and the German *Luftwaffe*."

Joseph Goebbels: "Our warmest sympathy. In Field Marshal Rommel the German Army loses one of its most successful commanders, whose name will be forever with the heroic two-year struggle of the *Afrika Korps*. Our deepest sympathy in your grief."

Hitler ordered a period of national mourning and that Rommel be buried with full military honors. The body lay in state in the town hall at Ulm, with Rommel's marshal's baton, helmet, sword, and jeweled decorations placed on a velvet cushion. A large crowd gathered in the square, which was festooned with banners and flags.

Field Marshal Gerd von Rundstedt, senior officer in the German Army, delivered the funeral oration. He stumbled over his prepared text in the name of the *Fuehrer*. "I have been called here by the *Fuehrer* to say farewell to his Field Marshal fallen on the field of honor [*sic!*] This tireless fighter in the cause of the *Fuehrer* and the Reich was imbued with the National Socialist spirit and it was this which gave him his power and has been the mainspring of all his actions. His heart belonged to the *Fuehrer.*"

This was the same Rommel who, only a few days earlier, had spoke openly of Hitler as "that damned fool!"

In March 1945 Frau Rommel received a letter from the director of the War Graves Commission informing her that the *Fuehrer* had ordered him to erect a monument to the late Field Marshal Rommel. He enclosed several designs by sculptors and asked for her reaction.

Frau Rommel made no reply to all this bloated hyprocrisy.

13*

MARTIN NIEMOELLER:
From U-Boat to Pulpit

═══════════

To announce God's word loudly and clearly, that is our service.

Man of War and Peace

IN WORLD WAR I HE WAS THE SKIPPER OF ONE OF THOSE DEEP-SEA sharks encased in an iron hull, a U-boat captain who caused great damage to Allied shipping. A naval officer of skill and determination, he was respected by those who served under him and admired by all who knew him. With his words "Up periscope," his crew automatically braced themselves for another triumph.

Martin Niemoeller was to become known throughout the world first for his resistance to Hitler and the Nazis and after 1945 for his controversial ecclesiastical movement. Emotional advocate of unpopular causes, he was known for his personal charm and for his strong Christian beliefs. His strength of character led him to speak out against the Nazis when others remained silent and to survive eight years in Hitler's concentration camps. There were strange contradictions in his career, but he qualifies, nevertheless, for any compendium of heroes in Naziland.

After his war service Niemoeller chose the calling of theologian and preacher of the Gospel. A superb pulpit orator, he attracted the attention and devotion of thousands of parishioners. As minister of the spiritual, he saw politics as alien to his profession. But he refused to stand aside when an Austrian demagogue emerged to claim that only he, not the divine power, could combine State and Nation. Though he never intended it, the popular preacher was transformed into an important political figure and his church became a center of opposition to Nazism.

Niemoeller was a dangerous enemy for the dictator. He was arrested, brought before the People's Court, and unaccountably set free. Undoubtedly, fear of his great popularity, of the number of his followers, may well have played a part in the decision, for many of his colleagues had disappeared into Nazi dungeons. After the verdict he was about to return to his home when he was arrested again at the back door of the courthouse and sent to a concentration camp.

That did not solve the problem for Hitler. Niemoeller was not the kind of man who could be forced to hold his tongue.

Patriot in Action

Friedrich Gustav Emil Martin Niemoeller was born in Lippstadt, Westphalia, on January 14, 1892, the son of Pastor Heinrich Niemoeller. He led an uneventful early life as the son of a Protestant minister. A passionate patriot, he decided on a career in the Imperial Navy and entered its service in 1910 as a midshipman.

Four years later the Great War exploded on an unbelieving world. Young Niemoeller enthusiastically greeted the opportunity of doing his share when the Fatherland was in danger from "attacks on all sides by nations jealous of Germany's power, prestige, and promise." Like millions of other Germans he was convinced that his country had been denied its proper place in the sun and he would fight for that goal.

Attracted by the glory of the submarine service, Niemoeller volunteered for U-boat duty. He first saw action in the North Sea. By this time the energetic officer, with his chiseled face, prominent nose, and unruly dark hair, had won the attention of his superiors in the submarine service. U-boat commanders were desperately needed and this young man with his curtness of speech and confident bearing earned the esteem of crews serving under him. In 1916 Niemoeller was ordered to the Mediterranean in command of his own U-boat.

Life aboard a German U-boat in those days of combat hinged around the character, personality, and ability of its skipper. The captain was responsible for the safety and well-being of his crew and neither side forgot it for a moment. It was at best a dirty business—cramped living quarters, foul odors, polluted air, personality conflicts. There were days of boredom and many moments of stark fear. There was always the satisfying euphoria following the captain's word that another enemy ship had been sent to the bottom of the sea.

In this atmosphere the parson's son turned out to be highly successful. Niemoeller was respected by his crew, admired by the Kaiser, and hailed as a hero by the German public. Few U-boat commanders during the war received more mention in official dispatches. His submarine inflicted such heavy damage on British shipping in the Mediterranean that the German press began to speak of him as "the scourge of Malta."

Kaiser William II, delighted with the exploits of his Westphalian U-boat commander, spoke of Niemoeller as "a national symbol of courage and daring." There were decorations, not only the Iron Cross but also the *Pour le Mérite*, the country's highest military order.

In his autobiography Niemoeller told the dramatic story of his work as a commerce destroyer in the Mediterranean:

Towards evening an airship comes in sight and we have to submerge until it has disappeared in the direction of Marseilles. It is high time for us to come up, as smoke is already reported on the horizon—apparently a big convoy coming from Marseilles. As darkness sets in, we lose sight of the smoke but the clear moonlight at 10 P.M. enables us to discern a number of vessels approaching, which we soon recognize as two large steamers and several patrol vessels.

At 10:30 P.M. we submerge to attack. The ships are clearly visible through the periscope and we are able to fire within a few minutes. Then I see one of the escort making at us with a huge white bow-wave. "Down periscope! Submerge to 60 feet!" We hear the propellers pass overhead. "Come up to 40 feet!"

The boat comes up like a wet dog shaking itself in the wake of the passing vessels. We resume the chase at 11:30 A.M., but it is doubtful whether our 12 1/2 knots will suffice to come up with the convoy. The engines are worked up to full power . . . avoid the remaining ships of the escort. "Full ahead both!" The boat vibrates as the engines work up to full power. There! the first explosion! A 300-foot column of smoke, flame and water shoots up into the dark sky. Now another! The same dreadful sight! Below us the sound of the gramophone is heard. As I stand on the hatch coaming, to get a good look, I tread on a hand—it is Topp, who stands by me, shivering in his pyjamas! He wanted to be in it, in spite of his fever and the frantic pain.

There is confusion among the escort: nobody appears to know which side the attack came from. The three patrol vessels on our side at once turn towards the steamers, while the two on the opposite side drop depth charges, which do not worry us in the slightest. When the fumes of the detonations dissipate, the first steamer has already disappeared, while the second has her upper deck awash. She sinks within a few minutes. We stop and remain stationary to watch developments. Searchlights flare up; W/T signals radiate through the night; the escorting ships pick up survivors; and towards five o'clock the five ships turn back to Marseilles. Their voyage ended earlier than they anticipated a few hours ago!*

Following this attack, Niemoeller and his crew headed homeward. His supply of oil had been reduced by a good third and he felt that his luck was running out. The U-boat steamed south following the course of the destroyed convoy. Seeing

*Martin Niemoeller, *From U-Boat to Concentration Camp* (London: Hodge, 1959), pp. 139-141.

nothing, Niemoeller altered course eastward toward Sardinia and home.

For Niemoeller the loss of the war was a traumatic shock. In November 1918 the stubborn and headstrong U-boat commander refused orders to hand his craft over to the British. Angry and distraught, he resigned his commission. Like millions of other Germans, he was disgusted with the "iniquitous Treaty of Versailles," which he regarded as an unfair stain upon the honor of his country. For Article 231 of the treaty, the famous (to Niemoeller "infamous") war-guilt clause, he had only contempt and revulsion. He was certain that the Fatherland had been mistreated by the victor powers.

During the war Niemoeller had dedicated himself to the task of killing as many enemy seamen as he could. With the calm of peace came a striking change in his attitude. He began to react against the kind of slaughter that had occupied him during the conflict. Enough of drowning, death, and crippling wounds. The man who had struck at the enemy as necessary for the life of the Fatherland now emerged as a convinced pacifist. The frustrated U-boat commander became a man of peace.

Road to Pacifism

Like other professional German officers who had served in the war, Niemoeller became disillusioned after the Armistice and seemed for a time to lose his way in life. Desperately seeking work, he turned to manual labor, at first on a farm and then in a factory. In the early 1920s he wrote his memoirs, which brought him little financial reward.

It was a most unsatisfactory existence for a man who had been absorbed in naval life. To pass the hours he began to read voraciously, especially in political economy and philosophy. He also sought to satisfy his continuing patriotism by joining one of the private military units seeking to win the battle of the streets against the Communists. He was sympathetic to the idea of a disciplined movement which would work to "clean up" German society. For that reason he even looked with favor in the early 1920s to the up-and-coming Nazi movement, which for a time appealed to him as an ardent German nationalist.

In 1927 he turned to theology in a move that was to change his life completely. So successful was he as former U-boat commander-turned-pastor that he was soon invited to Berlin-Dahlem, one of the most valued parishes in Germany. The wealthy residents of this suburb of Berlin, mostly retired industrialists, bankers, and officers, all highly conservative in political outlook, had not been noted for church attendance in the past, until their new Lutheran minister became their spiritual adviser.

In his new calling, Niemoeller devoted to his pastoral duties the same energy he had shown as a tough U-boat captain. He was not averse to political comment. Until the advent of Hitler to the chancellorship in 1933, Niemoeller, like most other pastors, again and again expressed his sympathy with the political aspirations of Hitler's National Socialist German Workers' Party. Many high Nazi leaders attended his church and he made them welcome.

But then came disenchantment. It soon became obvious that Hitler was moving toward dictatorship by his policy of coördination, which was designed to bring every facet of German life under totalitarian control. The *Fuehrer* was determined not only to further his anti-Semitic program but also to oppose Protestants and Catholics. His policy was to denounce Christianity as weak and inconsistent with the goals of the new Third Reich. Nazi belief would replace Protestantism and Catholicism with a new "Positive Christianity," with Adolf Hitler cast as the new godhead to replace the Trinity of Father, Son, and Holy Ghost.

For Pastor Niemoeller this was sacrilegious stupidity. He had agreed with the Nazis in their nationalist program designed to rescue the Fatherland from the terrible Treaty of Versailles. He was prepared to support the Third Reich in its new imperialist program. But Nazi assaults on his religious beliefs were too much for him. He spoke out boldly: "A Christendom that is built merely on race and blood is worse than paganism."

For the next several years Niemoeller, despite angry warnings from the *Gestapo,* continued his attacks on Nazi ideology. His parishioners at Dahlem, drawn by the fiery preaching of the former U-boat commander, were fascinated by his sermons denouncing Nazi ideology. "Heaven help us," he thundered, "if we make a *German* Gospel out of the Gospel, a *German* Church out of Christ's Church, *German* Christians out of Evangelical Churches."

Those words were part of a sermon Niemoeller preached. Calling his lecture "The Salt of the Earth," he urged his congregation to remember in silent intercession those who could not be in the audience that evening, "those who for the Gospel's sake are hampered in their freedom, or robbed of it." For five minutes he read a list of those who had been forbidden to speak, or evicted, or arrested. He reminded the *Fuehrer* about his "word of honor":

> And so what is happening to-day to our brothers and sisters brings us up against an unequivocal question: "Has the Church of Christ, in its members and officer-bearers, still the right to-day which the *Fuehrer* has confirmed with his word—with his word of *honor*—the right to allow us to defend ourselves against attacks on the Church, or are the people right who forbid us—the Christian community—to defend ourselves against unbelief and make it impossible for us to do so, and cast into prison the people who defend themselves?"

> Does the *Fuehrer's* word still hold good? Has the Church the right—and this right has been guaranteed it from ancient times—to collect alms in the congregation, or can the right to bring offerings in accordance with the will of Christ be forbidden it by the stroke of a pen on the part of a minister—or even of two ministers? . . . Let the light shine forth.

Blasphemous and treasonable words for the dictator. This loudmouthed, stubborn pastor had to be silenced.

Doctrinal Struggle

At first the Nazi regime treated the churches with great circumspection: Hitler had no desire to take on powerful theological opponents during the early months of power. For a short time he sought the way of appeasement. Many evangelical pastors remained nationalist and imperialist in sentiment and accepted the idea of heroic piety preached by Martin Luther. The *Fuehrer* counted on them to join a Christian faith "more suited to the times."

It soon became obvious, however, that the Nazi policy of "coördination" would have to include the clergy in its coils. The new regime opted for a Hitler-dominated church, a half-pagan version of what was called "Positive Christianity" or "German Christianity." The new ideology rejected the traditional concept of turning the other cheek and emphasized the idea of Christ driving the moneychangers from the temple. Hitler's version of Christianity would oppose Judaism, Marxism, Free Masonry, and cosmopolitanism. Again the negatives of nihilism.

The *Fuehrer* named a pliant follower, Ludwig Müller, as head of the new Reich Church designed to bring all Protestants together in one easily-ruled body. Evangelical theologian and crusading nationalist, Müller had been an Army chaplain assigned to the First Military Command in Königsberg, East Prussia, in the mid-1920s. There he became known for his preaching of an untrammeled patriotism, for sermons emphasizing the paramount duty of being a German, and for his strong anti-Semitic sentiment. His career blossomed after Hitler became Chancellor. In April 1933 he was appointed plenipotentiary for all problems concerning the Evangelical Church. On July 23, 1933, he was elected Reich Bishop by a national synod at Wittenberg, a gathering entirely under Hitler's control.

The *Fuehrer's* new German Faith movement quickly aroused opposition among theologians. In September 1933 some 4,000 clergymen formed the Pastors' Emergency League, which became the basis for a revived Christian movement. Bernhard Rust, Commissioner for Science, Art and Popular Education in Prussia, denounced "this first focus of resistance" in the Church and declared that it would not be tolerated.

The Pastors' Emergency League soon turned into the Confessional Church (*Bekenntniskirche*), a countermovement by Protestant theologians. The dissenters were led by Niemoeller and young theologian Dietrich Bonhoeffer. Niemoeller refused to accept the new Nazi church. "The nation," he said, "has no eternal being, though its everlastingness be repeated a thousand times." Identifying himself as an evangelical Christian, he spoke out openly against Hitler's *ersatz* German Christianity. He protested against deification of the State. "We are ready to give unto the world, without murmur, the things of the world. But the world asks for things that are God's, then we must manfully resist, lest we give the world the things that are God's, and for the sake of a comfortable life in a strange land lose our home." Christianity, Niemoeller said, was incompatible with the Nazi *Weltanschauung* (world view).

Led by Niemoeller and Bonhoeffer, thousands of pastors felt themselves obligated to offer religious resistance to Nazi control. Some 7,000 of the 17,000 Protestant pastors in Germany joined the Confessional Church. The rest remained silent or agreed with the *Fuehrer*. Hitler abandoned his attempt to rule the Church from within and shifted to brutal control from the outside. He would use his police apparatus to destroy all opposition to his regime.

Fanatical Storm Troopers exploded bombs in the vestry of Niemoeller's Dahlem church. The dissenting pastor was threatened with death. The former U-boat captain, who had faced death dozens of times in his wartime career, did not flinch. When Nazi-appointed Bishop Jaeger called on him for a "peace talk," Niemoeller ignored the invitation.

Perplexed parishoners watched in dismay as their pastors were hauled off by the *Gestapo* to Nazi dungeons and concentration camps. Hundreds of pastors were driven from their pulpits because they refused to preach according to Nazi orders. Niemoeller's sermon on June 19, 1937, proved to be his last under the Nazi Government. A week later *Gestapo* agents were waiting as he walked down the steps of his parish church at Berlin-Dahlem.

Niemoeller had spoken out loudly and boldly against a regime that would throttle his religion. His three years of dissent were to be followed by eight years of enforced silence.

Pastor in Prison

For Adolf Hitler, apotheosis of the little man, it was a deadly confrontation. He could not tolerate the existence of what he regarded as a dangerous preacher who threatened to explode the myths of Nazi ideology. The pastor was a war hero, but he was also an ever-present danger to National Socialism. It was important to silence him.

For Niemoeller the task was immediate and necessary. He must defend both Christianity and the Fatherland. "I have made great mistakes," he said from his Dahlem pulpit, "but I made them because I thought of the welfare of Germany. I did not know that the regeneration of a nation must go hand in hand with brutality, immorality and action against the will of God."

"Brutality, immorality and action against the will of God." Enraged by the pastor's description of his movement and angered by Niemoeller's increasing popularity, Hitler ordered his arrest. On July 1, 1937, Niemoeller was brought before the dreaded People's Court. He was charged with abuse of his pulpit, political agitation, and treason against the State and the German people.

A small residue of decency and humanity must have stayed in the hearts of several judges. The tribunal decided to set Niemoeller free and give him back to his parishioners. Those who voted in his favor may well have been motivated by fear of the pastor's popularity. Many of his colleagues were in jail or forbidden to preach. Niemoeller was acquitted of high treason, but was found guilty of abusing his pulpit for political purposes. He was given a token sentence and freed with a warning.

The irrepressible pastor went back to his preaching. Again the bold words directed against the Nazi state: "There is no man who can boast of having stood, with his help, by the Lord Jesus. There is no man who can boast of having made the Lord Jesus' death easier. Boasting stops before the cross. Nothing is left there but human malice, which seeks to hide itself behind a shred of virtue and is there starkly revealed in the innermost essence of our human nature. Before the cross all noble humanity—or what we call noble humanity—fails.''

So the dangerous pastor was still talking too much. He was arrested again and kept in Moabit Prison for seven months. Not cut off altogether from the outside world, he was allowed to write letters and receive members of his family. To a man of his energy, prison life must have been irksome, but he kept himself busy by preparing his defense. He was convinced that all the world would learn of the nature of the Hitler regime and its loathsome treatment of the Evangelical Church.

Nazi authorities were not anxious to try Niemoeller. They hoped that the rebellious preacher would submit or that his popularity would diminish. However, after he had been in jail for seven months, it was announced suddenly that he would be brought to trial.

The proceedings began on February 7, 1938, before a Special Court convened at Moabit Prison. There was world-wide interest, but foreign journalists who besieged the courtroom were denied entrance. No reports of the trial were allowed in the German press. In his defense Niemoeller reminded the court that he had voted for National Socialism in its early days and in 1933 had preached a sermon in support of it.

The prosecution in the proceedings held *in camera* charged that Niemoeller had damaged the State by his criticisms and that he had disobeyed orders of the Minister of the Interior by reading out names from his pulpit of persons who had resigned from the Church.

The verdict was expected—guilty.

Niemoeller was sentenced to seven months' imprisonment in a fortress and two fines of 500 and 1,500 marks. The punishment was for repeated violations of a law that had been introduced by Bismarck in the 1870s at the time of the *Kulturkampf* against the Roman Catholic Church. The ''pulpit clause'' of this law called for imprisonment of clergymen who discussed affairs of State at religious meetings in such a way as to disturb the peace. The court held that Niemoeller had already spent eight months in prison and that satisfied the proposed punishment of detention in a fortress.

Niemoeller was to be set free at midnight, but as he left the Court he was immediately rearrested by the *Gestapo*. The Secret Police took him away to their headquarters in the Alexanderplatz.

Protests from all over the world flowed into Berlin. Niemoeller's congregation at Dahlem sent a written petition to Hitler himself. The *Fuehrer* dictated a negative reply. Telegrams came to Hitler from the Archbishop of Canterbury, as well as from distinguished religious leaders in Sweden, France, and the United States. No effect.

The London *Times* reflected sentiment throughout the world:

> Dr. Niemoeller's trial and sentence must be considered as more than a personal question. He has never compromised with his conscience as to where he stands in the oldest struggle in the history of civilization, the struggle which raged in the Roman Empire, broke the medieval Empire, and defeated Bismarck. The modern conception of the totalitarian State is an absolute more rigid than that of earlier dictatorships. So, too, Christianity in the last resort is an absolute which postulates a recognized sphere of freedom.

For the next eight years, Niemoeller, in common with millions of other unfortunates, was to ensure a personal Golgotha in Hitler's concentration camps. He was more fortunate than most—he emerged alive from Nazi hellholes.

Concentration Camps

Niemoeller was sent first to Sachsenhausen concentration camp located north of Berlin near Oranienberg. There he became a symbol of "that other Germany, the good Germany." His life became more severe than that in prison before his trial. He was placed in solitary confinement as Hitler's "personal prisoner.'' The *Fuehrer* offered him freedom if he recanted, but he refused.

At Sachsenhausen Niemoeller wore a prisoner's uniform. He was allowed several books, including the English Prayer Book and a volume of Shakespeare in English. Once a fortnight he was allowed to write to his wife. In one of the few letters he received from her, he was comforted by her words: ''Even the Eskimos are praying for you.''

Visitors reported that Niemoeller seemed to be in good health, with his spirit unbroken despite long confinement. Before the first year of imprisonment was over, he wrote in a letter: ''Bodily I am all right. I am like a ship in a storm at sea, dragging her anchor, but the cable still holds.'' The worst of the situation was that he had no hope for release, no optimism that the angered *Fuehrer* would free him. For a time he shared a cell with several Roman Catholic priests, for whom he had such regard that it was said that he came close to converting to Rome.

Niemoeller remained the quintessential patriot. He was now in the concentration camp at Dachau. When the Nazis marched into Poland in September 1939, Niemoeller offered his services ''to fight in any capacity.'' But Hitler was adamant. He was well aware of Niemoeller's experience as a U-boat commander in the Great War and he needed every submarine skipper he could get, but he would not have the dissenter in the Nazi Navy. He rejected the offer. The egomaniac demanded 100% loyalty.

Throughout World War II, people all over the world held that ''the only good German is a dead German.'' That estimate did not apply to Niemoeller, who was defended everywhere as a decent human being who had denounced the bestialities of Nazism at great cost to himself. Everywhere there was interest in the clash of two personalities struggling for the soul of Germany—the representative of ruthless domination and the courageous pastor who refused to accept the tenets of Nazism. All over the world eyes were turned on Berlin.

In 1941, in the midst of the war, Niemoeller's final sermons were published in London in a book titled *The Gestapo Defied.*

An immediate best seller, the publication was noteworthy for an extraordinary foreword by brilliant novelist Thomas Mann. The Nobel Prize winner, the greatest German writer of the 20th century, steadfastly attacked Nazi policy. In Switzerland in 1933 when Hitler came to power, Mann refused to return to his homeland. He spoke out forcefully against the crimes of Hitlerism and appealed to "the other Germany to assert its dignity." In his preface Mann praised Niemoeller's sermons for their important psychological and significant radicalism. He had kind words for the former U-boat commander, whose unconditional obedience stemmed from his military traditions, a military virtue carried over into a new calling. "The fact that Hitler, who constantly harps on heroism, did not see or honor Niemoeller's soldierly qualities, makes his action against him particularly repulsive."

The foreword gave Mann an opportunity for a classic denunciation of Hitler:

> No trace of decency, no respect for human dignity and manly courage—such as his People's Tribunal had shown—existed in the breast of this incredibly vile wretch. Never has the slightest impulse of magnanimity stirred that depraved soul. His successes and dizzy rise to power from the pitiable plight of a bootless ne'er-do-well, which a topsy turvy fate had granted him, did not moderate his hatred or his seething vindictiveness, nor did it enrich his soul by so much as a spark of clemency and mercy, or justice to his prostrate enemies. To these he begrudges death—that, indeed, would be mercy. He inflicts upon them—and it delights his satanic and depraved heart—lifelong torture, physical humiliation and rape, the destruction of their personalities, the sapping of their brains, insanity, beggarly senility. It makes no difference whether it be a private citizen, a former official of the German Republic, heads of defeated nations, like Schuschnigg, or whole peoples and races, like the Czechs, Poles, and Jews.[*]

*Martin Niemoeller, *The Gestapo Defied*. Translated from the German by Jane Lymburn. (London: Hodge, 1941), p. iv.

Postwar Activities

Niemoeller remained Hitler's personal prisoner until the *Fuehrer's* suicide and the collapse of his boasted Thousand Year Reich. Niemoeller was released in 1945 when American Retroops found him in Italy.

One would expect a chastened Niemoeller after seven years of imprisonment. But the belligerent pastor was not tamed. He immediately set to work to bring the German Church back into the mainstream of European and world life. Again he became a center of controversy and stayed there for life.

Still the firebrand, Niemoeller denounced the Germans for their reluctance to accept responsibility for their behavior under Hitler. "The guilt exists," he said in an address at Frankfurt am Main. "There is no doubt about it—even if there were no other guilt than that of the six million gray urns containing the ashes of burnt Jews from all over Europe. And this guilt lies heavily upon the German people and the German name, even on Christendom. For in our world and in our name have these things been done." He insisted on sharing the guilt of the German people: "First they came for the Jews. I was silent. I was not a Jew. Then they came for the Communists. I was silent. I was not a Communist. Then they came for the trade unionists. I was silent. I was not a trade unionist. Then they came for me. There was no one left to speak for me." Niemoeller helped organize the Stuttgart Declaration of 1945, which confessed German war guilt.

At the same time Niemoeller raised his voice against the denazification program sponsored by the U.S. Military Government under Gen. Lucius D. Clay and implemented by Germans. He charged that the policy was sowing hatred and that the denazification process had become an instrument of revenge. He demanded that Lutheran pastors take no part in the denazification proceedings and that congregation members avoid volunteering as prosecution witnesses. "Hundreds of thousands," he said, "yield under the constant pressure to lie. The old system of guilt for kith and kin has returned. Tens of thousands have lost their work and their daily bread to await in internment camps either sentences or—long after sentence has been pronounced—their liberation.''

Shortly after the end of the war, Niemoeller became President of the Church's Office for Foreign Relations. In 1947 he served as President of the Church province of Hesse and Nassau. He declined the title of Bishop because of his view that ''it was not democratic.'' He went on frequent lecture tours to England, the United States, Australia, and elsewhere. Serving as a minister of global evangelism, he was received enthusiastically everywhere. Many listeners were charmed by his warm personality.

Niemoeller moved ran into controversy. Supporting the idea of a united Germany as a bridge between East and West, he went to Moscow in 1952 at the invitation of the Russian Orthodox Patriarch. Here he managed with some success to arrange for the release of German prisoners of war. He insisted that the Church could function under Communism, a view disputed as naîve by most colleagues. When he accepted a Lenin Peace Prize, he was denounced in the West German press. Yet, much of the *Ostpolitik* he advocated later became official policy of the Bonn Government.

In 1954, still politically active and attracted by the postwar ecumenical movement, Niemoeller emerged as a new religious leader. Influenced by his admiration for fellow-Catholic prisoners during the Hitler era, he began to turn his back on Lutheran dogmatism. He now had a change of heart. He made it known that he opposed the restoration of the German Church to what it had been before Hitler. He championed the World Council of Churches and became its treasurer. He announced that he had been converted to Christian pacifism. Attacking German nationalism and any kind of militarism, he called for a neutral, disarmed, and reunited Germany. With his sharp tongue he ridiculed the politics of nuclear deterrence. He was not interested in tactics. ''What would Jesus do?'' was for him the only important question. ''You cannot both love your enemies and exterminate them.''

Others inside the German Church were not impressed by Niemoeller's new ecumenical leadership. In 1956 they combined against him and threw him out of his position as President of the Church's Office of Foreign Relations. Niemoeller was unimpressed. He continued to emphasize his non-violent theology and went ahead with emotional rhetoric to champion the cause of the global ecumenical movement.

Flawed Hero?

Meanwhile, inside Germany Niemoeller's role as an anti-Nazi martyr was being challenged. His prestige began to suffer as more and more attacks were made upon his record. He became a center of bitter controversy. Some Germans found him to be a constant nuisance and dubbed him "Germany's most argumentative pastor," "the provocative Niemoeller," and "the difficult son of a difficult Fatherland." He was branded a fellow-traveller and an informer for Moscow because at times he seemed to be closer to the East than to the Federal Republic of Germany ("sired in Rome and born in Washington.") His enemies attacked his record, especially on anti-Semitism. It was charged that, although he was one of those who had disapproved the outright murder of Jews he had agreed to Jews being deprived of equal rights, outlawed, and thus placed in an atmosphere in which degradation and eventually extermination would be stages reached by degrees. Critics pointed out that in 1947 American Reform Rabbi Stephen S. Wise had denounced Niemoeller: "I am bound to declare that Niemoeller has not so borne himself throughout the unspeakable Hitler years as to merit the respect and confidence of the Christian peoples of America. When Hitler launched the movement destined to be the most disastrous in human history, the Rev. Niemoeller became his most enthusiastic supporter."

Other critics charged that far from representing the "mighty fortress for Christian humanity," Niemoeller had never really understood the menace of Hitlerism. They charged that he was given only a "light confinement" in concentration camps, that he had comparatively good treatment, and that his messages always reached the world outside. He remained the authoritarian, they said, who had little time for democratic niceties and who always remained the tough U-boat captain.

Inside Germany many of Niemoeller's fellow-countrymen were upset by his admission of collective German guilt. That was not the proper stance, they said, for a man one of whose four sons was killed on the Eastern Front. Others denounced his pacifism and especially his remark that "training soldiers is like running an academy for professional killers."

Others just as strongly defended the Protestant pastor by stressing his integrity and devotion to the Christian cause. Theologian Karl Barth, Niemoeller's mentor, called him "a knight on God's chessboard." Defenders spoke of him as "the spearhead of German Protestantism" and "the balance wheel in the clockwork of the Protestant Church." Far from being "a constant nuisance," they said, he was symbolic of the decent German. His enemies were motivated by day-to-day disputes on political issues and forgot that, as a theologian, he was merely "on the quest for a merciful God." Far from promoting the cause of anti-Semitism, they said, Niemoeller had never made a secret of the fact that he felt "sorry and ashamed" by Nazi attacks on Jews and regretted that "we have not done more." They pointed out that he had been dismissed from his ministry in 1933 because in a Christian magazine he had written an article opposing discrimination against Jews practiced by the new Hitler-appointed Church authorities. Moreover, Niemoeller had repeatedly denied that he was a Communist, and he had taken steps to forestall anticlerical measures by the East German Government. In their view it was unfair to call him "Germany's Red Dean."

Niemoeller died at Wiesbaden on March 6, 1984, after a long illness at the age of 92. Estimates about him differed to his dying day. But he is remembered in West Germany as "a courageous and incorruptible witness to the gospel." At first taken in by the nationalism of the Nazi movement, he later opposed it with courage and determination. Like other prophets he was never easy to live with, but most Germans accepted the authenticity of his preaching and the integrity of his faith.

In 1934 the recalcitrant U-boat captain turned pastor had spoken directly to Hitler in bold terms: "We are not worried about the Church; we are worried about the Third Reich."

"That," said Hitler, "is a worry you can leave to me."

Niemoeller was not willing to make that concession.

On balance, Niemoeller deserves the accolade of authentic German hero. It is not necessary to defend him. His record against the blight of Nazism speaks for itself.

14*

CARL VON OSSIETSKY:
Journalist

Every journalist who follows the dictators of his conscience in turbulent times knows that he is living dangerously. The best political journalism has always been written for and posted on walks at night.

An Honorable Profession

NO MATTER WHAT THE OBSTACLES, JOURNALISTS DEVOTE THEIR lives to the task of presenting their readers with the facts. German historian Leopold von Ranke set the standard for both historians and journalists—*was ist geschehen?* What happened? Conscientious reporters are indispensable professionals in civilized societies.

Civilized societies? The words cannot be applied to the twelve years of the Nazi era. Diminutive mouse-doctor Dr. Paul Joseph Goebbels used his propaganda machine to dictate the work of all reporters in the Third Reich. They became transmission belts for the lie. Nazi philosophy held that the more times a lie was repeated, the more the simple-minded public would accept it as gospel truth.

Yet, despite Hitler's iron-clad dictatorship there were some journalists who defied Nazism and refused to stain their profession by bowing to the dictator's will. They were honest and honorable men. They saw the central problem of their time as the defense and enrichment of an open and free society against indecent totalitarianism.

Such a man was journalist Carl von Ossietsky.

Critic-at-Large

There is a long tradition behind it. When ordinarily calm
Englishmen are overcome with emotion on any subject, no
matter how esoteric, they send letters to the editor of *The Times*.
Gilbert Murray, classical scholar at Oxford, best known for his
incomparable rendering of the classical plays of Euripides in
English verse and an energetic worker for international understanding, was so appalled by Nazi treatment of journalist Carl
von Ossietsky that he wrote a letter to *The Times* on January 13,
1937 (published January 16). Though cast in traditional British
understatement, the note revealed the outrage of British intellectuals at reports concerning the manipulation of a courageous
man:

To the Editor of *The Times*:

Sir: At a time when a more peaceful spirit seems to have
risen between Germany and her western neighbours one
cannot but remember an illustrious martyr to the cause of
peace who is still suffering. A few weeks ago Lord Allen in
your columns expressed his warm appreciation of the action
of the German Government in setting Herr von Ossietsky
free from his long imprisonment and allowing him to proceed to Oslo to receive the Nobel Prize. A recent report by
two English doctors who have attempted to visit him in
Berlin shows that this gratitude was premature. Ossietsky is
kept in a nursing home guarded by two members of the
"Gestapo" or secret police: he is not allowed out, and the
English doctors are not allowed to see him.

Herr von Ossietsky is not a criminal, not a Communist,
not an agitator, not a fanatic, only a steadfast and undaunted
worker for peace. He has committed no offense against the
Hitler Government. He has never even been charged. His
crime was that when the Republican Government was
secretly rearming in breach of its treaty he called attention
to the fact. He believes he did rightly, and most moralists,

from Plato to Kant, would agree with him: but if he did
wrong, he was abundantly paid for his wrong.

I hear that General Göring strove with him for two hours,
trying by threats and promises to make him refuse the Nobel
Prize; but in vain. He knew he had earned it by hard service,
and not all his years of suffering have broken the man's
courage. Unfortunately courage is an offence that most Governments find it hard to forgive.

Yours obediently,
GILBERT MURRAY
Yatacombe, Boar's Hill, Oxford, Jan. 13

Gilbert Murray's account was succinct and to the point. Behind the letter were thousands of cases of similar treatment by
dictators intent upon throttling dissent against the totalitarian
state. Ossietsky's story was special: on the one hand he aroused
the hatred of Hitler and on the other he earned global admiration
and award of the Nobel Peace Prize.

Fearless and outspoken, Ossietsky was a journalist who refused to remain silent in troublous times. He takes a place of
honor among those who struggled for human liberty and preservation of democratic principles in a slave state. In the long run
he was unsuccessful in his campaign for free opinion and freedom of the press during both the Weimar and Nazi eras. The
man was an authenic hero.

Ossietsky turned to pacifism during service in the Great War
of 1914-18. Like others, he was disgusted by the senseless
slaughter. In the postwar years he emerged as an anti-militarist
opposed to anything designed for national defense. The *Reichswehr*, he charged, was "a tool of murderers." He was scorned
by the rightist Prussian military who dreamed of a revival of
German power despite the strictures of the Treaty of Versailles.

The obstreperous journalist remained consistent in his
pacifism. Enemies in the Weimar Republic denounced him as
"a pamphleteer with a mordant pen." To Hitler and the Nazis
he was anathema. When he was awarded the Nobel Peace Prize
in 1936, he was condemned by the German Minister at Oslo, Dr.

Heinrich Sahm, who expressed his "astonishment and displeasure." The envoy's reaction was angry: "I can only say that this decision, for which the Nobel Committee is responsible, must be regarded as a deliberate demonstration against Germany." The outraged *Fuehrer* immediately ordered that no German in the future be allowed to accept the Nobel Prize.

But there were others who praised the fearless journalist. Novelist Thomas Mann again voiced the tenor of public opinion: "His person has become in the eyes of the world a symbol of the free and free-will spirit—with justice, for he has undergone what seemed to him to be good and human, and the end of this sick man has been hurried along by a search for vengeance or mercy."

Here was a man of peace mishandled in a way no bandit would have been treated. More than a theoretical apostle of peace, Ossietsky was willing to sacrifice himself at a time when war threatened on all sides. He rates the admiration of all human beings who value a sense of morality.

Path to Pacifism

Carl von Ossietsky was born in Hamburg on October 3, 1899, to Germanized descendants of a Polish Catholic family. His father, a merchant who belonged to the lesser Prussian nobility, died when the boy was two years old. His mother opened a small food store to earn a living, and skeptical of a school education, educated her son herself. Her second husband, a Hamburg sculptor, showed a lively understanding for the young lad and encouraged him in his ambition to become a writer.

At the age of 18, Carl, determined to earn his own bread, became an assistant clerk at the Hamburg District Court and later at the Land Registry Office. Looking forward to a career in journalism, he worked at his writing in his spare time. He first saw his words in print on February 25, 1914, when he wrote a letter to the editor of *Freies Leben (Free Life)*, in which he criticized an Army court-martial for having considered a drunken brawl as "military unrest" and having sentenced the involved soldiers to hard labor. Angered by the letter of this lowly court clerk, members of the court-martial had Ossietsky arrested, arraigned, and fined 200 marks for contempt of court.

One seldom criticized authorities in the Hohenzollern Empire. But young Ossietsky was not intimidated. He had no intention of keeping quiet in the face of injustice. He even dared to challenge a general of the armed forces. At the same time he began a serious study of the world's literature and tried to learn as much as he could about the nature of the world press. In 1913 he married an Englishwoman.

When war broke out in 1914, Ossietsky, already leaning toward pacifism, was conscripted and served as an infantryman through all four years. He witnessed at first hand the horrors of war on the Western Front. Like many others, his earlier pacifist sentiment hardened into hatred for all forms of militarism. He decided that from then on he would devote his entire personality and talents against anyone who would again seek to send the German people into such detestable slaughter. He would do all he could to support a free, democratic, responsible form of government in which the people themselves would decide whether or not they would go to war.

In 1920 Ossietsky was made secretary of the German Peace Society in Berlin, about whose work he had already learned during his army service. Two years later, together with several others, he founded the *Nie Wieder Krieg* (No More War) organization. He became foreign policy editor of the *Berliner Volks-zeitung (Berlin People's Paper)*. In 1924 he was one of the founders of the Republican Party, dedicated to the task of preventing the Weimar Republic from turning to the right.

In 1927 Ossietsky was appointed editor of *Die Weltbühne (The World Stage)*, a left-wing political weekly, after the death of its founder, Siegfried Jacobsohn. He soon gained a national reputation as champion of such causes as penal reform, rapprochement with France, and working-class unity. Before the war he had criticized the domestic and foreign policies of the Hohenzollern state; now he turned his polemical pen against right-wing politicians of the Weimar Republic. He charged that "the omnipotence of the generals" was devastating for the cause of peace and democracy. He used his acid pen especially against the rising National Socialist movement. Readers were intrigued by his elegant, aggressive writing style, and even more by his biting wit. He denounced rightist politicians and high officers in the *Reichswehr* as determined on a war of revenge and for their support of the up-and-coming Hitler. German chauvinism, he wrote, could only lead to disaster.

At the same time Ossietsky, as a defender of democracy, showed equal contempt for Germany's Communists. He regarded them as naïve tools of Russian Bolsheviks. "In the Red-Russian vocabulary," he wrote, "the word 'freedom' is not tolerated." He accused Moscow of trying to make "weak-minded followers and dumb servants of all European Communists." Despite his anti-Communist views, his enemies accused him of being favorable to Bolshevism. The rightist press usually described him as "a writer of Communist views."

During the first year of his editorship of *Die Weltbühne*, Ossietsky published an article by Berthold Jacobs accusing the authorities of protecting several members of the Armed Forces who had been charged with murder. Both Jacobs and Ossietsky were arrested, tried, found guilty, and sentenced to a fine and a short prison term. The two were soon released under an amnesty.

The embattled editor refused to remain silent in the face of what he regarded as dangerous policies of the government. He wrote scores of articles, editorials, and long essays notable for their trenchant irony and powerful polemics. This work culminated in a new conflict with the authorities. On March 12, 1929, he published an article by aircraft technician Walther Kreiser accusing the government of violating both the Weimar Constitution and the Treaty of Versailles by using money for military aircraft which had been appropriated for civil aviation. Titled *"Windiges aus der Luftwaffe"* ("Irregularities in the Aviation Sector"), the article criticized the budget of the *Reichswehr* (Armed Forces) Ministry and included some dangerous information: "But not all aircraft are always in Germany. Where are they? In the Soviet Union. Reports from there alluded to secret collusion between the *Reichswehr* and the Soviet Union which enabled German and Soviet generals to circumvent provisions of the Treaty of Versailles. Aircraft were not in Germany but on Russian airfields. They could not be found and counted by agents of the Western Powers.''

For the government that was treasonable information. But nothing was done for the moment.

Ossietsky insisted that he, too, opposed the Treaty of Versailles, but held that any changes should be brought about by open negotiations. Secret German rearmament, he warned, would only strengthen the aggressive forces inside Germany and lead to another catastrophe.

The journalist continued his attacks. In 1930, when the Reich's army budget was being considered again, he wrote that he was opposed to any increases. He wrote in *Die Weltbühne:* ''Everything is uncertain, everything except the tremendous superior strength of the United States. Europe has an anxiety neurosis and it is being shown in nervous outbreaks. Europe feels itself sold to American bankers and betrayed to the proletarians of Soviet Russia. At the present time, because it is less dangerous, Europe is silently inclined to place the blame for its sickness on a mysterious conspiracy of the Russians.''

The authorities were still rankled by the Kreiser article printed some two years before. In 1931 they suddenly indicted Ossietsky and Kreiser on the basis of a 1914 espionage law for high treason in betraying military secrets. The sensational trial was held before the Federal Supreme Court in Leipzig. The court held that the Kreiser article was certain to create a false impression among Allied nations that Germany was secretly rearming. In his defense Ossietsky insisted that all he had done was to attack the Government's handling of secret public funds and that he was well within his rights of criticism in a democracy.

Ossietsky and Kreiser were both found guilty and sentenced to eighteen months' imprisonment. Kreiser managed to escape to France, where he was granted asylum. Friends urged Ossietsky to flee in similar fashion. He refused. He saw his place as in Germany and he would remain there.

Bitterness in liberal circles. There were many large protest meetings. The hard-bitten journalist was accompanied to the prison door by such sympathetic friends as Lion Feuchtwanger, Ernst Toller, and Arnold Zweig.

The man of principle served nine months in prison. On December 22, 1932, the short-term government of Chancellor Kurt von Schleicher issued an amnesty decree. There was a question about the release of Ossietsky. Though Social Democrats hated him, they insisted that he, too, should benefit by the amnesty and pointed to a special paragraph in the amnesty decree which they said should be applied to him. Ossietsky was released.

More and more alarmed by Hitler's drive for power, Ossietsky's friends again urged him to seek refuge abroad, as had many of his political associates. Response negative. He would remain in Germany where he belonged. He was satisfied to stay there and be classified as an "enemy of the state." He resumed his work with *Die Weltbühne* and directed his polemical assaults toward Hitler—now only a month from power.

Ossietsky was aware of the nature of the rising Nazi flood. Unlike other Germans, he was not deceived by the temporary Nazi setback in the *Reichstag* elections of 1932. He understood how the German middle class had been attracted by Nazi bread-and-circuses. He prophesied in April 1931 that in a crisis the half-proletarian element inside the movement, meaning the *SA* Storm Troopers, would be defeated by reactionary bourgeois forces.

In the past Ossietsky had directed his ridicule against two older German institutions, the *Reichswehr* and the Social Democratic Party. Now, appalled by the excesses of Nazism, he took up his satirical pen against Hitler and the Nazis. He did not realize that because of his energetic opposition to the Nazi movement he would eventually lose the battle. Infuriated, Hitler ordered that the journalist be counted among his most dangerous enemies, and that he was to be throttled.

The Nazi leader was angered by an editorial in *Die Weltbühne* immediately before the Nazis came to power, in which Ossietsky prophesied that "the quiet of the graveyard will descend on this land." And further: "Soon we shall not be able to speak, but the cause will speak." Ossietsky knew what to expect from Hitler. "I shall remain here," he said, "and if they should imprison me I will serve the cause of peace better in prison than as a free man outside of Germany." Convinced of the purity of his motives, he was willing to accept imprisonment and the torture he knew went with it.

On February 28, 1933, the day after the sensational *Reichstag* fire, Ossietsky was arrested and sent to a military fortress. The spectacular conflagration enabled Hitler to remove scores of enemies from circulation. Among them, he included the journalist who had caused him much discomfort. A co-prisoner later reported that Ossietsky had been brutally beaten by his guards and that some of his teeth had been knocked out by a revolver butt. Standard operating procedure in Naziland.

Little was known of Ossietsky's fate after he disappeared into a Nazi dungeon. Eventually, international pressure forced the authorities to reveal that he had been transferred to Papenburg-Esterwegen concentration camp. It was impossible to elicit information about the charges on which he was being held. Under horrendous conditions Ossietsky contracted tuberculosis, from which he never recovered. Word leaked out that he was barbarously mistreated and was forced to do heavy field work. Again and again he was told that he could win his immediate release if only he would be sensible enough to sign a pledge that he had "revised" his beliefs. He refused.

A month after Ossietsky's imprisonment, Nazi authorities, annoyed by demonstrations in foreign cities on his behalf, allowed correspondents to visit him. Ossietsky informed the visiting journalists that his treatment was no different from that of anyone else taken into protective custody. He added that he had nothing "vital" to complain about. The reporters understood the veiled meaning.

"Case Ossietsky" took on international attention in early 1934 when a representative of the International Red Cross appeared unannounced at Papenburg and by threatening the Nazi warders with embarrassing consequences managed to see Ossietsky. The visitor reported to the foreign press that the prisoner was a thoroughly broken man, dangerously ill, and obviously mistreated.

Immediate world-wide reaction. Nazi authorities, anxious for foreign approval of their fledging regime, had to take notice when they saw the famous names of objectors. In London Harold Laski and Gilbert Murray spoke up on behalf of the German fighter for peace. Henry Wickham Steed, former editor of *The Times*, lecturer in European History at London University, and author of a book titled *Hitler: Whence and Whither?*, protested that in the *Reichstag* Fire trial Ossietsky was not allowed to appear as a witness and that the wildest accusations were made against him. "Now, in consequence of internment, with constant military exercises and insufficient food, he is at death's door. If it is too much to hope for his release, his claim to the sympathy of the civilized world ought not, I think, go unheeded."

Mention of the "civilized world" enraged Nazi authorities.

From France, Romain Rolland addressed a letter to the editor of *The New York Times,* asking that the foreign press get a statement from Ossietsky. The New York newspaper thereupon contacted its Berlin correspondent and requested that he visit the prisoner and asked if anything could be done for him. The visit took place. Ossietsky answered the question by shaking his head.

Toward the Nobel Prize

There was worse news for Nazi authorities already embarrassed by their prisoner. From various sources came reports that there was a move to nominate Ossietsky for the coming Nobel Peace Prize. In June 1934, from its headquarters in Paris, The German League for the Rights of Man proposed the name of Ossietsky for the award. On November 27, 1934, the Swiss newspaper *Baseler Nachrichten,* published an open letter signed by 60 prominent Swiss personalities: "Carl von Ossietsky is one of the most courageous and unbending, but also distinguished and noble German publicists who had become widely known across the borders of his own country. His fearless words and his unquenchable struggle for peace and justice have brought him the admiration of the whole peace-loving world. . . . Tens of thousands in all the countries of the world once again raise their voices for the freedom of Carl von Ossietsky. Countless organizations and important individuals have come out in support of his candidacy for the Nobel Peace Prize.''

In 1935 Harold Laski and Gilbert Murray in London and some fifteen representatives of American universities proposed Ossietsky's name for the prize. In 1936, members of the Swiss National Assembly, the Norwegian Labor Party, and Czechoslovakian parliamentarians joined the chorus for Ossietsky's nomination.

Consternation in Berlin! The Nobel Peace Prize for a traitor in the process of being "re-educated"? Impossible! This was most embarrassing.

Ossietsky had been transferred to Moabit Hospital in Berlin, where he was undergoing treatment by government physicians for his lung infection and heart disease. A few days before the decision by the Norwegian Nobel Committee in Oslo was due, Hermann Goering had prisoner Ossietsky brought to his office. With threats and flattery, Goering attempted to get Ossietsky to promise that if the announcement came in his favor he would turn down the award. If he did that, Goering said, he would be released, given financial security, and would not be troubled any more by the government.

Ossietsky said "No!" He was returned to his guarded hospital room.

Meanwhile, there were complications in Oslo. In mid-November 1936 Norwegian Foreign Minister Halvdan Koht and former Prime Minister and Foreign Minister Johann Ludwig Mowinckel resigned from the Nobel Peace Committee. The reason given officially by Koht was that he feared "an awkward situation" with the Nazi authorities might result if he participated in an award to a man held in a German concentration camp since 1933. Mowinckel explained his resignation: "Although I am not Foreign Minister, I am still my party's parliamentary leader. If Mr. Koht's position causes doubt as to the political integrity of the prize-awarding body, my position might also be open to misinterpretation."

The Nobel Committee met hastily and decided to accept the resignations, although it found Mowinckel's offer unnecessary. The committee then issued a report: "As the prize awarding might affect foreign nations' feelings and interests, it is reasonable that Foreign Minister Koht has resigned, but has never been asserted that leading politicians are barred from participating in the committee's meetings."

On November 16, 1936, the day of the resignations, private information reached Oslo and Copenhagen via Stockholm that Ossietsky had been liberated and was now convalescing in the Virchow Hospital in Berlin. It was reported that the journalist was suffering from a kidney ailment, heart disease, and tuberculosis. The news was that Ossietsky had pledged his word to German authorities that he would not leave Germany and would conduct himself as a loyal German citizen even if he did not embrace the National Socialist faith in all its implications. In the preceding six months there had been no mention in the German press of Ossietsky's name, with the exception of a small note reporting that he had been nominated by friends and admirers abroad as a candidate for the Nobel Peace Prize.

Nobel Award

The rumors had substance.

While still in custody, Ossietsky was awarded the Nobel Peace Prize for 1935. The stricken peace fighter in a country preparing for war had won an important skirmish. From his hospital bed he sent a short telegram to the President of the Prize Committee: "Thanks for the unexpected honor." It was a message which contributed to his loss of freedom for the remaining year-and-five-months of his life.

World reaction was predictably laudatory. There were demonstrations in major capitals to praise the action of the Nobel Prize Committee. Among them was a mass meeting in Cooper Union, New York City, to honor Ossietsky. Columbia University President Nicholas Murray Butler sent a message to the audience: "One of the two distinct and widely separate types of public service has been the ground for the award of the

Nobel Peace Prize. The first is definite formulation and execution of public policy, which strengthens the foundations on which peace must rest. The other is forward facing and courageous appeal to public opinion to support such policies. Ossietsky has assuredly deserved consideration because of his outspoken support despite almost every type of calumny and persecution of ideas of peace and of the public policies which make for peace.''

New York's Mayor Fiorello La Guardia spoke in his usual colorful and dramatic fashion. It was easy, he said, for anyone to champion any cause in any country, but it took a man to do it in Nazi Germany. ''A martyr to his ideals, Ossietsky has become an apostle of peace through the award. Never before has the award been made under such dramatic circumstances. Imagine the consternation of Hitler's cabinet when it was announced. This was more embarrassing to the Hitler government than all the demonstrations of the whole world. It focuses attention on the contrast between the philosophy of peace and happiness and that brute force, oppression and intolerance.''

Educator John Dewey declared that Ossietsky had become the outstanding hero of peace in modern times and perhaps any time. He described the award as the greatest blow to Nazi prestige. He hoped that it might mark the beginning of the end of the Nazi Government's hold not only on its own country but also the United States, where some Americans were being misled by propaganda on what Hitler had done in Germany. ''Norway is to be praised for challenging the conduct of Hitler not only on racial persecution but also persecution of all who dare to say a good word for peace for the republican form of government.''

Other distinguished Americans, including theologians Reinhold Niebuhr of the Union Theological Seminary and Harry Emerson Fosdick, joined the chorus of approval for Ossietsky and disgust for Hitler and Nazism. Messages were read from British journalist Sir Norman Angell and physicist Albert Einstein. The famous scientist described Ossietsky as ''the most admirable of the few outstanding personalities in Nazi Germany who have put the interests of humanity above that of national egoism.''

"Scandal" in Berlin

Rage in Nazi Germany

Announcement of the Nobel award was received by the Nazi Government with a barrage of criticism. In the uproar the German Foreign Office officially called it "preposterous and fatal": "The award of the Nobel Prize to a notorious traitor is such a brazen challenge and insult to the new Germany that it will be followed by an appropriate, unequivocal answer." Within hours Foreign Minister Constantin von Neurath instructed Dr. Heinrich Sahm, the German Minister at Oslo, to express to the Norwegian Government the Reich's astonishment and displeasure over the award. The statement pointed out that while the Norwegian Government was not directly involved, nevertheless the award was made by a Norwegian national representation "and constitutes a conscious and deliberate insult to Germany." Dr. Sahm was also instructed to issue the threat that "the German Government reserves the right to draw all the implications of this event."

The controlled German press followed with almost hysterical denunciations of the Nobel Prize Committee, Norway, and the Norwegians. The semi-official *Diplomatische Korrespondenz* reported angrily: "The Norwegian nation cannot really be congratulated on having representatives who make a spectacle of such a viewpoint. These Norwegian delegates of the people have done their land a sorry service. If they were not to believe that the German people had been publicly insulted through a bizarre burlesque then we must believe that they either shared with Ossietsky the desire to enslave and defame Germany, or that they share the same viewpoint as the traitor they have honored."

Der Angriff (Attack), organ of Dr. Paul Joseph Goebbels, Reich Minister for Public Enlightenment and Propaganda, charged that the award did not further peace but misunderstanding, and that it was contrary to Alfred Nobel's intention when he created the prize. Other newspapers charged that giving the Nobel Prize "to such a notorious traitor was a shameful challenge to the New Germany, which certainly will be followed by a deserved reply."

Norwegians were not intimidated by the barrage of Nazi criticism. President H. Olden of the Norwegian Peace Union was unimpressed: "The prize award was just and correct. I salute the decision with joy." Martin Tranmael, editor of the daily newspaper *Arbeiderblad (Workers' Journal)* and a member of the Nobel Prize Committee, said that the award to Ossietsky was a slap in the face at fascism: "Mr. Ossietsky is a symbol not only of the peace ideal but also of anti-fascism. He was chosen for his work for peace, which is almost identical with democracy." Other Norwegian newspapers pointed out that the prize was awarded not by the Norwegian Government but by a private organization over which it had no control in a democratic state. Only in rightist newspapers was there any criticism. The *Aftenpost* claimed that the authority and respect of the Nobel Committee and the Peace Prize institution had been gravely shattered by this "mistake" and feared that good relations with Germany were endangered.

Hitler himself was enraged by the announcement. He was so incensed that he issued a decree forbidding any German to accept a Nobel Prize in the future, and that thereafter special 100,000-mark prizes for art, literature, and science would replace Nobel Prizes for Germans.

The world was unimpressed.

A Matter of Money

Global attention was soon focussed on two special aspects of the Nobel award. Would Ossietsky be allowed to go to Oslo for the formal presentation? And what about the money—the $39,303 prize, at that pre-inflation era a considerable amount of cash? Would the virtually imprisoned journalist be permitted to collect it?

As for the trip to Oslo—"No!" There was no chance that Hitler would let Ossietsky go to Norway, again defame the Third Reich, and then refuse to return to his homeland. Moreover, the journalist, now in a nursing home in north Berlin and in worsening condition, might not survive the trip. Doctors reported that the excitement of the award had a bad effect on the patient's health, but Ossietsky said that his condition was good enough for the journey. Meanwhile, Goebbels assured Ossietsky that he would be granted the right to journey to Oslo.

But *Gestapo* agents saw to it that Ossietsky did not leave the nursing home. He did not go to Oslo.

And then the matter of money. As a German citizen, Ossietsky was obliged by law to offer the proceeds to the *Reichsbank,* which would welcome the foreign exchange and give Ossietsky the equivalent in reichsmarks. But soon there was mystery surrounding the whereabouts of the money. There were transfer difficulties. At first the *Kristiania Bank og Kreditkasse* in Oslo refused to yield the money.

Evidently abandoning all hope of going to Oslo, Ossietsky was said to have instructed a Berlin attorney named Dr. Kurt Warnow to act as his agent. Warnow apparently did not practice law, had no office in Berlin, and his name appeared on no official register.

Warnow sent a German woman, who gave the name of Mrs. Alexandra Kuruzberger, to Oslo with a power of attorney supposedly signed by Ossietsky authorizing her to transfer the money to a German bank after deducting $200 in cash for expenses. The mystery woman, who said she was a secretary to Warnow and acting on his instructions, refused to see any reporters of the Norwegian press. Suspicious Oslo newsmen charged that she was actually acting on behalf of Nazi authorities to seize the Nobel money.

In any event, bank officials decided to withhold payment on the ground that the prize had been deposited in the name of Ossietsky and could not be handed to any other person.

In February 1937 there were press reports that Ossietsky was the victim of a swindler and that he had lost all but 16,000 marks of the Nobel money. It was also reported that Warnow, by a confidence trick, had turned the bulk of the fortune over to a woman and that for embezzling the Ossietsky fund he had been sentenced to two years at hard labor.

When reporters interviewed him in August 1937, Ossietsky informed them that the entire prize sum of 97,000 marks had been turned over to him without interference by the government and that, in fact, government officials had kept him from losing considerable amounts through bad investments by an attorney he had at first appointed to collect and administer the fund. Finding that his money was endangered, he had appealed through his doctor for State intervention and had been granted help, including the naming of his doctor as administrator.

At this time Ossietsky appeared to be recovering slowly from his illnesses. Supervision by the secret police was removed after he gave his word that he would not engage in any kind of pacifist or Communist agitation and that he would not lecture or write on political subjects. The press reported that he was planning to become a medical photographer. He informed interviewers that he hoped that authorities would allow him to spend some time in the Swiss Alps during the following autumn, and he was optimistic about the permission should he promise to return to Germany. He said that the announcement of the Nobel Peace Prize came as a distinct shock to him at a time when he was running a high fever and his life was dangerously threatened. He feared difficulties with the authorities and for a time considered refusing to accept the award. He decided finally that if he did refuse it would be said abroad that he had been forced to decline and, therefore, he would serve his country best by accepting it.

Sad and tragic optimism. In the spring of 1938, the tuberculosis from which he was suffering reached his brain, resulting in meningitis. He died on May 4, 1938, at the age of 49.

Journalist as Hero

Carl von Ossietsky lost his struggle for peace but he won the admiration of the world for his courage against hopeless odds. He contributed much to a burdened humanity. German novelist Thomas Mann honored him for his stand against "the beginning of evil." At the Nobel Prize ceremony in Oslo, Professor

Frederik Stang praised the absent prizewinner: "Ossietsky is not only a symbol; he is a deed, and he is a man."

Ossietsky was not forgotten in the postwar German Federal Republic and its democratic milieu. In late 1978 the new four-year-old University of Oldenbourg, with some 4,700 students, sued the state for the right to name itself Ossietsky University in honor of the pacifist victim of Nazi torture. The dispute developed into a conflict between conservative residents of the north German city and liberal students of the new university. Students charged that an element of the confrontation was the older generation's refusal to come to terms with the Nazi past. "Ossietsky symbolizes the socially committed causes the university espouses," said a student spokesman.

The authorities of Lower Saxony sided with the town and vetoed the name change. Its position was that naming a state institution for any historical figure was "no longer timely" and that it was "a relapse into outdated traditions." Students replied with irony that the town had an army barracks named for Gen. Paul von Hindenburg. In defiance of the edict they insisted on retaining Ossietsky's name adorning the tower of the university library.

Iconoclast Ossietsky would have enjoyed the uproar.

Index

THE BEST IN WAR BOOKS

__DEVIL BOATS: THE PT WAR AGAINST JAPAN
William Breuer 0-515-09367-X/$3.95
A dramatic true-life account of the daring PT
sailors who crewed the Devil Boats—outwitting
the Japanese.

__PORK CHOP HILL S.L.A. Marshall
0-515-08732-7/$3.95
A hard-hitting look at the Korean War and the
handful of U.S. riflemen who fought back the
Red Chinese troops.
"A distinguished contribution to the literature
of war."—New York Times

__THREE-WAR MARINE Colonel Francis Fox Parry
0-515-09872-8/$3.95
A rare and dramatic look at three decades
of war—World War II, the Korean War, and
Vietnam. Francis Fox Parry shares the
heroism, fears, and harrowing challenges of
his thirty action-packed years in an
astounding military career.